LAW OF S
AND VALUATIONS

by

John Murdoch LLB ACIArb
*Senior Lecturer in Law
Reading University*

and

Paul Murrells
*Solicitor
Surveyors Indemnity Management Services
Tunbridge Wells*

1995

Estates Gazette

A member of Reed Business Publishing

The Estates Gazette Limited
151 Wardour Street, London W1V 4BN

ISBN 0 7282 0251 4

© John Murdoch and Paul Murrells 1995

Typesetting by Amy Boyle Word Processing, Rochester, Kent
Printed in Finland at Werner Söderström Osakeyhitö

To Sandi and Rosemary

Preface

The idea of suing a surveyor or valuer for negligence is hardly a new one. Indeed, it is now more than a century since a valuer was first held liable to a lender, in respect of a valuation which was commissioned and paid for by the borrower. A highly controversial ruling, certainly – the *Yianni* of its day, perhaps – but, like *Yianni*, one which has now become firmly established as one of the crosses which every practitioner must bear.

Surveyors and valuers, then, have long been potentially liable to their clients and to certain third parties for incompetent work. However, the last few years have seen an enormous increase in that liability, in terms of both the number of claims made and the sheer size of those claims. At one end of the spectrum, house buyers appear ever more ready to bring legal proceedings against mortgage valuers; at the other, the collapse of the commercial property market in the late 1980s has left a number of firms facing actions by lending institutions in which the damages claimed run into tens of millions of pounds.

Naturally, all this activity in the courts has raised issues as to the legal basis (and the limits) of professional liability, and a number of critical questions have been addressed. How, for example, should a house buyer's damages be assessed? To what extent can a valuer be held responsible for a falling market? How long does a professional's liability last? Can that liability be restricted or excluded? Is it affected by unreasonable conduct by a lender client? All these issues, and many more, have occupied the attention of the courts during the past decade.

Surprisingly, given the pace of legal development in this area, there appears to have been little attempt to subject it to systematic legal analysis. True, the property professions have on occasion been given a chapter in books which cover a wider field, and some of the more important decided cases have been the subject of critical appraisal in both legal and property journals. However, we believe that the time is now ripe for a detailed examination of the liability of surveyors and valuers, including the important practical matter of the professional indemnity insurance by which it is underpinned, and this book is the result of our belief.

Liability for negligence is normally said to depend upon the three elements of duty, breach and damage, and this formulation has also determined the shape of the book. The first two chapters explore the scope of a surveyor's or valuer's legal duty of care and skill (together with the question of fees, in an attempt to lighten the general gloom)! The next three chapters are concerned with what constitutes a breach of that duty, both generally and in the specific context of particular kinds of professional work. There follow two chapters on the extent of liability, again dealing both with general legal questions (such as remoteness of damage) and with more specific issues concerning the assessment of damages for certain claimants such as house buyers and lenders.

The parameters of liability thus established, the book deals with various legal mechanisms by which it may be reduced or avoided. These include limitation periods, disclaimers and the possibility of attributing a share of the blame to someone else, either the plaintiff or a third party. Finally, we consider the principles governing professional indemnity insurance, without which there would surely be no professional work at all.

In all these areas, our aim has been not only to provide an analysis of legal principle but also to point out particular dangers for practitioners and to suggest ways in which they may be avoided. To this end, we have attempted to state the law on the basis of materials available to us on 31 October 1994.

The task of producing this book has given us good reason to feel grateful to several people. To Malcolm Stitcher of counsel, for alerting us to a number of interesting issues both in and out of court; to our publishers, for their customary courtesy and efficiency in meeting some tight deadlines; and, last but not least, to our respective wives, for tolerance in the face of those irritating absences from home and hearth which authorship invariably requires.

Note:

The cut-off date of October 31 1994 mentioned above serves to exclude at least two later developments which readers may wish to note. First, the judgment of Judge Thornton OR in the case of *Bradford & Bingley Building Society* v *Thorne* was handed down on November 14 1994. This judgment is of particular interest in that the judge, while following the orthodox judicial line (that a negligent valuer was not liable to a mortgage lender for losses caused by a falling property market), broke new ground in holding the valuer liable for loss of the "cushion" against market falls which the lender would have had if a non-negligent valuation of the property had been given. Whether future courts will pick up this ball and run with it remains to be seen; in any event, it appears likely that the whole "falling markets" issue will be considered by the Court of Appeal during 1995.

A second recent development is of higher authority and is potentially of even greater significance. On January 13 1995 the Court of Appeal reversed the decision of the trial judge in *First National Commercial Bank plc* v *Humberts* (which we discuss at p183). Their lordships' ruling (which is briefly reported at [1995] EGCS 1) was that a mortgage lender cannot be said to have suffered loss in consequence of a negligent over-valuation until the value of the property falls below the amount of the mortgagor's outstanding debt. The limitation period on a claim in tort by the lender against the valuer accordingly runs from this date, and not (as the trial judge had held) from the date of the mortgage loan.

St Valentine's Day 1995   John Murdoch
Paul Murrells

ERRATUM

The following should be added at the end of the text on p31, after "The House of Lords ruled unanimously in favour of"

concurrent liability in terms which leave no doubt that the decision

CONTENTS

Preface v
Table of Cases xiii
Table of Statutes xxiii

CHAPTER 1 The surveyor/valuer and the client 1

A Introduction 1
B Identifying a contract 3
    Surveyor/valuer and client 3
    Mortgagee and house buyer 7
C Duties to the client 10
    Contract terms 10
    Experts and arbitrators 13
D Remuneration of surveyors and valuers 22
    Express agreement as to fees 22
    Implied agreement as to fees 23
    Forfeiture of fees 25
E Liability to the client in tort 28
    The concurrent liability problem 28
    Surveyors and valuers 30
    The problem solved 31

CHAPTER 2 The surveyor/valuer and third parties 34

A Development of liability to third parties
    for negligence 34
B Basis of liability to third parties for negligence 36
C Liability of borrower's valuer to mortgage 41
D Liability of mortgage valuer to house buyer 44
    Position of valuer 45
    Position of mortgage lender 53
E Liability of vendor's surveyor to purchaser 59
F Liability to vendor for "down-valuation" 61
G Liability to mortgagor on sale of repossessed property .. 63
H Liability for independent determinations 64
I Other cases 64

J	Firm's liability for valuer's torts	66
	Employee's negligence	66
	Employee's disobedience and fraud	67
	Partnerships	69

CHAPTER 3 The meaning of professional negligence 71

A	Introduction	71
B	Specialists	73
C	Inexperienced practitioners	74
D	Confirmation of instructions	75
	Surveys	75
	Valuations	79
E	Proof of negligence	81
	The role of experts	81
	Expert evidence	83
	Applications for summary judgment	87

CHAPTER 4 The surveyor's standard of care 89

A	Structural survey	89
	Method of reporting	91
	Damp, rot, woodworm and timber defects	93
	Roof defects	97
	Subsidence	100
	Defects in services	106
B	Home Buyers' Survey and Valuation	107

CHAPTER 5 The valuer's standard of care 109

A	Accuracy	110
	The nature of valuation	110
	The "bracket"	111
B	Valuation methods	114
	General	114
	RICS/ISVA Guidance Notes	117
	Legal knowledge	122
C	Types of valuation	123
	Mortgage valuations of residential property	123
	Valuations by independent experts	129
	Other valuations	130

CHAPTER 6 Damages – general principles 132

A The causing of loss 132
    Causation in fact and law 132
    Reliance 135
    Remoteness of damage 138
B Limits on liability 139
    Mitigation 139
    Collateral benefits 141
C Interest on damages 144

CHAPTER 7 The assessment of damages 146

A Purchaser 146
    The basic measure 146
    Incidental items of loss 154
    Damages for "inconvenience" 157
    Personal injury 163
B Lender 164
    The basic measure 164
    Incidental items of loss 168
    Interest 170
    Offsets against damages 173
    The borrower's covenant 174
C Vendor 176
D Other claimants 177

CHAPTER 8 Defences to liability 180

A Limitation periods 180
    Claims in contract 180
    Claims in tort 181
    Latent damage 185
    Personal injuries 192
    Contribution claims 193
    Fraud and concealment 194
B Exemption clauses and disclaimers 196
    Types of disclaimer 196
    General effectiveness of disclaimers 199
    The Unfair Contract Terms Act 201

CHAPTER 9 Sharing the blame 213

A Contributory negligence 213
  General principles 213
  Scope of the Law Reform (Contributory Negligence) Act 214
  Professional negligence cases 216
  Contributory negligence by house buyers 218
  Contributory negligence by commercial lenders 220
B Contribution among wrongdoers 228

CHAPTER 10 Professional indemnity insurance 233

A The general background 233
B The nature of PI insurance 233
C Invalid claims 235
  Material non-disclosure 235
  Non-compliance with policy terms and conditions 238
D PI insurance and third party rights 241
E Fraud 243
F Current problems 244

Index 247

Table of cases

A

Addis v Gramophone Co [1909] AC 488 158
Ailsa Craig Fishing Co Ltd v Malvern Fishing Co Ltd
  [1983] 1 All ER 101 199
Al Saudi Banque v Clarke Pixley [1990] Ch 313 37,40
Alcock v Wraith (1991) 59 BLR 16 57
Allen v Ellis & Co [1990] 1 EGLR 170 .... 99, 137, 139, 163, 192, 201, 219
Alliance & Leicester Building Society v Edgestop Ltd
  (No. 1) [1994] 2 All ER 38 216
  (No. 2) June 28 1993, Chancery Division, unreported 84
  (No. 3) [1994] 2 EGLR 229 .... 34, 67, 69, 70, 84, 195
Allied Trust Bank Ltd v Edward Symmons & Partners [1994]
  1 EGLR 165 .... 5, 43, 119, 165
American Express International Banking Corporation v Hurley [1985]
  3 All ER 564 64
Anglia Hastings & Thanet Building Society v House & Son (1981)
  260 EG 1128 .... 31, 230
Anns v Merton London Borough Council [1978] AC 728 .... 47, 48
Arenson v Casson, Beckman, Rutley & Co
  [1977] AC 405, HL 14, 15, 16, 17, 18, 19
  [1973] Ch 346, CA (sub nom Arenson v Arenson) 15
Argyll (Duchess of) v Beuselinck [1972] 2 Lloyds Rep 172 74
Assured Advances Ltd v Ashbee & Co [1994] EGCS 169 173
Axa Equity & Law Home Loans Ltd v Goldsack & Freeman [1994] 1
  EGLR 175 .... 5, 113, 168, 226
Axa Equity & Law Home Loans Ltd v Hirani Watson [1994] EGCS 90
  .... 109, 116, 168

B

Baber v Kenwood Manufacturing Co. [1978] 1 Lloyd's Rep 175 21
Banque Bruxelles Lambert SA v John D Wood Commercial Ltd [1994]
  2 EGLR 108 ...... 6, 43, 72, 113, 116, 117, 136, 138, 141, 142, 143, 164, 167,
                              168, 170, 172, 173, 174, 183, 216, 218, 221, 222
Banque Keyser Ullman SA v Skandia (UK) Insurance Co [1991] 2 AC 249 ... 167
Barclays Bank plc v Fairclough Building Ltd Times, May 11 1994 215
Baxter v FW Gapp & Co Ltd
  [1939] 2 KB 271; [1939] 2 All ER 752, CA 167, 168, 169, 171
  [1938] 4 All ER 457 .... 11, 74, 110, 115, 116
Beaton v Nationwide Building Society [1991] 2 EGLR 145 .... 7, 53, 57, 128, 210
Beaumont v Humberts [1990] 2 EGLR 166 .... 4, 40, 80, 113, 130, 178
Bell v Peter Browne & Co [1990] 2 QB 495 .... 29, 181, 183
Bell Hotels (1935) Ltd v Motion (1952) 159 EG 496 .... 28, 130, 177
Belvedere Motors Ltd v King (1981) 260 EG 813 .... 19, 20

Bere v Slades [1989] 2 EGLR 160 .... 53, 126
Beresforde v Chesterfield BC [1989] 2 EGLR 149 .... 8, 58, 59
Bigg v Howard Son & Gooch [1990] 1 EGLR 173 .... 28, 100, 145, 157, 161
BNP Mortgages Ltd v Barton Cook & Sams February 18 1994, Official
  Referees' Business, unreported 114
BNP Mortgages Ltd v Chadwick Bird July 1994, Official Referees'
  Business, unreported 172
BNP Mortgages Ltd v Goadsby & Harding Ltd [1994] 2
  EGLR 169 .... 71, 117, 168, 243
Bolam v Friern Hospital Management Committee [1957] 2 All ER 118 71
Bolton v Puley (1982) 267 EG 1160 159
Bourne v McEvoy Timber Preservation (1975) 237 EG 496 .... 41, 61
Broadoak Properties Ltd v Young & White [1989] 1 EGLR 263 .... 156, 158
Brunsden v Humphrey (1884) 14 QBD 141 193
Buckland and Garrard v Pawson & Co (1890) 6 TLR 421 25
Buckland v Watts (1968) 208 EG 969 .... 28, 154, 155
Burgess v Purchase & Sons (Farms) Ltd [1983] 2 All ER 4 21

C
Campbell v Edwards [1976] 1 All ER 785 .... 14, 19, 21
Campbell v Meacocks [1993] CILL 886 .... 182, 188, 189
Canada Steamship Lines Ltd v R [1952] AC 192 199
Cann v Willson (1888) 39 ChD 39 .... 34, 35, 36, 42, 44
Caparo Industries plc v Dickman [1990] 2 AC 605 .... 29, 37, 38, 40
Cemp Properties (UK) Ltd v Dentsply Research & Development Corporation
  [1989] 2 EGLR 192 .... 60, 62
China & South Sea Bank Ltd v Tan Soon Gin [1990] 1 AC 536 64
Chong v Scott Collins & Co (1954) 164 EG 662 28
CIL Securities Ltd v Briant Champion Long [1993] 2 EGLR 164 .... 31, 179
Collard v Saunders (1972) 221 EG 797 .... 156, 163
Commercial Financial Services Ltd v McBeth & Co January 15 1988, Court
  of Session, unreported 42, 200, 206
Commercial & General Acceptance Ltd v Nixon (1981) 152 CLR 491 63
Computastaff Ltd v Ingledew Brown Bennison & Garrett (1983)
  268 EG 906 .... 60, 62, 231
Conn v Munday (1955) 166 EG 465 28
Corfield v DS Bosher & Co [1992] 1 EGLR 163 179
Corisand Investments Ltd v Druce & Co (1978) 248 EG 315 .... 28, 43, 109, 110,
                                                    115, 123, 145, 165, 169, 172, 173
County Personnel (Employment Agency) Ltd v Alan R Pulver [1987] 1 All
  ER 289; [1986] 2 EGLR 246 .... 149, 179
Craneheath Securities Ltd v York Montague Ltd [1994] 1 EGLR 159
  .... 5, 42, 119, 227
Cross v David Martin & Mortimer [1989] 1 EGLR 154 .... 10, 98, 102, 108,
                                                           140, 156, 161
CTI v Oceanus Mutual Underwriting Association (Bermuda) [1984] 1 Lloyd's
  Rep 476 237
Cuckmere Brick Co Ltd v Mutual Finance Ltd [1971] Ch 949 .... 63, 176

Curran v Northern Ireland Co-Ownership Housing Association Ltd (1986)
8 NIJB 1 .... 47, 55, 57

D

Daisley v BS Hall & Co (1972) 225 EG 1553 .... 101, 152, 153
Darlington BC v Waring & Gillow (Holdings) Ltd [1988] 2 EGLR 159 21
Davies v Idris Parry [1988] 1 EGLR 147 .... 47, 127, 205, 210, 217, 218
Davies v Swan Motor Co (Swansea) Ltd [1949] 2 KB 291 214
Davis v Sprott & Sons (1960) 177 EG 9 35
Debenham v King's College, Cambridge (1884) 1 TLR 170 24
Derry v Peek (1889) 14 App Cas 337 .... 35, 244
Donoghue v Stevenson [1932] AC 562 35
Downsview Nominees Ltd v First City Corporation Ltd [1993] AC 295 64
Drew v Josolyne (1888) 4 TLR 717 24
Drinnan v CW Ingram & Sons 1967 SLT 205 .... 139, 159, 164, 193
Duncan v Gumleys [1987] 2 EGLR 263 146
Duquemin v Reynolds (1987) JLR 259 128

E

Eagle Star Insurance Co Ltd v Gale and Power (1955) 166 EG 37 174
Eley v King & Chasemore [1989] 1 EGLR 181 .... 78, 99, 103
English Exporters (London) v Eldonwall [1973] Ch 415 83
ERAS EIL appeals (Re) [1992] 2 All ER 82 .... 29, 186
Esso Petroleum Co Ltd v Mardon [1976] QB 801 29
European Partners in Capital (EPIC) Holdings BV v Goddard & Smith [1992]
2 EGLR 155 .... 42, 87, 88
Ezekiel v McDade
[1994] EGCS 194, CA 155, 158, 159, 163
[1994] 1 EGLR 255 .... 120, 163

F

Faraday v Tamworth Union (1917) 86 LJCh 436 24
Farthing v Tomkins (1893) 9 TLR 566 24
Felton v Gaskill Osbourne & Co [1993] 2 EGLR 176 .... 182, 190
First National Commercial Bank plc v Humberts (1993) 10 Const LJ 141 183
Fisher v Knowles (1982) 262 EG 1083 .... 10, 31, 77
Footner v Joseph (1859) 3 LCJ 233; 5 LCJ 225 24
Ford v White & Co [1964] 2 All ER 755 153
Forsikringsaktieselskapet Vesta v Butcher [1989] AC 852, HL 29
[1988] 2 All ER 43, CA; [1986] 2 All ER 488 215
Forster v Outred & Co [1982] 2 All ER 753 183
Francis v Harris [1989] 1 EGLR 45 23
Freeman v Marshall & Co (1966) 200 EG 77 .... 41, 66, 74, 157
Fryer v Bunney (1982) 263 EG 158 .... 94, 157, 158

G

Garland v Ralph Pay and Ransom (1984) 271 EG 106 .... 63, 176
Gibbs v Arnold Son & Hockley [1989] 2 EGLR 154 ...... 53, 120, 126, 156, 157
Goodwin v Phillips June 17 1994, Official Referees' Business, unreported ... 162

GP & P Ltd v Bulcraig & Davis [1988] 1 EGLR 138 228
Graham & Baldwin v Taylor, Son & Davis (1965) 109 SJ 793 25
Gran Gelato Ltd v Richcliff (Group) Ltd [1992] Ch 560; [1992] 1 EGLR
  297 .... 60, 62
Greater Nottingham Co-operative Society Ltd v Cementation Piling &
  Foundations Ltd [1989] QB 71 30
Green v Ipswich BC [1988] 1 EGLR 239 .... 47, 124, 210
Gross Fine & Krieger Chalfen v Clifton (1974) 232 EG 837 24
Gurd v A Cobden Soar & Son (1951) 157 EG 415 .... 3, 44, 101

H

Hacker v Thomas Deal & Co [1991] 2 EGLR 161 .... 31, 95, 158, 159
Hadden v City of Glasgow DC 1986 SLT 557 .... 8, 9, 48, 57, 200
Halford v Brookes [1991] 3 All ER 559 .... 189, 190
Halifax Building Society v Edell [1992] Ch 436 .... 7, 57
Hardy v Wamsley-Lewis (1967) 203 EG 1039 .... 93, 154, 155
Harmer v Cornelius (1858) 5 CB (NS) 236 11
Harris v Wyre Forest DC
  [1990] 1 AC 831; [1989] 1 EGLR 169, HL 9, 31, 37, 39, 44, 48, 49, 50,
      51, 52, 54, 56, 57, 81, 125, 203, 204, 205, 206, 207, 208, 209, 210, 211
  [1988] QB 835; [1988] 1 EGLR 132, CA 37, 48, 54, 55, 204
Hayes v Dodd [1990] 2 All ER 815 161
Heatley v William H Brown Ltd [1992] 1 EGLR 289   31, 78, 145, 155, 156, 158, 163
Hedley Byrne & Co Ltd v Heller & Partners Ltd [1964] AC 465 .... 29, 32, 34, 36,
                                          40, 42, 45, 54, 199, 200, 217
Henderson v Merrett Syndicates Ltd [1994] 3 All ER 506 .... 31, 32, 33
Henley v Cloke & Sons [1991] 2 EGLR 141 .... 53, 111, 127, 128, 158, 210
Heywood v Wellers [1976] QB 446 .... 26, 159
Hill v Debenham Tewson and Chinnocks (1958) 171 EG 835 .... 28, 156, 157
Hingorani v Blower (1975) 238 EG 883 .... 102, 154
Hipkins v Jack Cotton Partnership [1989] 2 EGLR 157 .... 105, 150, 158
Hiron v Pynford South Ltd [1992] 2 EGLR 138 29
HIT Finance Ltd v Lewis & Tucker Ltd [1993] 2 EGLR 231 . 42, 137, 145, 164, 168,
                                    169, 170, 171, 172, 223, 224, 225, 226
Hooberman v Salter Rex [1985] 1 EGLR 144 .... 97, 152, 158
Hood v Shaw (1960) 176 EG 1291 156
Horbury v Craig Hall & Rutley [1991] EGCS 81 .... 31, 182, 188, 190, 191
Howard v Horne & Sons [1990] 1 EGLR 272 .... 31, 108, 152
Hunter v J & E Shepherd 1992 SLT 1096 156
Hutchinson v Harris (1978) 10 BLR 19 .... 27, 28, 161

I

Investors in Industry Ltd v South Bedfordshire District Council [1986] 1 All
  ER 787 81
Iron Trades Mutual Insurance Co Ltd v JK Buckenham Ltd [1990] 1 All
  ER 808 186

J

Jarvis v Swan Tours Ltd [1973] 1 QB 233 159

JEB Fasteners Ltd v Marks Bloom & Co [1983] 1 All ER 583 135
Jenkins v Betham (1855) 15 CB 167 122
Johnson v Ribbins (1975) 235 EG 737 . . . . 63, 115
Jones v Sherwood Computer Services plc [1992] 2 All ER 170 21
Jowitt v Woolwich Equitable Building Society December 14 1987, Official
 Referees' Business, unreported 129

K

Kelner v Baxter (1866) LR 2 CP 174 65
Kendall Wilson Securities v Barraclough [1986] 1 NZLR 576 . . . . 66, 136, 225
Kenney v Hall, Pain & Foster (1976) 239 EG 355 . . . 6, 23, 75, 134, 136, 137, 177
Kerridge v James Abbott & Partners [1992] 2 EGLR 162 . . . . 11, 62, 82, 96
Kitney v Jones Lang Wootton [1988] 1 EGLR 145 . . . . 31, 183, 184
Knight v Lawrence [1991] 1 EGLR 143 178
Kofi Sunkersette Obu v Strauss & Co [1951] AC 243 22
Kooragang Investments Pty Ltd v Richardson & Wrench Ltd [1982] AC
 462 . . . . 68, 70
K/S Norjarl A/S v Hyundai Heavy Industries Co Ltd [1992] QB 863 14

L

Lancashire & Cheshire Association of Baptist Churches Inc v Howard
 & Seddon Partnership [1993] 3 All ER 467 29
Langham House Developments Ltd v Brompton Securities Ltd (1980) 256
 EG 719 20
Laserbore Ltd v Morrison Biggs Wall Ltd [1993] CILL 896 83
Last v Post (1952) 159 EG 240 28
Lawrence v Hampton & Sons (1964) 190 EG 107 101
Le Lievre v Gould [1893] 1 QB 491 . . . . 35, 40, 42
Lee v Thompson [1989] 2 EGLR 151 . . . . 29, 183
Leigh v Unsworth (1972) 230 EG 501 . . . . 31, 101
L'Estrange v F Graucob Ltd [1934] 2 KB 394 199
Liesbosch v Edison [1933] AC 449 162
Lister v Romford Ice and Cold Storage Co Ltd [1957] AC 555 29
Lloyd v Butler [1990] 2 EGLR 155 . . . . 53, 127
Lloyd v Grace, Smith & Co [1912] AC 716 67
London & South of England Building Society v Stone (1983) 267 EG 69 . 31, 140,
 173, 174, 175, 176
Love v Mack (1905) 92 LT 345 . . . . 5, 35, 42, 114
Lowy v Woodroffe, Buchanan and Coulter (1950) 156 EG 375 198
Lucas v Ogden [1988] 2 EGLR 176 31
Luxmoore-May v Messenger May Baverstock [1990] 1 All ER 1067; [1990]
 1 EGLR 21 72

M

Macey v Debenham Tewson & Chinnocks [1993] 1 EGLR 149 113
McCullagh v Lane Fox & Partners Ltd [1994] 1 EGLR 48 . . . . 60, 62
McIntyre v Herring Son & Daw [1988] 1 EGLR 231 . . . . 31, 71, 80
McNaughton (James) Papers Group Ltd v Hicks Anderson & Co [1991]
 2 QB 113 . . . . 38, 40

Manson v Baillie (1855) 2 Macq 80 23
Marder v Sautelle and Hicks [1988] 2 EGLR 187 .... 142, 143
Mariola Marine Corporation v Lloyd's Register of Shipping [1990] 1 Lloyd's
  Rep 547 40
Martin v Bell-Ingram 1986 SLT 575 .... 48, 156, 158, 201
Master (Andrew) Hones Ltd v Cruikshank and Fairweather [1980] RPC 16 73
Matto v Rodney Broom Associates [1994] 2 EGLR 163 .... 78, 105, 106, 111
Mayer v Pluck (1971) 223 EG 219 62
Melrose v Davidson & Robertson 1993 SLT 611 .... 9, 53, 212
Michael v Ensoncraft Ltd [1990] EGCS 156 161
Midland Bank Trust Co Ltd v Hett, Stubbs & Kemp [1979] Ch 384 ... 29, 32, 181
Miller v Beal (1879) 27 WR 403 23
Miller (Thomas) & Co v Richard Saunders & Partners [1989] 1
  EGLR 267 .... 132, 133, 134
Miro Properties Ltd v J Trevor & Sons [1989] 1 EGLR 151 .... 41, 65, 66
Mondel v Steel (1841) 8 M&W 858 27
Moneypenny v Hartland (1826) 1 C & P 352 .... 26, 28
Moore (DW) & Co Ltd v Ferrier [1988] 1 All ER 400 29
Morgan v Perry (1973) 229 EG 1737 .... 102, 139, 144, 152, 154, 156
Mortgage Express Ltd v Bowerman & Partners [1994] 2 EGLR 156 168
Moss v Heckingbottom (1958) 172 EG 207 .... 77, 90, 158
Mount Banking Corporation Ltd v Brian Cooper & Co [1992] 2
  EGLR 142 .... 5, 43, 82, 111, 112, 114, 115, 133, 165
Muldoon v Mays of Lilliput [1993] 1 EGLR 43 113

N

Nash v Eli Lilly & Co [1993] 4 All ER 383 189
Nash v Evens & Matta [1988] 1 EGLR 130 .... 47, 124
National Bank of Greece SA v Pinios Shipping Co (No. 1) [1990] 1 AC 637 ... 29
National Justice Compania Saviera SA v Prudential Insurance Co Ltd,
  "The Ikarian Reefer" [1993] CILL 838 .... 83, 85
Nikko Hotels (UK) Ltd v MEPC plc [1991] 2 EGLR 103 21
Nitrigin Eireann Teoranta v Inco Alloys Ltd [1992] 1 All ER 854 29
Normid Housing Association Ltd v Ralphs & Mansell Ltd (1988)
  43 BLR 18 .... 241, 242
North Eastern Co-operative Society Ltd v Newcastle upon Tyne CC [1987]
  1 EGLR 142 .... 18, 20
Nyckeln Finance Co Ltd v Stumpbrook Continuation Ltd [1994] 2
  EGLR 143 .... 5, 31, 72, 113, 117, 137, 140, 164, 168, 216, 217, 222
Nykredit Mortgage Bank plc v Edward Erdman Group Ltd October 1 1993,
  Mayor's and City of London Court, unreported 5, 31, 43, 140, 145, 172, 176, 225

O

Odder v Westbourne Park Building Society (1955) 165 EG 261 ...... 35, 45, 55
Old Gate Estates Ltd v Toplis [1939] 3 All ER 209 .... 35, 65, 115
Olley v Marlborough Court Ltd [1949] 1 KB 532 199
Oswald v Countrywide Surveyors Ltd [1994] EGCS 150 .... 96, 145, 154, 162
Overseas Tankship (UK) Ltd v Morts Dock and Engineering Co Ltd,
  The Wagon Mound [1961] AC 388 138

Table of Cases xix

P

Palacath Ltd v Flanagan [1985] 2 All ER 161; [1985] 1 EGLR 86 ..... 17, 18, 19
Pan Atlantic Insurance Co Ltd v Pine Top Insurance Co [1994] 3 All ER 581 .. 237
Parker v South Eastern Ry (1877) 2 CPD 146 199
Parker-Tweedale v Dunbar Bank plc [1991] Ch 12 64
Parsons v Way and Waller Ltd (1952) 159 EG 524 155
Peach v Iain G Chalmers & Co [1992] 2 EGLR 135 .... 4, 53, 82, 128
Pepler v Roger Stevens & Chance October 6 1989, Queen's Bench
  Division, unreported 105
Perry v Sidney Phillips & Son
  [1982] 3 All ER 705, CA 140, 148, 149, 150, 151, 152, 159, 153, 155
  [1982] 1 All ER 1005 148
Perry v Wilson October 20 1993, Queen's Bench Division,
  unreported 113, 119, 130
Pfeiffer v E & E Installations [1991] 1 EGLR 162 .... 31, 107
Philips v Ward [1956] 1 All ER 874 ...... 147, 148, 149, 150, 151, 152, 153, 155
Pickering v Sogex Services (UK) Ltd (1982) 262 EG 770 22
Picton Jones & Co v Arcadia Developments Ltd [1989] 1EGLR 43 22
Pinnock v Wilkins Times, January 29 1990 145
Pirelli General Cable Works Ltd v Oscar Faber & Partner [1983] 2 AC 1 29
P K Finans International (UK) Ltd v Andrew Downs & Co Ltd [1992] 1
  EGLR 172 .... 43, 118, 135, 227
Pontsarn Investments Ltd v Kansallis-Osake-Pankki [1992] 1 EGLR 148 21
Post Office v Norwich Union Fire Insurance Society Ltd [1967] 2 QB 363 242
Predeth v Castle Phillips Finance Co Ltd [1986] 2 EGLR 144 .... 79, 118
Private Bank & Trust Co Ltd v S (UK) Ltd [1993] 1 EGLR 144 ...... 5, 111, 113

R

Rajdev v Becketts [1989] 2 EGLR 144 178
Reeves v Things & Long [1993] NPC 159 146
Rich (Marc) & Co AG v Bishop Rock Marine Co Ltd [1994] 3 All ER 686 37
Robbie v Graham & Sibbald [1989] 2 EGLR 148 .... 53, 211
Roberts v J Hampson & Co [1989] 2 All ER 504; [1988] 2 EGLR 181 .... 48, 105,
                                                124, 125, 126, 158, 210
Rona v Pearce (1953) 162 EG 380 137

S

Saif Ali v Sidney Mitchell & Co [1980] AC 198 72
Safeway Food Stores Ltd v Banderway Ltd (1983) 267 EG 850 20
Samuels (BM) Finance Group plc v Countrywide Surveyors Ltd June 15 1994,
  Official Referees' Business, unreported 144
Scholes v Brook (1891) 63 LT 837: affirmed (1892) 64 LT 674 . 5, 35, 42, 116, 228
Secretary of State for the Environment v Essex, Goodman & Suggitt [1985]
  2 EGLR 168 .... 31, 182, 230
Shacklock v Chas Osenton, Lockwood & Co (1964) 192 EG 819 176
Shankie-Williams v Heavey [1986] 2 EGLR 139 .... 41, 60, 138
Shaw v Halifax (SW) Ltd [1994] 2 EGLR 95 .... 154, 157, 158
Sheldon v RHM Outhwaite (Underwriting Agencies) Ltd [1994] 4 All ER 481 .. 196
Simple Simon Catering Ltd v Binstock Miller & Co (1973) 228 EG 527 153

Sinclair v Bowden Son and Partners (1962) 183 EG 95 158
Sincock v Bangs (Reading) (1952) 160 EG 134 .... 28, 90
Singer & Friedlander Ltd v John D Wood & Co (1977) 243 EG 212 . 42, 109, 110,
111, 112, 115, 165
Smith v Carter 1994 SCLR 539 .... 41, 128
Smith v Eric S Bush
 [1990] 1 AC 831; [1989] 1 EGLR 169, HL 9, 31, 37, 39, 44, 48, 49
  50, 51, 52, 54, 56, 57, 81, 125, 203, 205, 206, 207, 208, 209, 210, 211
 [1988] QB 743; [1987] 1 EGLR 157, CA 47, 48, 204
Smith v South Wales Switchgear Co Ltd [1978] 1 All ER 18 199
Spencer-Ward v Humberts [1994] EGCS 129 .... 188, 189, 190
Spring v Guardian Assurance plc [1994] 3 All ER 129 37
Standard Chartered Bank Ltd v Walker [1982] 3 All ER 938 64
Stevenson v Nationwide Building Society (1984) 272 EG 663 ..... 7, 57, 210, 211
Steward v Rapley [1989] 1 EGLR 159 .... 150, 151
Stewart v HA Brechin & Co 1959 SC 306 76
Strover v Harrington [1988] 1 EGLR 173 .... 77, 78, 82, 106, 228
Summers v Congreve Horner & Co (Independent Insurance Co Ltd,
 Third Party) [1992] 2 EGLR 152 .... 239, 240
Sutcliffe v Sayer [1987] 1 EGLR 155 79
Sutcliffe v Thackrah [1974] AC 727 .... 14, 15, 16
Swingcastle Ltd v Alastair Gibson
 [1991] 2 AC 223; [1991] 1 EGLR 157, HL 43, 145, 169, 170, 171, 172
 [1990] 3 All ER 463; [1990] 2 EGLR 149, CA 170, 173
Syrett v Carr & Neave [1990] 2 EGLR 161 .... 78, 95, 150, 157, 158, 161

T

Tai Hing Cotton Mill Ltd v Liu Chong Hing Bank Ltd [1986] AC 80 30
Taylor v Brewer (1813) 1 M&S 290 22
Taylor v Yielding (1912) 56 SJ 253 20
Templer v M'Lachlan (1806) 2 Bos & Pul (NR) 936 27
Tenenbaum v Garrod [1988] 2 EGLR 178 79
Thorman v New Hampshire Insurance Co (UK) Ltd (1987) 39 BLR 41 ... 233, 234
Tilley & Noad v Dominion Insurance Co Ltd [1987] 2 EGLR 34 238
Tipton & Coseley Building Society v Collins [1994] EGCS 120 59
Tomlin v Luce (1888) 41 ChD 573; (1889) 43 ChD 191 63
Tremayne v T Mortimer Burrows and Partners (1954) 165 EG 232 157
Treml v Ernest W Gibson and Partners (1984) 272 EG 68 .... 142, 145, 156, 158

U

UBAF Ltd v European American Banking Corporation [1984] QB 713 183
UCB v Dundas & Wilson 1989 SLT 243 .... 39, 230
United Bank of Kuwait v Prudential Property Services Ltd [1994] 2
 EGLR 100 .... 5, 31, 43, 167, 168, 225
Upchurch (Nigel) Associates v Aldridge Estates Investment Co Ltd [1993]
 1 Lloyd's Rep 535 242
Upsdell v Stewart (1793) Peake 255 24
Upstone v GDW Carnegie & Co 1978 SLT 4 152
Uxbridge Permanent Building Society v Pickard [1939] 2 KB 248 67

V

Victoria Laundry (Windsor) Ltd v Newman Industries Ltd [1949] 2 KB 528 ... 138

W

Wallshire Ltd v Aarons [1989] 1 EGLR 147 .... 19, 20, 129, 130
Walker v Giffen Couch & Archer [1988] EGCS 64 161
Ward v McMaster [1985] IR 29 .... 7, 47, 57
Warwick (The University of) v Sir Robert McAlpine (1988) 42 BLR 11 85
Watts v Morrow
    [1991] 4 All ER 937; [1991] 2 EGLR 152, CA .. 91, 92, 145, 149, 150, 153, 155,
                                                      156, 158, 159, 160, 163
    [1991] 1 EGLR 150 .... 90, 91, 92, 149, 150
Way v Latilla [1937] 3 All ER 759 23
Weedon v Hindwood, Clarke & Esplin (1974) 234 EG 121 .... 123, 176
Westlake v Bracknell DC [1987] 1 EGLR 161 .... 7, 31, 47, 57, 158, 195, 196
West Midland Baptist Trust Association (Incorporated) v Birmingham
    Corporation [1970] AC 874, HL 123
    [1968] 2 QB 188, CA 123
Whalley v Roberts & Roberts [1990] 1 EGLR 164 ..... 53, 81, 126, 158, 159, 219
Whitehouse v Jordan [1981] 1 All ER 267 86
Whitley (FG) & Sons Co Ltd v Thomas Bickerton [1993] 1 EGLR 139 . 31, 178, 184
Whitty v Lord Dillon (1860) 2 F & F 67 .... 26, 28
Wilkie v Scottish Aviation Ltd 1956 SC 198 24
Wilson v Baxter Payne & Lepper [1985] 1 EGLR 141 .... 31, 145, 158
Wimpey Construction (UK) Ltd v Poole [1984] 2 Lloyd's Rep 299 73
Wolff v Vanderzee (1869) 20 LT 350 63
Wooldridge v Stanley Hicks & Son (1953) 162 EG 513 .... 3, 45
Woolwich Building Society v Taylor Times, May 17 1994 .... 242, 243

Y

Yianni v Edwin Evans & Sons [1982] QB 438 .... 1, 3, 39, 45, 46, 47, 48, 49, 50,
                                              52, 54, 123, 124, 203, 218, 219

Z

Zubaida v Hargreaves [1993] 2 EGLR 170 .... 19, 20

Table of statutes

Administration of Justice Act 1970
   s1 59
Arbitration Act 1979
   s1 20

Building Societies Act 1962
   s30 210
   (Repealed by Building Societies Act 1986)
Building Societies Act 1986
   s83 7
   Schedule 12, Part III, para 1(a) 8
   Schedule 12, Part III, para 3 8

Civil Liability (Contribution) Act 1978 226
   s1 194
   s1(1) 193, 229
   s1(2) 194, 229
   s1(3) 194, 230
   s1(4) 229
   s2(1) 230
   s2(3) 230
   s4 214
   s6(1) 229

Fire Precautions Act 1971 123

Judgments Act 1838 .... 144, 145

Latent Damage Act 1986 .... 184, 185, 188
   s4(1)(a) 185
   s4(1)(b) 186
Law Reform (Contributory Negligence) Act 1945
   s1 .... 213, 214
Law Reform (Married Women and Tortfeasors) 1935 230
Law Reform (Miscellaneous Provisions) (Scotland)
   Act 1990
   s68 211
Leasehold Reform Act 1967 80

Limitation Act 1980 29
  s2 .... 181, 184, 185, 192
  s3 180
  s5 180
  s8 180
  s10 229
  s10(1) 194
  s11(1) 192
  s11A(3) 180
  s14 192
  s14A 185, 186, 188, 189, 190, 191, 192, 195
  s14A(5)to(8) 186
  s14A(9)&(10) 187
  s14B 184, 185, 195
  s14B(1) 191
  s14B(2) 191
  s17 180
  s32 .... 194, 195, 196
  s33 192

Marine Insurance Act 1906
  s18 (1) 235

Partnership Act 1890
  ss5-8 12
  s10 69

Sale of Goods Act 1979
  s53 27
Supply of Goods and Services Act 1982
  s13 .... 11, 16, 72
  s14(1) 12, 72
  s14(2) 12
  s15(1) 23
  s15(2) 23
  s18(1) 11
Supreme Court Act 1981
  s35A(1) 144, 170

Third Parties (Rights Against Insurers) Act 1930 241
  s1 242
  s2 242

Unfair Contract Terms Act 1977	9, 48, 50, 200, 203, 207, 211
s1(1)	201
s1(3)	201
s2(1)	201
s2(2)	202, 204
s11(1)	202
s11(3)	202
s11(4)	203
s11(5)	202
s13(1)	205
s14	201

CHAPTER 1

The surveyor/valuer and the client

A Introduction

Of the various legal relationships which may arise in the course of professional work, that which exists between the adviser and the client is undoubtedly the centrepiece. However, it is important to appreciate that the word "client" in this context has a specific and legally significant meaning; it is the person or organisation to whom the adviser undertakes *by way of a contract* to provide professional services in return for some reward. Thus, while a mortgage valuer instructed by a building society might regard the prospective house buyer, no less than the building society, as a client (and might be encouraged in this by certain judicial remarks),[1] this is not what we mean by the term. Nor do we regard a person who instructs a *firm* of surveyors to inspect a property as the "client" of the individual employee who carries out this task. The client of that individual surveyor is the firm by which he or she is employed; the person who commissions the survey is a client only of the firm itself.[2]

Where a legal question arises concerning any survey or valuation, a primary task is to identify and examine any contract under which the work is carried out. The contents of that contract, or indeed its very existence, control a number of issues, of which the following are perhaps the most significant:

i The right of a surveyor or valuer to receive a fee for professional services will in practice depend upon proof of some contractual undertaking by the client (express or implied) to pay for them.
ii Before 1963, the law of tort did not provide a remedy for anyone suffering financial loss as a result of placing reliance upon negligent advice. The only person entitled to claim damages in respect of such advice was the person who had contracted (and, presumably, paid) for it. In consequence, as will be seen, plaintiffs in a number of earlier cases sought to argue that they

---

1 See, for example, *Yianni* v *Edwin Evans & Sons* [1982] QB 438 at p 456, *per* Park J.
2 See further pp12–13.

had been brought into a contractual relationship with the negligent valuer or surveyor on whose report they had relied, for example through the agency of some intermediary.

iii Although, as will be seen in the next chapter, a surveyor or valuer carrying out professional work may now owe a duty of care in tort to third parties, that duty can only be defined by reference to the contract under which the work in question is carried out. Thus, for example, where it is alleged that a surveyor has failed to detect and report on a particular defect in a property, it is essential to discover from the surveyor's terms of engagement both the type of inspection which was to be undertaken and any specific limitations which may have been agreed as to the scope of that inspection. Only in the light of that information is it possible to say whether the overlooking of the defect amounted to negligence on the surveyor's part.

iv Apart from its significance in describing the services to be provided, the contract between surveyor and client may also contain terms which seek to exclude or limit liability for negligence. The extent to which such terms can be effective is considered later.[1]

v A marked feature of recent professional negligence litigation concerning valuers (and, to a lesser extent, surveyors) has been the number of attempts by defendants to raise the defence of contributory negligence, by arguing that the plaintiff's decision to rely on the valuer's report was unreasonable. This matter is considered in detail in a later chapter;[2] for the moment we may simply note the *possibility* that the defence may be unavailable in cases where the plaintiff brings an action for breach of contract rather than for the tort of negligence.

For all these reasons, it may be of great importance both to identify the parties to the contract under which a survey or valuation is undertaken, and to analyse the terms, both express and implied, of that contract.

---

1 See pp196–212.
2 See pp213–227.

B Identifying a contract

1 Surveyor/valuer and client

As noted above, the legal position before 1963 was that a claim in respect of professional negligence leading to financial loss was available only to a client, that is to say, a person to whom the professional adviser was joined in a contractual relationship. Not surprisingly, therefore, arguments as to whether such a contract existed lay at the centre of many reported cases. However, once the law recognised that non-clients might in any event be owed a duty of care in tort, the question of a contractual relationship declined in importance and, no doubt as a consequence of this, the point received less close attention in court. Indeed, in many of the more recent cases it is impossible to tell from the judgment whether the plaintiff's claim was brought in contract or in tort; nor, if it succeeded, on what basis the defendant was held liable.

These general developments in the law may be illustrated by two particular groups of cases involving surveyors and valuers. First, there are those in which a mortgage valuation commissioned by a lender is shown to and relied upon by the purchaser. That this might create a duty of care *in tort* between the mortgage valuer and the purchaser was not recognised until the case of *Yianni* v *Edwin Evans & Sons*.[1] Prior to that decision, the purchaser could only succeed by proving the existence of a contract and, not surprisingly, many attempted to do so.

In *Gurd* v *A Cobden Soar & Son*,[2] the necessary contract was established by virtue of the fact that the defendant surveyors, who had been instructed by the mortgagee (an insurance company), insisted on payment of an additional fee from the purchaser for allowing the latter to see a copy of their report. In *Wooldridge* v *Stanley Hicks & Son*,[3] the defendants were instructed by a bank (the prospective mortgagee) in a letter, which included an express request *from the purchaser* to pay particular attention to any signs of dry rot or woodworm. This, it was held, was enough to make the purchaser their client for this limited purpose (although the judge did not consider whether the defendants would have been entitled

---

1 [1982] QB 438; see p45.
2 (1951) 157 EG 415.
3 (1953) 162 EG 513.

to charge the purchaser a fee for this service). Interestingly, however, the defendants were held to owe no duty to the purchaser in respect of their basic inspection of the property and were consequently not liable for failing to discover a bulge in a flank wall. The court refused to find that the bank had acted as agent for the purchaser in commissioning the inspection.

These cases may be contrasted with the more recent decision of the Court of Appeal in *Beaumont v Humberts*,[1] which concerned the purchase by the plaintiff of a historic house in a Dorset village. The defendants there carried out both a full survey for the plaintiff and a mortgage valuation for his mortgagees (though they were instructed by the mortgagees to account directly to the plaintiff for this). When the plaintiff brought an action for damages in respect of the insurance reinstatement value given in the mortgage valuation report, the Court of Appeal held by a majority that the defendants owed the plaintiff a duty of care *in tort* in respect of this.[2] What is significant in the present context, however, is that the possibility of a contractual relationship was not even mentioned.

Similar indifference as to the contractual situation may be seen in *Peach v Iain G Chalmers & Co*,[3] where a house purchaser brought an action in respect of a negligent mortgage valuation. The judge, in describing how the valuation had been commissioned, stated:

The [lending bank] suggested that a valuation of the property be obtained and put Mr Peach in touch with the defenders ... It seems that Mr Peach directly instructed the defenders to prepare the report. He certainly paid for it but the defenders may have regarded the [lending bank] as their clients, for they had standing arrangements to provide the bank with reports and valuations for lending purposes.

This uncertainty as to which of the parties was the surveyors' client remained unresolved in the judgment, for the court simply held them liable to the purchaser in tort.

The second group of cases mentioned above consists of those in which a survey or valuation is commissioned by a borrower with the intention that it will be shown to and relied upon by prospective lenders. Here also, the courts in a number of early cases displayed

---

1 [1990] 2 EGLR 166.
2 See p40.
3 [1992] 2 EGLR 135.

some ingenuity in discovering a contractual relationship. In *Scholes v Brook*,[1] for example, such a contract was held to exist notwithstanding that the valuer's fees were paid by the mortgagor, nor that the identity of the mortgagee was not originally revealed to the valuer. In *Love v Mack*,[2] where the defendant valuer was instructed by an insurance company (which originally intended to underwrite the mortgage loan) and was paid by the mortgagor, it was held that there was no contract between the valuer and the mortgagee. However, Kekewich J was in no doubt that, had the instructions come from the mortgagee instead of the insurance company, a different decision would have been reached.

In this area, too, most of the recent cases pay little attention to contractual issues, except where it is quite clear that the valuer has been instructed by the lending institution; where this is so, the plaintiff's case is usually, though not always,[3] pleaded as both breach of contract and negligence.[4] What is more common is to find that the valuer, having acted originally on instructions from the borrower, agrees to readdress a valuation to the lender. Where this is done, the court normally assumes without discussion that a duty of care (presumably in tort) is owed.[5] It is unusual for a contractual relationship to be established, although such a contract was held to exist in *Mount Banking Corporation Ltd v Brian Cooper & Co*,[6] where the lenders' request for a valuation crossed in the post with the valuer's report.

The only serious attempt in recent years to establish a contract between a lending institution and a valuer instructed by the borrower was that which took place (unsuccessfully) in *Banque*

---

1 (1891) 63 LT 837; affirmed (1892) 64 LT 674.
2 (1905) 92 LT 345.
3 See *Axa Equity & Law Home Loans Ltd v Goldsack & Freeman* [1994] 1 EGLR 175.
4 See, for example, *Nykredit Mortgage Bank plc v Edward Erdman Group Ltd* (October 1 1993, Mayors and City of London Court, unreported); *United Bank of Kuwait v Prudential Property Services Ltd* [1994] 2 EGLR 100; *Nyckeln Finance Co Ltd v Stumpbrook Continuation Ltd* [1994] 2 EGLR 143.
5 See, for example, *Private Bank & Trust Co Ltd v S (UK) Ltd* [1993] 1 EGLR 144; *Allied Trust Bank Ltd v Edward Symmons & Partners* [1994] 1 EGLR 165; *Craneheath Securities Ltd v York Montague Ltd* [1994] 1 EGLR 159.
6 [1992] 2 EGLR 142.

Bruxelles Lambert SA v *Eagle Star Insurance Co Ltd*.[1] That case concerned three separate valuations undertaken by John D Wood & Co for the plaintiffs, each upon the clear understanding that responsibility for the valuers' fees lay with the borrowers (who were indeed duly invoiced by the valuers). According to Phillips J, this factor was crucial:

Despite this, it is the plaintiffs' case that they entered into a contract with the defendants under which the defendants undertook to produce a valuation and the plaintiffs implicitly agreed to pay the defendants' reasonable fees for so doing. This I find inherently unlikely. Valuations of commercial properties are expensive and I find it hard to believe that a valuer would enter into a contract to produce one without express agreement as to the amount of his fees, or the basis on which they would be calculated. I find it even more unlikely that a bank in the position of the plaintiffs would make itself liable for the valuer's fees.

In view of the modern courts' general lack of concern as to whether a contract exists between the parties, the decision of Goff J in *Kenney* v *Hall, Pain & Foster*[2] comes as something of a surprise. That case arose after an employee of the defendant estate agents told the plaintiff, to whom he was trying to sell a house, that the plaintiff's existing property was worth in the region of £100,000. The plaintiff thereupon instructed the defendants to put his house on the market at that price and, having taken a bridging loan, purchased another property. When it transpired that the defendants' estimate was hopelessly over-optimistic, the plaintiff (who had been brought to the verge of bankruptcy by his expenditure) claimed damages for negligence. It seems almost indisputable that these facts would have supported a duty of care in tort, but the judge was not satisfied with this approach:[3]

When an estate agent is asked to place a value on property with a view to sale he will, in the absence of a contrary intention, be entitled to charge for such valuation; though if he is instructed thereafter to act as agent for the vendor on the sale of the property, the valuation will ordinarily be treated as

---

1 [1994] 2 EGLR 108; 31 EG 68; 32 EG 89. The plaintiffs hoped thereby to prevent their own contributory negligence from leading to a reduction in the damages recovered: see p215.
2 (1976) 239 EG 355.
3 (1976) 239 EG 355 at p 429.

part of the services rendered towards the earning of the commission in the event of a successful sale, in which event a separate fee for the valuation will be waived ... It follows that the valuations given to the plaintiff ... constituted services rendered to him pursuant to a contract, which was subject to the usual implied terms ...

2 Mortgagee and house buyer

One aspect of this contractual question which has not yet been resolved by the courts concerns the nature of the relationship which exists between a house buyer and a lending institution. That relationship will undoubtedly ripen into a contract if and when a mortgage loan is offered and accepted; however, it does not follow from this that there is a contract between the parties at that earlier stage of their relationship when any mortgage valuation which may be commissioned by the lender is carried out.

In most of the cases in which a mortgagee has been sued by the house buyer over a negligent valuation, the courts have appeared to assume without argument that any claim is based in tort,[1] even where it is clear that the house buyer has paid the mortgagee a fee in respect of that valuation.[2] For example, the crucial question is sometimes said to be whether the mortgagee can be held *vicariously* liable for the negligence of the individual valuer, rather than *directly* liable for breach of a contractual duty which has been personally undertaken. So too, disclaimers are commonly treated as non-contractual notices rather than as contract terms.[3]

Some support (albeit somewhat inferential) for the "no contract" view may also be found in *Halifax Building Society* v *Edell*,[4] where Morritt J was called upon to consider the scope of the Ombudsman Scheme, which was set up under the Building Societies Act 1986.[5] His lordship held that a House Buyer's Report and Valuation or a full structural survey, if carried out by an employee of a building society in connection with an application from an existing borrower for a further advance, would fall within the jurisdiction of the

---

1 *Westlake* v *Bracknell District Council* [1987] 1 EGLR 161; *Beaton* v *Nationwide Building Society* [1991] 2 EGLR 145.
2 *Stevenson* v *Nationwide Building Society* (1984) 272 EG 663; *Ward* v *McMaster* [1985] IR 29.
3 See *Beaton* v *Nationwide Building Society* [1991] 2 EGLR 145 at p 151.
4 [1992] Ch 436.
5 Section 83.

Ombudsman, since it would be done pursuant to a contract between the building society and the house buyer.[1] However, in relation to a basic mortgage valuation the "contract" argument was not even considered; it was held that negligence in such a case would be within the jurisdiction of the Ombudsman for a quite different reason, namely that it would constitute "maladministration" on the society's part.[2] (It may be pointed out in passing that, in cases where negligence by an in-house valuer thus falls within the Ombudsman scheme, this may provide a borrower with an attractive alternative to taking legal action, something which may involve considerable expense.)

The clearest judicial denial that a mortgage valuation forms part of a contract between mortgagor and mortgagee is to be found in the Scottish case of *Hadden* v *City of Glasgow District Council*.[3] In considering certain disclaimers which were contained in a local authority's mortgage application forms, Lord Cowie was pressed by counsel to treat these as exemption clauses and thus to apply strict rules of interpretation to them. However, the judge ruled that such an approach would be unjustified:

In my opinion, the present case does not fall into the category of contract cases. There was no contract between the parties when the particulars of the home loans scheme were given to the pursuers or even when the offer of a loan containing the "memorandum relating to advances," was sent to the pursuers. These were the documents which contained the relevant conditions and provisions which govern the present case and, in my opinion, they made it clear that the defenders were disclaiming any duty of care to the pursuers in certain respects, and they were not attempting to exempt themselves from liability under a contract.

Support for the counter-argument, that a valuation *is* carried out under a contract between mortgagor and mortgagee, is less easy to find. However, some weight might be attached to the statement of Lord Templeman in *Smith* v *Eric S Bush*; *Harris* v *Wyre Forest*

---

1 Building Societies Act 1986, Schedule 12, Part III, para 1(a).
2 *Ibid*, Schedule 12, Part III, para 3.
3 1986 SLT 557. Serious doubts were also expressed by Parker LJ in *Beresforde* v *Chesterfield Borough Council* [1989] 2 EGLR 149.

District Council[1] that "the statutory duty of the council to value the house did not in my opinion prevent the council coming under a *contractual or tortious* duty to [the plaintiffs], who were cognisant of the valuation and relied on the valuation".[2]

The strongest authority for this view is to be found in another Scottish case which, like *Hadden*, concerned the effect of disclaimers. In *Melrose* v *Davidson & Robertson*[3] the plaintiffs, who were seeking a mortgage loan from a building society, completed an application form which contained a disclaimer of liability on the part of whichever independent mortgage valuer might be instructed to inspect the property. The form also stated that the purchasers would pay a fee to the building society and would receive a copy of the valuer's report. When the plaintiffs brought an action for negligence against the valuer concerned, it was necessary to decide whether the disclaimer formed part of a contract since, at that time, the application of the Unfair Contract Terms Act in Scotland was limited to contract terms.[4]

In considering this question, the Scottish appeal court was faced by two separate arguments on behalf of the plaintiffs. It was first claimed that the society, by issuing the application form, made an offer to consider any application which was made in accordance with its terms, and that this offer was accepted when the plaintiffs signed and returned the application form. The court rejected this suggestion, on the ground that the society had given no undertaking to consider any application and could thus be under no obligation to do so. However, the three judges unanimously accepted the plaintiffs' second line of argument, namely that a contract was created at the moment when the plaintiffs returned the mortgage application to the society. The court expressly acknowledged that, since the society was under no duty to consider the plaintiffs' application, it was equally under no positive duty to them to obtain such a valuation. However, it was held that, if the society decided to commission a valuation of the property and consequently obtained a report from the valuer, the society would

---

1 [1990] 1 AC 831 at p 847; [1989] 1 EGLR 169. Lord Griffiths (at p 865) also appeared to envisage a contractual obligation of some kind.
2 Emphasis supplied.
3 1993 SLT 611.
4 See p211.

then be obliged to send it to the plaintiffs, who would in turn be obliged to pay the prescribed fee. These mutual obligations, albeit contingent, were sufficient to bring about a contract.

C Duties to the client

1 Contract terms
(a) Position of the surveyor/valuer

In considering what legal duty is owed by a surveyor or valuer to a client, the contract between them is of primary importance. The law does not require this contract to be made in any particular form – it may be written or oral, or even inferred from conduct – but there are obvious advantages in ensuring either that the contract itself is made in writing or that written evidence (such as a confirming letter) is available to establish the terms of an oral contract.

In theory at least, the standard of care and skill which a surveyor or valuer is required to show will be governed by the terms of the contract under which he or she is engaged. In practice, it is very unlikely that this contract will refer specifically to such standards, unless it is for the purpose of excluding or restricting the duty which would normally be owed.[1] However, this is not to say that a person's express terms of engagement are irrelevant to claims for professional negligence; those terms may be of considerable importance in defining the precise scope of the services to be provided, information without which the idea of "negligence" can have no substance.[2] Thus, for example, while a surveyor may be judged by the same *standard* of care and skill in all areas of professional activity, the courts recognise that what is required by that theoretical standard will differ according to whether what is undertaken is a mortgage valuation, a structural survey or some intermediate type of inspection.[3]

Where (as is usually the case) the contract is silent as to the standard of care and skill demanded, it is necessary for a term to be implied, and the nature of that implied term is well established.

---

1 See pp196–212.
2 The relevance of instructions in this context is considered at pp75–80.
3 See *Fisher* v *Knowles* (1982) 262 EG 1083; *Cross* v *David Martin & Mortimer* [1989] 1 EGLR 154.

As was stated by Willes J in *Harmer* v *Cornelius*:[1]

When a skilled labourer, artisan or artist is employed, there is on his part an implied warranty that he is of skill reasonably competent to the task he undertakes ... The public profession of an art is a representation and undertaking to all the world that the professor possesses the requisite ability and skill.

An example of the application of this general principle to the specific case of a mortgage valuation may be found in the judgment of Goddard LJ in *Baxter* v *FW Gapp & Co Ltd*:[2]

His duty was, first, of all, to use reasonable care in coming to the valuation which he was employed to make and he must be taken to have held himself out as possessing the experience and skill required to value the particular property.

In seeking to describe the hypothetical surveyor or valuer against whom a particular defendant's work is measured for the purposes of a professional negligence action, the courts have used a range of adjectives which include "average", "reasonable", "competent" and "prudent". Nothing however turns on the various formulations; there is only one standard, which was well expressed by Judge Hordern QC in *Kerridge* v *James Abbott & Partners*:[3]

[The defendant] was obliged to survey the property to the standard of a reasonably competent surveyor exercising due skill, care and diligence and possessing the necessary knowledge and experience.

It should be noted that the general principles outlined above now have statutory support. It is provided by the Supply of Goods and Services Act 1982, section 13 that:

In a contract for the supply of a service where the supplier is acting in the course of a business,[4] there is an implied term that the supplier will carry out the service with reasonable care and skill.

---

1 (1858) 5 CB (NS) 236 at p 246.
2 [1938] 4 All ER 457 at p 459.
3 [1992] 2 EGLR 162.
4 "Business" for this purpose includes a profession: section 18(1).

For the sake of completeness, it may also be pointed out that, by section 14(1) of the 1982 Act:

Where, under a contract for the supply of a service by a supplier acting in the course of a business, the time for the service to be carried out is not fixed by the contract, left to be fixed in a manner agreed by the contract or determined by the course of dealing between the parties, there is an implied term that the supplier will carry out the service within a reasonable time.[1]

(b) Position of the employer

The foregoing discussion of contractual duties is based on the assumption that there is a direct contractual relationship between a client and the particular surveyor or valuer who carries out professional work on the client's behalf. In reality, of course, this will frequently not be so; the client is likely to instruct a *firm* of surveyors and, where this is done, there will be no contractual link between the client and any individual employee of the firm. Nor, where surveyors or valuers operate as a company, are individual directors regarded as parties to the firm's contracts. However, in the case of a partnership, contracts entered into in the normal course of business are binding on all the partners.[2]

Where a firm is instructed, it is the firm itself which will owe a duty of reasonable care and skill to the client. It is suggested moreover that this duty is clearly one which is not fulfilled merely by entrusting its performance to an employee of the firm, even where that employee is selected, instructed and supervised with all reasonable care. The duty of care is "non-delegable" in the sense that negligence by the employee concerned will in itself render the firm guilty of a breach of contract to the client.

A question which does not appear to have arisen for judicial decision in the surveying context is whether this contractual duty of care is non-delegable in the further sense of making the firm, as contracting party, responsible for the negligence of any other person (ie not an employee) to whom it entrusts performance. Such a situation might arise, for example, in respect of a "consultant" whose relationship with the firm is not a contract of employment; it might also come about where a firm, having taken instructions from

---

1 A "reasonable time" is a question of fact: section 14(2).
2 Partnership Act 1890, sections 5–8.

a client, finds it necessary to subcontract the work to a specialist. This question is potentially of considerable importance because, while an employer is vicariously liable in tort for the negligence of individual employees, there is no such liability in respect of independent contractors; hence, if the firm is to be held liable for those who are not its employees, it can only be on the basis of a non-delegable duty of the type now under discussion.

There does not appear to be a single solution to the question of liability in such cases; everything turns on the nature of the term which is to be implied into the contract between firm and client, and this in turn will depend upon the nature of the work, the dealings between the parties and the surrounding circumstances. Nevertheless, it is suggested that a firm which holds itself out as competent to provide professional services of a particular type should in normal circumstances be treated as having undertaken legal responsibility for the standard of those services, regardless of the precise arrangements which it makes to secure their performance.

There is, however, an important qualification. Where a *mortgagee*, having commissioned a valuation of residential property, makes that valuation and/or the valuer's report available to a house purchaser (charging the purchaser a fee in the process), the mortgagee will be held responsible to the purchaser for the negligence of an employee but not for the negligence of an independent valuer.[1] The justification for this is presumably that, even if the valuation is provided as part of the contract between the mortgagee and the purchaser,[2] it is not such a central purpose of that contract that the mortgagee may be regarded as undertaking personal (ie non-delegable) responsibility for the way in which it is carried out.

2 Experts and arbitrators

The duty of care and skill which a surveyor or valuer normally owes to the client may require qualification in one particular area of professional work, namely that of expert determinations. Such determinations occur where two contracting parties, whose interests conflict, agree that they will submit an actual or potential dispute to an independent third party with appropriate expert knowledge and,

---

1 See pp53–59.
2 This question is considered at p7–10.

further, that they will treat the decision of that third party as binding upon them. In some cases the procedure adopted will constitute a formal submission of the dispute to arbitration; in others the third party will be, not an arbitrator, but merely an "independent expert".

In the field of real property, the most common example of this practice is to be found in rent reviews. Many commercial leases provide for the rent payable to be reviewed at predetermined intervals in accordance with specified principles, and for this process to be carried out, if landlord and tenant are unable to reach agreement, by an independent third party (often one appointed by the President of a professional body such as the RICS or the ISVA). However, this is not the only use which may be made of such third-party determinations; a surveyor might equally be asked to determine the surrender value of a lease[1] or the market value of property which the parties have agreed in principle to buy and sell.[2]

The analysis of the legal relationships arising in these cases which is most widely accepted[3] is that what is originally a bilateral contract (such as a lease) between the parties in dispute is converted by the appointment of the independent third party (whether as arbitrator or expert) into a trilateral contract.[4] Given this analysis, one might expect the law simply to regard the surveyor concerned as having two clients instead of the usual one and as owing a duty of care and skill to each of those clients. However, this straightforward approach would take no account of the somewhat special treatment which the law accords those who, by exercising an independent decision-making function, occupy a position resembling that of a judge.

The problem was succinctly stated by Lord Salmon in the leading case of *Sutcliffe* v *Thackrah*:[5]

It is well settled that judges, barristers, solicitors, jurors and witnesses enjoy an absolute immunity from any form of civil action being brought against

---

1 See *Campbell* v *Edwards* [1976] 1 All ER 785.
2 See *Arenson* v *Casson, Beckman, Rutley & Co* [1977] AC 405.
3 Though not universally: see *Mustill & Boyd on Commercial Arbitration* (2nd ed, 1989) pp 220-223.
4 *K/S Norjarl A/S* v *Hyundai Heavy Industries Co Ltd* [1992] QB 863 at p 885, *per* Sir Nicolas Browne-Wilkinson, V-C.
5 [1974] AC 727 at p 757.

them in respect of anything they say or do in court during the course of a trial ... Since arbitrators are in much the same position as judges, in that they carry out more or less the same functions, the law has for generations recognised that public policy requires that they too shall be accorded this immunity to which I have referred. The question is – does this immunity extend beyond arbitrators properly so called, and if so, what are its limits?

In a number of cases prior to 1974, the courts had given a liberal answer to this question by conferring immunity on all those who, without being formally appointed as arbitrators, undertook to make a decision which would be binding on two persons with conflicting interests. In *Arenson* v *Arenson*,[1] for example, the Court of Appeal held that the auditors of a private company, who had determined the value of its shares for the purpose of a sale between existing shareholders, could not be made liable for a negligent undervaluation. The reason for this was explained by Buckley J:[2]

Where a third party undertakes the role of deciding as between two other parties a question, the determination of which requires the third party to hold the scales fairly between the opposing interests of the two parties, the third party is immune from an action for negligence in respect of anything done in that role.

This wide statement of principle was, however, strongly disapproved by the House of Lords in *Sutcliffe* v *Thackrah*,[3] following which an appeal in *Arenson* itself led to the decision of the Court of Appeal in that case being overturned by the House of Lords.[4] Their lordships in those two cases examined the whole basis on which immunity from suit is conferred and, although the speeches contain considerable differences of emphasis, the consensus view appears to be that what matters is not so much the formal status (arbitrator or expert) given to the decision-maker but rather the function which he or she is appointed to perform. Indeed, the idea that immunity is linked to the settlement of disputes by judicial or quasi-judicial means led to suggestions[5] that even a

---

1 [1973] Ch 346.
2 At p 370.
3 [1974] AC 727.
4 *Arenson* v *Casson, Beckman, Rutley & Co* [1977] AC 405.
5 [1977] AC 405 at p 431, *per* Lord Kilbrandon, p 440, *per* Lord Salmon and p 442, *per* Lord Fraser.

formally appointed arbitrator might not have immunity in a case where what is required is merely an expert opinion and not a "judicial" process. Notwithstanding such remarks, however, it is suggested that an arbitrator would still be immune in such circumstances, a view which gains some support from the fact that the statutory implication of a duty of care and skill in contracts for services[1] is specifically excluded in relation to "services rendered by an arbitrator".[2]

As for those independent decision-makers who are not appointed as arbitrators in the formal sense, it is now settled that immunity can only arise where they are "quasi-arbitrators", that is, where they are acting as arbitrators in an informal sense. Precisely what distinguishes a "quasi-arbitrator" from a "mere valuer" is not entirely clear, but a reasonable picture emerges from the speeches in the two cases. As Lord Morris put it in *Sutcliffe* v *Thackrah*:[3]

There may be circumstances in which what is in effect an arbitration is not one that is within the provisions of the Arbitration Act. The expression quasi-arbitrator should only be used in that connection. A person will only be an arbitrator or quasi-arbitrator if there is a submission to him either of a specific dispute or of present points of difference or of defined differences that may in future arise and if there is agreement that his decision will be binding.

The emphasis placed by Lord Morris on the presence of a "dispute" was echoed in *Arenson* v *Casson, Beckman, Rutley & Co*[4] by Lord Simon, who also criticised the term "quasi-arbitrator" as tending to confuse the issue. Having stressed the significant distinction between deciding a dispute and merely answering a question, Lord Simon continued:[5]

There may well be other indicia that a valuer is acting in a judicial role, such as the reception of rival contentions or of evidence, or the giving of a reasoned judgment. But in my view the essential prerequisite for him to claim immunity as an arbitrator is that, by the time the matter is submitted to him for decision, there should be a formulated dispute between at least two parties which his decision is required to resolve. It is not enough that parties

---

1 Supply of Goods and Services Act 1982, section 13; see p11.
2 Supply of Services (Exclusion of Implied Terms) Order 1985 (SI 1985 No 1).
3 [1974] AC 727 at p 752.
4 [1977] AC 405.
5 [1977] AC 405 at p 424.

who may be affected by the decision have opposed interests – still less that the decision is on a matter which is not agreed between them.

Lord Wheatley, having denied that an all-embracing formula could be found on which to base the crucial distinction, sought instead to identify the main indicators that a person was carrying out the kind of "judicial function" which would attract immunity:[1]

The indicia are as follows: (a) there is a dispute or difference between the parties which has been formulated in some way or another; (b) the dispute or difference has been remitted by the parties to the person to resolve in such a manner that he is called on to exercise a judicial function; (c) where appropriate, the parties must have been provided with an opportunity to present evidence and/or submissions in support of their respective claims in the dispute; and (d) the parties have agreed to accept his decision.

The question whether an independent surveyor conducting a rent review might satisfy these requirements, and thus be immune from liability for negligence, arose for decision in the case of *Palacath Ltd v Flanagan*.[2] The lease in that case provided for five-yearly rent reviews to be carried out by an "independent surveyor" appointed either by the parties or (upon their failure to agree) by the President of the RICS. The lease further provided that, in determining the rent (upon certain stated assumptions), the surveyor:

(1) will act as an expert and not as an arbitrator; (2) will consider any statement of reasons or valuation or report submitted to him as aforesaid but will not be in any way limited or fettered thereby; (3) will be entitled to rely on his own judgment and opinion.

The defendant surveyor, on being appointed by the President of the RICS under these provisions, carried out an inspection of the premises (without the parties or their representatives, although he had stated his willingness for them to be present). He also invited and received from each party a written submission, which was shown to and commented on by the other party. Having completed this process, the defendant published his determination of the rent, at a figure which the plaintiff landlords claimed was unreasonably

---

1 [1977] AC 405 at p428.
2 [1985] 2 All ER 161; [1985] 1 EGLR 86.

low. They duly brought an action for negligence against the surveyor, who claimed to have acted as a "quasi-arbitrator" and thus to be immune from liability.

In dealing with the availability of this defence as a preliminary issue, Mars-Jones J confessed that he had at one time thought that the case contained all the indicia identified by Lord Wheatley in *Arenson* v *Casson, Beckman, Rutley & Co.*[1] However, on further reflection the judge concluded that the ultimate test was whether the defendant was obliged to act wholly or in part on the evidence and submissions made by the parties, or whether he was entitled to act solely on his own expert opinion. When the procedure adopted by the defendant was submitted to this test, there could be only one result:[2]

I am satisfied that the provisions of [the rent review clause] were not intended to set up a judicial or quasi-judicial machinery for the resolution of this dispute or difference about the amount of the revised rent. Its object was to enable the defendant to inform himself of the matters which the parties considered were relevant to the issue. He was not obliged to make any finding or findings accepting or rejecting the opposing contentions. Nor indeed, as I see it, was he obliged to accept as valid and binding on him matters on which the parties were agreed. He was not appointed to adjudicate on the cases put forward on behalf of the landlord and the tenant. He was appointed to give his own independent judgment as an expert, after reading the representations and valuations of the parties (if any) and giving them such weight as he thought proper (if any). That being so, there can be no basis for conferring immunity on the defendant in respect of a claim for damages for negligence in and about giving that independent expert view.

Surprisingly perhaps, *Palacath Ltd* v *Flanagan*[3] appears to be the only reported case in which an independent surveyor has sought immunity as a quasi-arbitrator. It may be that the question was intended to arise in *North Eastern Co-operative Society Ltd* v *Newcastle upon Tyne City Council*,[4] but the pleadings (which merely sought a declaration as to the capacity in which an independent surveyor had acted) did not make this clear. Scott J was

---

1 [1977] AC 405 at p 428; see p17.
2 [1985] 2 All ER 161 at p 166; [1985] 1 EGLR 86.
3 [1985] 2 All ER 161; [1985] 1 EGLR 86.
4 [1987] 1 EGLR 142.

accordingly not prepared to consider the question of public interest immunity, but confined himself to declaring that the surveyor was not an arbitrator. The judge also refused to rule positively on whether the surveyor was an "expert" or a "quasi-arbitrator", on the ground that these terms had no particular significance.

These cases aside, it has been generally assumed by both litigants and judges that, in considering the legal position of the independent surveyor, the only important question is whether the surveyor is acting as an expert or as an arbitrator; the separate category of "quasi-arbitrator" seems largely to have been ignored. This is certainly the impression given by the judgment of Lord Denning MR in *Campbell* v *Edwards*,[1] which was delivered just two weeks after *Arenson* v *Casson, Beckman, Rutley & Co*[2] had been decided by the House of Lords. In considering the effects of that decision, Lord Denning was in no doubt:[3]

Previously, for over 100 years, it was thought that when vendor and purchaser agreed that the price was to be fixed by a valuer, then the valuer was in the position of a quasi-arbitrator and could not be sued for negligence. It is now clear that he owes a duty to both parties to act with reasonable care and skill in making his valuation.

The assumption that only an arbitrator is immune from liability in negligence approach may also be seen in a number of cases involving rent reviews. In *Belvedere Motors Ltd* v *King*[4] and *Wallshire Ltd* v *Aarons*[5] it was accepted without argument that an independent expert surveyor owes a duty of care to the landlord, while in *Zubaida* v *Hargreaves*[6] it was stated by the judge (again without apparent argument) that a duty of care to the tenant was "well established". However, none of these surveyors in fact incurred liability, for none was found to have acted negligently in determining the rent.

In the light of these decisions, the crucial question is clearly "expert or arbitrator?", and the answer to this question is to be

---

1 [1976] 1 All ER 785.
2 [1977] AC 405.
3 [1976] 1 All ER 785 at p 788.
4 (1981) 260 EG 813.
5 [1989] 1 EGLR 147.
6 [1993] 2 EGLR 170.

found by construction of the terms of the relevant lease. Many leases provide expressly that an independent surveyor is to act "as an expert and not as an arbitrator", and surveyors appointed on such terms have not normally sought to argue the contrary.[1] Nevertheless, it should be noted that such words, though highly persuasive, are not conclusive; as Greer LJ stated in *Taylor* v *Yielding*:[2] "You cannot make a valuer an arbitrator by calling him so, or vice versa".

In the absence of express provision, the whole of the lease may be relevant in indicating the intention of the parties as to the status of the independent surveyor. Thus, in *Langham House Developments Ltd* v *Brompton Securities Ltd*,[3] the fact that the previous clause of the lease provided for certain other disputes to be settled by arbitration was enough to convince Megarry V-C that what the rent review provision envisaged was determination by an independent expert. In *North Eastern Co-operative Society Ltd* v *Newcastle upon Tyne City Council*,[4] a clause was interpreted as meaning that the independent surveyor would not be an arbitrator if appointed (as he was) by agreement of the parties, but would be an arbitrator if appointed by the President of the RICS on their failure to reach agreement. And in *Safeway Food Stores Ltd* v *Banderway Ltd*,[5] where a clause provided for the appointment of an "umpire" by the parties' valuers, it was held that such an umpire would be an expert rather than an arbitrator.

The possibility of claiming damages for negligence from an independent expert has assumed a higher degree of importance in recent years, as the courts have made it increasingly difficult for a party to challenge the expert's determination in any other way. Whereas the award of an arbitrator is subject to a (limited) right of appeal on a point of law,[6] the decision of an expert is virtually unimpeachable, except where the expert's appointment is itself

---

1 See, for example, *Belvedere Motors Ltd* v *King* (1981) 260 EG 813; *Palacath Ltd* v *Flanagan* [1985] 2 All ER 161; [1985] 1 EGLR 86; *Wallshire Ltd* v *Aarons* [1989] 1 EGLR 147; *Zubaida* v *Hargreaves* [1993] 2 EGLR 170.
2 (1912) 56 SJ 253.
3 (1980) 256 EG 719.
4 [1987] 1 EGLR 142.
5 (1983) 267 EG 850.
6 Arbitration Act 1979, section 1.

invalid (eg because it it out of time).¹ As Lord Denning MR explained in *Campbell* v *Edwards*:²

It is simply the law of contract. If two persons agree that the price of property should be fixed by a valuer on whom they agree, and he gives that valuation honestly and in good faith, they are bound by it. Even if he has made a mistake they are still bound by it. The reason is because they have agreed to be bound by it.

In making this point, Lord Denning raised (though without deciding) the possibility that a "speaking" valuation which contained patent errors might be open to challenge, and this view was actually applied by Nourse J in *Burgess* v *Purchase & Sons (Farms) Ltd*.³ However, the latter decision was overruled by the Court of Appeal in *Jones* v *Sherwood Computer Services plc*,⁴ where it was held that there is no significant distinction between speaking and non-speaking valuations; both are equally binding upon the parties, except where there is evidence of fraud or collusion.

The current status of expert determinations was neatly summarised by Knox J in *Nikko Hotels (UK) Ltd* v *MEPC plc*:⁵

If parties agree to refer to the final and conclusive judgment of an expert an issue which either consists of a question of construction or necessarily involves the solution of a question of construction, the expert's decision will be final and conclusive and, therefore, not open to review or treatment by the courts as a nullity on the ground that the expert's decision on construction was erroneous in law, unless it can be shown that the expert has not performed the task assigned to him. *If he has answered the right question in the wrong way, his decision will be binding. If he has answered the wrong question, his decision will be a nullity.*⁶

---

1 See *Darlington Borough Council* v *Waring & Gillow (Holdings) Ltd* [1988] 2 EGLR 159.
2 [1976] 1 All ER 785 at p 788: see also *Baber* v *Kenwood Manufacturing Co* [1978] 1 Lloyd's Rep 175.
3 [1983] Ch 216.
4 [1992] 2 All ER 170.
5 [1991] 2 EGLR 103 at p 108; followed in *Pontsarn Investments Ltd* v *Kansallis-Osake-Pankki* [1992] 1 EGLR 148.
6 Emphasis supplied.

D Remuneration of surveyors and valuers

1 Express agreement as to fees

The right of a surveyor or valuer to be paid by a client for professional services is dependent upon the contract under which those services are carried out. If that contract makes express provision as to the amount of remuneration and the circumstances in which it is to be paid, the parties will be bound by this, even if the result is that the professional receives less than the objective value of the services[1] or even nothing at all.[2] It may also be noted (although the problem arises more frequently in the context of agency work) that agreement as to fees should precede the formation of the contract for services. If this is not done, a subsequent "confirming letter" which sets out a basis for charging may not be binding upon the client (though of course the client may accept the proposal by conduct).[3]

An important restriction upon the freedom of the parties to agree whatever remuneration terms they wish concerns professional services rendered in connection with litigation. An agreement by a client to pay a "contingency fee" for such services (ie a fee dependent upon success in the litigation) is unlawful, under the ancient doctrine of champerty, and is therefore unenforceable. However, this principle is confined to activities which may genuinely be described as "litigation in a court of law". In *Pickering* v *Sogex Services (UK) Ltd*[4] the plaintiff surveyor was engaged to seek, by negotiations with the district valuer, a reduction in the rateable value of the client's property, on the basis that the surveyor's fee would be a percentage of the rates saved (if any). This agreement was held to be lawful, even though the agreement which was reached with the district valuer was then formally recorded at the local valuation court; the process of negotiation could not be described as "litigation", nor was the local valuation court a "court of law" for this purpose. A similar decision was reached in *Picton Jones & Co* v *Arcadia Developments Ltd*,[5] where the plaintiff surveyors were to

---

[1] *Kofi Sunkersette Obu* v *Strauss & Co* [1951] AC 243.
[2] *Taylor* v *Brewer* (1813) 1 M & S 290.
[3] See Murdoch *The Law of Estate Agency and Auctions* (3rd ed, 1994) pp 174–177.
[4] (1982) 262 EG 770.
[5] [1989] 1 EGLR 43.

be paid a "success fee" if they secured planning permission and certain other statutory permits for their developer clients. This agreement was held to be valid and enforceable, notwithstanding that it breached a (then current) RICS rule.

2 Implied agreement as to fees

Where there is no express agreement as to fees, a professional adviser who seeks payment must establish an implied agreement for remuneration. This seldom presents any difficulty in practice, since the courts have always regarded a request for professional services as raising a strong presumption that they are to be paid for.[1] Indeed, this presumption is now supported by statute, for section 15(1) of the Supply of Goods and Services Act 1982 provides:

Where, under a contract for the supply of a service, the consideration for the service is not determined by the contract, left to be determined in a manner agreed by the contract or determined by the course of dealing between the parties, there is an implied term that the party contracting with the supplier will pay a reasonable charge.[2]

When called upon to decide what charge would be reasonable, a court will endeavour to ascertain and give effect to the intention of the parties. Most unusually, in *Francis* v *Harris*[3] the Court of Appeal found this to be an impossible task, as the evidence of what the parties had intended to be the basis of a surveyor's fees was completely unclear. The court was accordingly forced reluctantly to order a new trial.

In a normal case, however, a judge will be sufficiently satisfied as to the parties' intentions to reach a conclusion as to a reasonable level of remuneration for services rendered. In carrying out this task, the courts have almost invariably related their assessment to the time and trouble expended, and have resisted strongly any suggestion that fees for professional services (as opposed to

---

1 See, for example, *Manson* v *Baillie* (1855) 2 Macq 80; *Miller* v *Beal* (1879) 27 WR 403; *Way* v *Latilla* [1937] 3 All ER 759; *Kenney* v *Hall, Pain & Foster* (1976) 239 EG 355.
2 What is a reasonable charge is a question of fact: Supply of Goods and Services Act 1982, section 15(2).
3 [1989] 1 EGLR 45.

remuneration for bringing about a particular *result*, such as a transaction or a grant of planning permission) should be based on the value of property to which those services relate. Examples of claims of this kind which the courts have rejected include those of an architect for designing a building (whether the building is subsequently erected[1] or not[2]), and of an estate agent for merely carrying out a valuation.[3]

A number of cases have arisen out of attempts by surveyors to argue that a professional scale of charges such as "Ryde's scale" may be taken as a measure of reasonable remuneration for acting as an expert witness, or otherwise assisting the client, in court or arbitration proceedings. A suggestion that this was the custom met with a scathing response from Lord Kenyon CJ in *Upsdell* v *Stewart*:[4] "As to the custom offered to be proved, the course of robbery on Bagshot Heath might as well be proved in a court of justice"! Other judges, while less vehement, have taken the same line.[5] Thus in *Drew* v *Josolyne*,[6] Lord Coleridge CJ said that he would never award a fee assessed as a percentage of the sum in dispute, while in *Faraday* v *Tamworth Union*,[7] Younger LJ explained: "I will not be the first to sanction judicially a basis of remuneration which, at its best, may create an unconscious bias in the mind of the witness remunerated, and, at its worst, may be attended by much more serious results". In each of these cases, the court insisted that an assessment based on the surveyor's time and trouble was appropriate.

Notwithstanding this strong line of authority, there appear to be two situations in which, even without an express agreement, a person supplying professional services may succeed in claiming remuneration on a different basis. The first of these is where it is possible to prove a binding custom to this effect. As was noted by Lord Clyde in *Wilkie* v *Scottish Aviation Ltd*:[8]

---

1 *Footner* v *Joseph* (1859) 3 LCJ 233; 5 LCJ 225.
2 *Farthing* v *Tomkins* (1893) 9 TLR 566.
3 *Gross Fine & Krieger Chalfen* v *Clifton* (1974) 232 EG 837.
4 (1793) Peake 255.
5 See, for example, *Debenham* v *King's College, Cambridge* (1884) 1 TLR 170.
6 (1888) 4 TLR 717.
7 (1917) 86 LJCh 436 at p 439.
8 1956 SC 198 at p 205.

If a person employs a professional man to perform some service and makes no inquiry as to the basis upon which the professional man is to be remunerated for this service, it is not unreasonable that he should pay for the service on the usual and customary basis. It is not open to him to complain that he is unaware of it, if he has never even taken the trouble to ascertain it before engaging another to do work for him without specifying a precise fee.

In order for a custom to bind a client, either the custom must be a reasonable one or, whether it is reasonable or not, it must be known to the client at the time when the professional services are requested. An example of the latter is *Buckland and Garrard* v *Pawson & Co*,[1] where a surveyor succeeded in claiming fees based on the value of property on proving that the client was himself a surveyor and had frequently been remunerated on this basis in the past.

The second situation in which a reasonable sum may exceed what would be justified on a "time and trouble" costing is where this is justified by the value to the client of the services provided. In *Graham & Baldwin* v *Taylor, Son & Davis*,[2] for example, an architect was retained to assist a firm of surveyors who were themselves acting for property developers in connection with a planning application. After the application had been rejected, the architect, by his sole efforts, produced an amended scheme which satisfied both the clients and the local authority. When the architect claimed reasonable remuneration for his services, it was held that this need not be assessed entirely on the basis of the amount of time spent on the work; a somewhat higher award was justified in view of the fact that the architect had, through inspiration based on professional expertise and experience, achieved the result which the clients wanted.

3 Forfeiture of fees

A question which occasionally arises in the context of a professional negligence action is whether the negligent adviser, in addition to paying damages to the client, also loses any entitlement to be paid for the advice in question. The answers given by the

---

1 (1890) 6 TLR 421.
2 (1965) 109 SJ 793.

courts to this question have not been entirely consistent; however, it is suggested that the applicable legal principles are in fact fairly clear.

The starting point is that, where negligence is such as to render professional services completely worthless, the client is under no obligation to pay for those services, and may indeed recover any payments already made on the basis that there has been a total failure of consideration.[1] In *Whitty* v *Lord Dillon*,[2] for example, the defendant engaged the plaintiff to give a "rough valuation" of the timber on a certain estate. The plaintiff erroneously included saplings, which do not fall within the definition of "timber", in his calculations, with the result that his valuation was inaccurate by some 40 to 50%. It was held that the defendant was not liable to pay the plaintiff the agreed fee, since the work was of no value to him.

Where, notwithstanding a professional adviser's negligence, the services which he or she has provided retain at least some value to the client, it appears that the latter cannot refuse to pay for those services. In *Moneypenny* v *Hartland*[3] a surveyor, instructed to design a bridge and estimate the cost of constructing it, negligently failed to investigate the ground where the foundations were to be placed and consequently gave a wildly inaccurate estimate. It was held that the surveyor, while forfeiting his fee for the estimate, remained entitled to be paid for the design, since the client could still make use of this. In so ruling, Best CJ explained:[4]

Unless that negligence or want of skill has been to an extent that has rendered the work useless to the defendants, they must pay him, and seek their remedy in a cross action. For if it were not so, a man, by a small error, might deprive himself of his whole remuneration.

It seems clear from *Moneypenny* v *Hartland* that, where a professional adviser carries out a number of separately identifiable services for a client, negligence which renders some but not all of the services worthless may justify the client in refusing to pay fees for those affected, while remaining liable for the remainder. A much

---

1 *Heywood* v *Wellers* [1976] QB 446.
2 (1860) 2 F & F 67.
3 (1826) 1 C & P 352.
4 (1826) 1 C & P 352 at p 378.

more difficult question, however, is whether (in cases where such severance is impossible or unrealistic), the client may nevertheless be entitled to pay a reduced fee on the ground that negligence has rendered the services, not completely worthless, but simply *worth less*. Such an argument has long been available in contracts for the sale of goods, where the buyer may obtain a reduction in the price to take account of defects.[1] Moreover, in *Mondel* v *Steel*[2] this principle, known as the defence of "abatement", was extended beyond pure sales to transactions which contain a work element, such as building contracts. Nevertheless, it was acknowledged by Parke B in *Mondel* v *Steel* that "the same practice has not, however, extended to all cases of work and labour, as, for instance, that of an attorney (*Templer* v *M'Lachlan*[3]) unless no benefit whatever has been derived from it".

The availability of abatement as a defence to claims for payment for professional services arose specifically in *Hutchinson* v *Harris*,[4] which concerned an action for negligence brought by the client of an architect. Although the matter had neither been pleaded nor argued at trial, the Court of Appeal gave detailed consideration to the defence of abatement and (having considered the old cases cited above) concluded that this defence could not be used to justify a reduction of fees for services which had been substantially, albeit negligently, performed. In so deciding, the court pointed out the danger that a contrary decision might well lead to over-compensation of the client. If the client were awarded damages to cover all losses flowing from the professional person's negligence, and also avoided payment of the full agreed fee, he or she would in effect (at least in financial terms) have received those services at a reduced fee or even for nothing.

Despite the large number of reported professional negligence actions involving surveyors and valuers, the principles discussed above have arisen for decision on relatively few occasions. It is not immediately obvious why this should be so, although it may be that, where the size of the fee is insignificant compared with the damages claimed, the parties simply do not make an issue of it:

---

1 See the Sale of Goods Act 1979, section 53.
2 (1841) 8 M & W 858.
3 (1806) 2 Bos & Pul (NR) 936.
4 (1978) 10 BLR 19.

either the surveyor waives a claim for fees or, if these have already been paid, the client does not press for their return. Even where a claim or counterclaim in respect of charges has actually been made, this has frequently been expressly conceded by the client[1] or has on occasion been accepted by the court without apparent argument.[2]

There remain a few reported cases in which a negligent surveyor has been deprived of fees. In *Hill v Debenham Tewson & Chinnocks*,[3] for example, the defendants' counterclaim for fees was rejected on the ground that their report to the client was "worthless".[4] So too in *Chong v Scott Collins & Co*,[5] where the defendants were ordered to return a fee which the client had already paid, it was said that the defendants' "failure to deliver a document on which a proper decision could be arrived at is a total failure of consideration". Finally, in *Sincock v Bangs (Reading)*[6] and *Buckland v Watts*,[7] where the survey of which the client complained was only one of a range of services carried out by the defendants, it was held that the part of the agreed fee which related to the survey was to be forfeited, but that the defendants remained entitled to the balance.

E Liability to the client in tort

1 The concurrent liability problem

"Professional negligence", as described in the earlier parts of this chapter, consists of the breach by a professional adviser of a duty of care which is owed to the client as an express or implied term of the contract between them. The question which now arises for discussion is whether the client may, instead of pursuing that

---

1 See, for example, *Last v Post* (1952) 159 EG 240; *Bell Hotels (1935) Ltd v Motion* (1952) 159 EG 496; *Corisand Investments Ltd v Druce & Co* (1978) 248 EG 315; *Bigg v Howard Son & Gooch* [1990] 1 EGLR 173.
2 As in *Conn v Munday* (1955) 166 EG 465.
3 (1958) 171 EG 835.
4 Citing *Moneypenny v Hartland* (1826) 1 C & P 352 and *Whitty v Lord Dillon* (1860) 2 F & F 67.
5 (1954) 164 EG 662.
6 (1952) 160 EG 134; doubted by Stephenson LJ in *Hutchinson v Harris* (1978) 10 BLR 19 at p 32.
7 (1968) 208 EG 969.

contractual claim, base an action on the tort of negligence. That question, which has provoked considerable argument during the last 30 years but which has only very recently received an authoritative answer, is significant for a number of reasons. The most important of these is that the law imposes different limitation periods on the two types of claim, so that a client may well seek to sue in tort at a time when an action for breach of contract would undoubtedly be barred under the Limitation Act 1980.[1]

Concurrent liability in contract and tort has long been established in certain areas, for example in the principle that a person injured at work through the negligence of the employer may choose to sue the employer in tort (rather than for breach of an implied term in the contract of employment).[2] However, its potential significance in professional negligence cases remained relatively slight until the decision of the House of Lords in *Hedley Byrne & Co Ltd* v *Heller & Partners Ltd*,[3] which extended the tort of negligence to cover financial loss resulting from reliance on negligent advice. Since that decision the question has been raised in a large number of cases involving solicitors, surveyors, valuers, architects and other advisers, the results of which might be summarised as a victory for the principle of concurrent liability,[4] though with a healthy undercurrent of judicial dissent.[5]

Opponents of concurrent liability have relied in the main upon two arguments: that the rights and obligations of contracting parties ought in principle to be controlled exclusively and exhaustively by the agreement which they themselves have made; and that, since certain legal rules (notably those governing limitation of actions)

---

1 See pp180–196.
2 See *Lister* v *Romford Ice and Cold Storage Co Ltd* [1957] AC 555.
3 [1964] AC 465.
4 Eg *Esso Petroleum Co Ltd* v *Mardon* [1976] QB 801 at p 819; *Midland Bank Trust Co Ltd* v *Hett, Stubbs & Kemp* [1979] Ch 384; *Pirelli General Cable Works Ltd* v *Oscar Faber & Partners* [1983] 2 AC 1; *DW Moore & Co Ltd* v *Ferrier* [1988] 1 All ER 400; *Forsikringsaktieselskapet Vesta* v *Butcher* [1989] AC 852; *Bell* v *Peter Browne & Co* [1990] 2 QB 495; *Caparo Industries plc* v *Dickman* [1990] 2 AC 605 at p 619; *Nitrigin Eireann Teoranta* v *Inco Alloys Ltd* [1992] 1 All ER 854; *Lancashire and Cheshire Association of Baptist Churches Inc* v *Howard & Seddon Partnership* [1993] 3 All ER 467.
5 See *Lee* v *Thompson* [1989] 2 EGLR 151 at p 153; *National Bank of Greece SA* v *Pinios Shipping Co (No 1)* [1990] 1 AC 637 at p 650; *Re ERAS EIL appeals* [1992] 2 All ER 82; *Hiron* v *Pynford South Ltd* [1992] 2 EGLR 138.

differ as between contract and tort, to permit concurrent liability must inevitability breed inconsistency and confusion in the law. These arguments were most clearly and authoritatively expressed by Lord Scarman, who delivered the unanimous judgment of the Privy Council in *Tai Hing Cotton Mill Ltd* v *Liu Chong Hing Bank Ltd*:[1]

Their lordships do not believe that there is anything to the advantage of the law's development in searching for a liability in tort where the parties are in a contractual relationship. This is particularly so in a commercial relationship. Though it is possible as a matter of legal semantics to conduct an analysis of the rights and duties inherent in some contractual relationships including that of banker and customer either as a matter of contract law when the question will be what, if any, terms are to be implied or as a matter of tort law when the task will be to identify a duty arising from the proximity and character of the relationship between the parties, their lordships believe it to be correct in principle and necessary for the avoidance of confusion in the law to adhere to the contractual analysis: on principle because it is a relationship in which the parties have, subject to a few exceptions, the right to determine their obligations to each other, and for the avoidance of confusion because different consequences do follow according to whether liability arises from contract or tort, eg in the limitation of action.

Notwithstanding the authoritative source of this passage, it must be said that the balance of subsequent authority, like the preceding case law, has continued to favour concurrent liability in principle, while recognising that a contractual relationship might still have some impact upon a tort claim. In particular, *Tai Hing* itself has been treated, not as ruling out concurrent liability altogether, but as deciding that, where the mutual obligations of two parties are governed by a contract between them, the law of tort cannot be used to import any more extensive obligations into their relationship.[2]

2 Surveyors and valuers

Although the issue of concurrent liability is obviously one of great practical importance in actions concerning surveyors and valuers,

---

1 [1986] AC 80 at p 107.
2 See, for example, *Greater Nottingham Co-operative Society Ltd* v *Cementation Piling & Foundations Ltd* [1989] QB 71.

it must be said that such actions have contributed very little to the debate. True, judicial remarks in support of concurrent liability[1] have far outweighed those against.[2] However, in the few reported cases where the ability to claim in tort was crucial to the success of a client's action, the possibility that such a claim might not be available does not appear to have been explicitly considered.[3] Moreover, in most of the cases where the client has adopted the common practice of pleading both breach of contract and tort, the court has simply held the surveyor or valuer liable without identifying the basis of that liability.[4]

3 The problem solved

The foregoing discussion may now be regarded as little more than a historical footnote, in the light of the recent decision of the House of Lords in *Henderson v Merrett Syndicates Ltd*.[5] That case concerned a large number of negligence actions brought by members of insurance syndicates ("names" at Lloyd's) against the underwriting agents who managed those syndicates. In relation to some of these actions, the limitation period for a claim in contract had clearly expired and, when the plaintiffs sought to sue in tort, the defendants argued that the presence of a contract ruled out such a claim. The House of Lords ruled unanimously in favour of

---

1 Eg *Leigh v Unsworth* (1972) 230 EG 501; *McIntyre v Herring Son & Daw* [1988] 1 EGLR 231; *Howard v Horne & Sons* [1990] 1 EGLR 272; *Smith v Eric S Bush*; *Harris v Wyre Forest District Council* [1990] 1 AC 831 at p870; [1989] 1 EGLR 169; *Pfeiffer v E & E Installations* [1991] 1 EGLR 162; *CIL Securities Ltd v Briant Champion Long* [1993] 2 EGLR 164; *Nyckeln Finance Co Ltd v Stumpbrook Continuation Ltd* [1994] 2 EGLR 143 at p146.
2 See *Heatley v William H Brown Ltd* [1992] 1 EGLR 289; *Nykredit Mortgage Bank plc v Edward Erdman Group Ltd* (October 1 1993, Mayors and City of London Court, unreported).
3 See *Anglia Hastings & Thanet Building Society v House & Son* (1981) 260 EG 1128; *Secretary of State for the Environment v Essex, Goodman & Suggitt* [1985] 2 EGLR 168; *Westlake v Bracknell District Council* [1987] 1 EGLR 161; *Kitney v Jones Lang Wootton* [1988] 1 EGLR 145; *Horbury v Craig Hall & Rutley* [1991] EGCS 81; *Whitley (FG) & Sons Co Ltd v Thomas Bickerton* [1993] 1 EGLR 139.
4 See, for example, *Fisher v Knowles* (1982) 262 EG 1083; *London & South of England Building Society v Stone* (1983) 267 EG 69; *Wilson v Baxter Payne & Lepper* [1985] 1 EGLR 141; *Lucas v Ogden* [1988] 2 EGLR 176; *Hacker v Thomas Deal & Co* [1991] 2 EGLR 161; *United Bank of Kuwait v Prudential Property Services Ltd* [1994] 2 EGLR 100.
5 [1994] 3 All ER 506.

will govern, not only underwriting agents and names, but all relationships between professionals and their clients.

The leading judgment of their lordships was delivered by Lord Goff, who carried out an extensive and erudite analysis of both the legal principles involved and the relevant case law.[1] Crucial to this analysis was his lordship's view of *Hedley Byrne* v *Heller*:[2]

The fundamental importance of this case rests in the establishment of the principle upon which liability may arise in tortious negligence in respect of services (including advice) which are rendered for another, gratuitously or otherwise, but are negligently performed – viz, an assumption of responsibility coupled with reliance by the plaintiff which, in all the circumstances, makes it appropriate that a remedy in law should be available for such negligence. For immediate purposes, the relevance of the principle lies in the fact that, as a matter of logic, it is capable of application not only where the services are rendered gratuitously, but also where they are rendered under a contract.

From this viewpoint, the decision (with which the other members of the House of Lords expressed agreement) was inevitable:[3]

In the present case liability can, and in my opinion should, be founded squarely on the principle established in *Hedley Byrne* itself, from which it follows that an assumption of responsibility coupled with the concomitant reliance may give rise to a tortious duty of care irrespective of whether there is a contractual relationship between the parties, and in consequence, unless his contract precludes him from doing so, the plaintiff, who has available to him concurrent remedies in contract and tort, may choose that remedy which appears to him to be the most advantageous.

In the light of this decision, there can be no doubt that a client will be able in the vast majority of cases to take advantage of the more generous limitation periods provided by the law of tort. However, one should not overlook the qualification to which Lord Goff alluded, namely that the contract between the parties *might* preclude a tort claim. This point was indeed made more explicit by Lord Browne-Wilkinson, who delivered the only other reasoned judgment in the

---

1 The judgment of Oliver J in *Midland Bank Trust Co Ltd* v *Hett Stubbs & Kemp* [1979] Ch 384 was strongly endorsed.
2 [1994] 3 All ER 506 at p 526.
3 [1994] 3 All ER 506 at p 533.

case:[1]

The existence of an underlying contract (eg as between solicitor and client) does not automatically exclude the general duty of care which the law imposes on those who voluntarily assume to act for others. But the nature and terms of the contractual relationship between the parties will be determinative of the scope of the responsibility assumed and can, in some cases, exclude any assumption of legal responsibility to the plaintiff for whom the defendant has assumed to act ... I can see no good reason for holding that the existence of a contractual right is in all circumstances inconsistent with the co-existence of another tortious right, provided that it is understood that the agreement of the parties evidenced by the contract can modify and shape the tortious duties which, in the absence of contract, would be applicable.

---

1 [1994] 3 All ER 506 at p 544.

CHAPTER 2

The surveyor/valuer and third parties

In this chapter we examine the extent to which a surveyor or valuer may be held liable to third parties (ie persons other than clients) for financial losses caused by the inadequate performance of professional services. Since, by definition, there is no contractual link between the surveyor and a third party, it follows that any action brought by the latter must lie in tort. And, although other torts (notably that of deceit[1]) may in theory be applicable, it is the tort of negligence which is in practice most likely to be invoked.

A Development of liability to third parties for negligence

The possibility of liability to non-clients, for losses suffered by them in reliance on professional advice, is generally traced to the 1963 decision of the House of Lords in *Hedley Byrne & Co Ltd* v *Heller & Partners Ltd*.[2] It may therefore come as something of a surprise that the first recorded instance of a valuer incurring such liability arose as long ago as 1888. In *Cann* v *Willson*[3] the owner of certain property, who wished to raise money by mortgaging it, commissioned a valuation of the property from the defendant and instructed him to send this report directly to the solicitors acting for the intended mortgagee. The solicitors, having made clear to the defendant the purpose for which the valuation was required, passed the information to their client, who relied on it in agreeing to lend on the security of the property. When the mortgagor defaulted and the property proved to be worth much less than the defendant's valuation of it, the plaintiff sued the defendant for the money which had been lent and lost. Chitty J upheld this claim on two alternative grounds: that the defendant's "recklessness" was sufficient to constitute fraud and (more importantly in the present context) that the circumstances were such as to impose a duty on the defendant

---

1 See *Alliance & Leicester Building Society* v *Edgestop Ltd (No 3)* [1994] 2 EGLR 229; p69.
2 [1964] AC 465.
3 (1888) 39 ChD 39.

to use reasonable care in preparing his report.

Not surprisingly, perhaps, *Cann v Willson* proved to be too far ahead of its time. Chitty J's extended view of what might constitute fraud was soon overturned by the House of Lords in *Derry v Peek*,[1] and their lordships' decision in that case was also seen by judges as denying that there could ever be liability in tort for financial loss resulting from a negligent statement. In consequence, Romer J in *Scholes v Brook*[2] regarded *Cann v Willson* as an extremely doubtful decision, and it was soon specifically overruled. The Court of Appeal in *Le Lievre v Gould*[3] declined merely to distinguish *Cann v Willson*,[4] but emphatically declared it to be no longer law.

For the next three-quarters of a century, English law reverted to the orthodox view, namely that a surveyor or valuer's duty of care was owed only to those with whom there was a contractual relationship. In the absence of such a contract, it mattered not that the defendant actually knew that an identified plaintiff intended to rely on a report, as where a report was commissioned by a mortgagor to show to the mortgagee.[5] Nor did it make any difference that the defendant's fee for professional services would ultimately (though indirectly) be paid by the plaintiff, as in the common case of a house buyer paying for a mortgage valuation.[6] Moreover, the revolutionary decision of the House of Lords in *Donoghue v Stevenson*[7] appeared to be of no assistance to the plaintiff in this context, for it was held that this applied only to cases of physical injury; it could not therefore be extended to cover financial losses suffered by one who entered into some transaction in reliance on a negligently prepared report.[8]

The hardship and apparent injustice which might result from these restrictive principles was not alleviated until after 1963, when the House of Lords reached its seminal decision in *Hedley Byrne & Co*

---

1 (1889) 14 App Cas 337.
2 (1891) 63 LT 837; affirmed (1892) 64 LT 674.
3 [1893] 1 QB 491.
4 Which it might easily have done on the ground of foreseeability: see p40.
5 *Scholes v Brook* (1891) 63 LT 837 (where the plaintiff in fact succeeded in establishing the existence of a contract); *Love v Mack* (1905) 92 LT 345.
6 *Odder v Westbourne Park Building Society* (1955) 165 EG 261; *Davis v Sprott & Sons* (1960) 177 EG 9.
7 [1932] AC 562.
8 *Old Gate Estates Ltd v Toplis* [1939] 3 All ER 209.

Ltd v *Heller & Partners Ltd*.[1] It was there held that, provided certain conditions were satisfied, liability in tort for negligent statements could arise in respect of financial loss as well as physical injury or damage. More specifically, their lordships stated that *Cann* v *Willson* had been correctly decided after all, a ruling which clearly opened the way for a range of claims against surveyors and valuers.

B Basis of liability to third parties for negligence

The House of Lords in *Hedley Byrne* v *Heller* unanimously agreed that a duty of care in respect of words must be more narrowly defined than that in respect of deeds, in view of the risk that a defendant might otherwise be exposed to liability "in an indeterminate amount for an indefinite time to an indeterminate class". This risk arose because, as Lord Pearce pointed out:[2] "Words are more volatile than deeds. They travel fast and far afield. They are used without being expended and take effect in combination with innumerable facts and other words." In recognition of this, the House stated that a duty of care would not automatically arise merely because a defendant could foresee that the plaintiff might rely on what was said; it would arise only where there was a "special relationship" between the parties.

In seeking to describe those attributes which would render a relationship "special" for this purpose, the House of Lords did not speak with one voice. Lord Devlin, for example, took a restrictive line by insisting that the relationship must be "equivalent to contract".[3] However, one idea which appeared to gain majority support was that of a "voluntary assumption of responsibility" by the defendant. Thus, in contrast with physical acts, in respect of which the law simply *imposed* a duty of care, it appeared that words would come within the tort of negligence only where the person uttering them made it clear that some responsibility for their accuracy was being undertaken.

If the law were really to insist on a voluntary assumption of responsibility in any subjective sense before imposing a duty of care on a defendant, this would have a number of important

---

1 [1964] AC 465.
2 [1964] AC 465 at p 534.
3 [1964] AC 465 at p 528.

consequences, not least that the mere presence of a disclaimer would probably be sufficient to indicate that no such responsibility was being assumed. An argument to this effect was indeed accepted by the Court of Appeal in *Harris* v *Wyre Forest District Council*,[1] where it enabled a local authority to avoid liability for a negligent in-house mortgage valuation. However, when that case reached the House of Lords,[2] the Court of Appeal's decision was reversed, and Lord Griffiths explained[3] that the phrase "voluntary assumption of responsibility" was not to be interpreted literally. It could, he said, "only have real meaning if it is understood as referring to the circumstances in which the law will deem the maker of the statement to have assumed responsibility to the person who acts on the advice". This more realistic approach has since been cited with approval on several occasions, notably by the House of Lords in *Caparo Industries plc* v *Dickman*[4] and *Spring* v *Guardian Assurance plc*.[5]

Having thus rejected the idea of "voluntary assumption of responsibility" as the test of a duty of care in respect of statements, Lord Griffiths suggested[6] that the true legal principle is that a duty of care will be imposed "if it is foreseeable that if the advice is negligent the recipient is likely to suffer damage, that there is a sufficiently proximate relationship between the parties and that is it just and reasonable to impose the liability". It now appears that this threefold test, which is commonly used by the courts in other cases where the existence of a duty of care is disputed, is regarded as perfectly applicable to negligent statements, and that it is not thought necessary to have different tests for words and deeds. Indeed, the Court of Appeal recently adopted it as the appropriate test in a case where reliance on a survey, which had been negligently carried out by a marine surveyor employed by a classification society, was alleged to have led to physical damage (loss of cargo in a shipwreck).[7]

---

1 [1988] QB 835; [1988] 1 EGLR 132.
2 *Smith* v *Eric S Bush; Harris* v *Wyre Forest District Council* [1990] 1 AC 831.
3 [1990] 1 AC 831 at p 862.
4 [1990] 2 AC 605 at pp 628, 637.
5 [1994] 3 All ER 129.
6 [1990] 1 AC 831 at p 865.
7 *Marc Rich & Co AG* v *Bishop Rock Marine Co Ltd* [1994] 3 All ER 686: see also *Al-Saudi Banque* v *Clarke Pixley* [1990] Ch 313 at p332.

Practitioners may object that, while it is all very well to speak in terms of "foreseeability", "proximity" and what is "just and reasonable", these vague expressions give little indication as to what may be regarded as important in particular factual situations. Such objectors may find greater assistance in the assertion of Lord Oliver in *Caparo Industries plc v Dickman*,[1] that a duty of care is typically held to exist where:

(1) the advice is required for a purpose, whether particularly specified or generally described, which is made known, either actually or inferentially, to the adviser at the time when the advice is given;
(2) the adviser knows, either actually or inferentially, that his advice will be communicated to the advisee, either specifically or as a member of an ascertainable class, in order that it should be used by the advisee for that purpose;
(3) it is known, either actually or inferentially, that the advice so communicated is likely to be acted on by the advisee for that purpose without independent inquiry; and
(4) it is so acted on by the advisee to his detriment.

This passage received close scrutiny in *James McNaughton Papers Group Ltd v Hicks Anderson & Co*,[2] a case which, like *Caparo*, concerned the negligent auditing of company accounts. Neill LJ, adopting an approach which may well be followed in future negligent statement cases, suggested that the question of a duty of care should be examined under a series of (overlapping) headings:

(1) the purpose for which the statement was made;
(2) the purpose for which the statement was communicated;
(3) the relationship between the adviser, the advisee and any relevant third party;
(4) the size of any class to which the advisee belongs;
(5) the state of knowledge of the adviser; and
(6) reliance by the advisee.

Lord Oliver, in the passage from *Caparo v Dickman* cited above, makes repeated reference to what the adviser knows "actually or inferentially". This raises an important issue in the present context,

---

1 [1990] 2 AC 605 at p 638.
2 [1991] 2 QB 113 at pp125–127.

namely whether the law draws any distinction between a surveyor or valuer who *actually* knows that a report will be relied upon by a non-client and one who merely *ought* to realise that this is likely to happen. If there is no such distinction, there might be some substance in the fears which are sometimes expressed by practitioners of potential liability to anyone who in fact relies on a report, even one which is passed on by a third party or is discovered lying on a desk in the adviser's office. However, such a conclusion might be open to the objection that it would effectively base a duty of care on foreseeability alone, and would thus ignore the other relevant factors of "proximity" and "just and reasonableness".

Common sense suggests that a plaintiff seeking to establish a duty of care will be on stronger ground where the defendant can be proved to have actual knowledge. Indeed, while a Scottish court has held it sufficient for a plaintiff to allege that valuers "knew or ought to have known" of likely reliance by a particular plaintiff,[1] most of the cases discussed in the remainder of this chapter have concerned a valuer or surveyor who in fact knew that a third party was likely to place reliance on their report. Moreover, some indication of the task facing a plaintiff who cannot prove actual knowledge may be found in the speech of Lord Griffiths in *Smith* v *Eric S Bush*; *Harris* v *Wyre Forest District Council*.[2] His lordship, in holding that a valuer instructed by a mortgagee owed a duty of care to a house buyer who relied on his report, was at pains to emphasise the limits of that ruling:[3]

I would certainly wish to stress that, in cases where the advice has not been given for the specific purpose of the recipient acting upon it, it should only be in cases when the adviser knows that there is a high degree of probability that some other identifiable person will act upon the advice that a duty of care should be imposed. It would impose an intolerable burden upon those who give advice in a professional or commercial context if they were to owe a duty not only to those to whom they give the advice but to any other person who might choose to act upon it.

---

1 *UCB* v *Dundas & Wilson* 1989 SLT 243.
2 [1990] 1 AC 831; [1989] 1 EGLR 169.
3 [1990] 1 AC 831 at p865: see also *Yianni* v *Edwin Evans & Sons* [1982] QB 438 at p456; p47.

It is worth emphasising at this point that, while foreseeability alone is not enough to establish a duty of care, lack of foreseeability will prove fatal to any claim. This point was acknowledged by the Court of Appeal in *Beaumont* v *Humberts*,[1] where the judges were in fact divided on the question of whether the defendant should have realised that his report would be relied upon by the plaintiff. It also formed the basis of the decision in *Le Lievre* v *Gould*,[2] where the defendant surveyor was employed by a builder to issue a series of certificates as to the progress of certain building works. Without the defendant's knowledge (either actual or constructive), the builder passed on these certificates to the plaintiff, a mortgagee of the land in question, who thereupon advanced instalments of the mortgage loan. In these circumstances it was held by the Court of Appeal that no duty of care was owed by the defendant to the plaintiff, a decision which was subsequently approved by a majority of the House of Lords in *Hedley Byrne & Co Ltd* v *Heller & Partners Ltd*.[3]

If there is a single thread running through the cases on negligent statements which have been decided since *Hedley Byrne* v *Heller*, it is perhaps the importance which the courts attach to whether the relevant statement was made with a particular identifiable transaction in mind. It is, for example, precisely because a company's audited accounts may be relied on by so many different persons for so many different purposes that the courts have refused to treat the auditors as owing a duty of care to individual shareholders[4] or creditors.[5] Similarly, while it is reasonably foreseeable that a prospective purchaser of a yacht may rely on the vessel's latest classification survey in deciding whether or not to purchase, it has been held that there is not sufficient proximity between the surveyor and the purchaser to impose a duty of care.[6] By contrast, where a survey or valuation is carried out on behalf of an identified individual, the courts have usually been prepared to extend the surveyor's duty of care to a limited company controlled

---

1 [1990] 2 EGLR 166.
2 [1893] 1 QB 491.
3 [1964] AC 465.
4 *Caparo Industries plc* v *Dickman* [1990] 2 AC 605; *James McNaughton Papers Group Ltd* v *Hicks Anderson & Co* [1991] 2 QB 113.
5 *Al-Saudi Banque* v *Clark Pixley* [1990] Ch 313.
6 *Mariola Marine Corporation* v *Lloyd's Register of Shipping* [1990] 1 Lloyd's Rep 547.

by that individual.[1] So too, where the prospective purchaser of a flat arranged for a valuation to be carried out and submitted to a building society, a Scottish court had little hesitation in holding that the valuer's duty of care extended to an individual (of whom he knew nothing) who entered the scene as a joint purchaser.[2]

A useful example of the modern judicial approach to a surveyor's duty of care, and a reminder that "proximity" means more than "foreseeability", may be found in the decision of the Court of Appeal in *Shankie-Williams* v *Heavey*.[3] That case arose when the defendant, who traded as a "dry rot surveying specialist", was instructed to inspect a ground-floor flat in a house which had recently been converted into three flats. The defendant's instructions came from the developer responsible for the conversion, but he knew that the developer wanted a report which could be shown to a prospective purchaser. In these circumstances it was held that the defendant owed a duty of care to a purchaser of the ground-floor flat which he had inspected, although that purchaser's claim failed for other reasons.[4] However, he owed no duty of care to the purchaser of the first-floor flat, who claimed to have assumed that, if there was no evidence of dry rot on the ground floor, the rest of the house would likewise be free from infestation.

For the remainder of this chapter we turn to consider how the general principles described above have been applied by the courts to specific areas in the work of surveyors and valuers.

C Liability of borrower's valuer to mortgagee

Where a proposal to lend money on the security of property is under consideration, it is highly likely that reliance will be placed on a professional valuation of the property in question. If it transpires that the property has been overvalued, the lender may well be exposed to considerable financial risk, since part at least of the loan

---

1 See, for example, *Freeman* v *Marshall & Co* (1966) 200 EG 777; *Miro Properties Ltd* v *J Trevor & Sons* [1989] 1 EGLR 151; p65.
2 *Smith* v *Carter* 1994 SCLR 539.
3 [1986] 2 EGLR 139. See also *Bourne* v *McEvoy Timber Preservation* (1975) 237 EG 496.
4 See p138.

will be unsecured. The extent to which the lender may have redress against a negligent valuer in this situation is something which has exercised the English courts for more than a hundred years.

A number of reported cases around the turn of the century arose out of mortgage loans made by private individuals (usually at the suggestion of their solicitors). Not surprisingly, as the law then stood, the line which was almost invariably taken by the courts[1] was that a valuer owed no duty of care to anyone other than a client. Hence, unless the mortgagee could establish the existence of a contract with the valuer concerned,[2] an action for negligence was doomed to failure.[3]

In recent years, the legal relationship of valuer and mortgagee has fallen to be reconsidered in the light of the legal developments brought about by the decision of the House of Lords in *Hedley Byrne & Co Ltd v Heller & Partners Ltd*.[4] Today, of course, the lending of money on the security of land and buildings is almost exclusively a function of financial institutions, and a number of successful negligence actions have been brought by those institutions against the valuers on whose reports they relied in deciding to lend. In all these cases, it appears to have been assumed by all parties that a duty of care is owed, provided only that the valuer is aware of the purpose for which the valuation is required and that it has not been provided to the client under an explicit condition that it is not to be shown to or relied on by any other party.[5] Even where the existence of a duty of care is not explicitly conceded by the defence,[6] this assumption is so much a feature of the case law that, while the evidence may occasionally show that a contractual relationship exists between the valuer and

---

1 See, however, *Cann v Willson* (1888) 39 ChD 39: p34.
2 As in *Scholes v Brook* (1891) 63 LT 837; affirmed (1892) 64 LT 674.
3 See, for example, *Le Lievre v Gould* [1893] 1 QB 491; *Love v Mack* (1905) 92 LT 345.
4 [1964] AC 465; see p35.
5 See the Scottish case of *Commercial Financial Services Ltd v McBeth & Co* (January 15 1988, Court of Session, unreported).
6 As it was in *Singer & Friedlander Ltd v John D Wood & Co* (1977) 243 EG 212; *HIT Finance Ltd v Lewis & Tucker Ltd* [1993] 2 EGLR 231; *Craneheath Securities Ltd v York Montague Ltd* [1994] 1 EGLR 159.

the mortgagee,[1] some of the judgments do not even address this issue, on the basis that there will in any event be liability in tort.[2]

In almost all the reported cases of this kind, it is clear that the valuer concerned knew the actual identity of the proposed mortgagee; it is common practice among institutional lenders to require any report originally commissioned by the mortgagor to be readdressed to the mortgagee. Even without such specific knowledge, however, the existence of a duty of care has not been put in issue. Thus, a duty of care has been conceded by valuers in respect of valuations which they addressed to "the lending principals" and sent either to solicitors[3] or to mortgage brokers.[4]

It appears that there is only one modern case in which the existence of a commercial mortgage valuer's duty of care has been contested, and even there the valuers accepted that they owed a duty to the mortgagee. In *Banque Bruxelles Lambert SA* v *Eagle Star Insurance Co Ltd*,[5] the plaintiffs made a number of very large loans to companies on the security of commercial properties. In each case the property concerned represented the company's only asset and, before making the loan, the plaintiffs relied on a valuation carried out by John D Wood & Co. In addition, the plaintiffs required insurance cover against the risk of default by the company in repaying the loan, and the relevant mortgage indemnity guarantee policies were issued by Eagle Star, which also relied on the valuations in agreeing to become involved. When, following a collapse of the property market, the borrower companies became insolvent, it was alleged that the properties on which the loans were secured had been negligently overvalued. It was held that, in carrying out those valuations, John D Wood & Co owed a duty of care, not only to the mortgagees (which they conceded), but also to Eagle Star (which they had strenuously denied).

---

1 See, for example, *Mount Banking Corporation Ltd* v *Brian Cooper & Co* [1992] 2 EGLR 142; *European Partners in Capital (EPIC) Holdings BV* v *Goddard & Smith* [1992] 2 EGLR 155; *Nykredit Mortgage Bank plc* v *Edward Erdman Group Ltd* (October 1 1993, Mayors and City of London Court, unreported); *United Bank of Kuwait* v *Prudential Property Services Ltd* [1994] 2 EGLR 100.
2 See, for example, *PK Finans International (UK) Ltd* v *Andrew Downs & Co Ltd* [1992] 1 EGLR 172; *Allied Trust Bank Ltd* v *Edward Symmons & Partners* [1994] 1 EGLR 165.
3 *Corisand Investments Ltd* v *Druce & Co* (1978) 248 EG 315.
4 *Swingcastle Ltd* v *Alastair Gibson* [1991] 2 AC 223; [1991] 1 EGLR 157.
5 [1994] 2 EGLR 108.

Authoritative support for the above description of a mortgage valuer's legal position (and a substantial obstacle in the way of any defendant who might seek to deny the existence of a duty of care) may now be found in the speech of Lord Templeman in *Smith v Eric S Bush*; *Harris v Wyre Forest District Council*.[1] Having referred to *Cann v Willson*,[2] his lordship concluded:[3]

> A valuer who values property as security for a mortgage is liable either in contract or in tort to the mortgagee for any failure on the part of the valuer to exercise reasonable skill and care in the valuation. The valuer is liable in contract if he receives instructions from and is paid by the mortgagee. The valuer is liable in tort if he receives instructions from and is paid by the mortgagor but knows that the valuation is for the purpose of a mortgage and will be relied on by the mortgagee.

D Liability of mortgage valuer to house buyer

The type of third-party liability which has generated the greatest degree of controversy within the surveying profession is one which may be incurred in relation to the purchase of residential property. Such purchases are commonly financed, either wholly or in part, by a loan on mortgage, and an institutional mortgagee such as a bank, building society or local authority will routinely require a professional valuation of the property to ensure that it is sufficient security for the intended loan. The question which then arises is whether the purchaser of the property, having relied either on the valuer's report or on the mere fact that the valuation has been carried out, has any redress in the event of a negligent over-valuation.

Prior to the developments in the tort of negligence described earlier in this chapter, a claim by a purchaser against the mortgagee's valuer could not succeed unless the evidence showed that there was a contractual relationship between them. This might be so where, for example, the purchaser paid an additional fee for a copy of the valuer's report,[4] or where the valuer received a specific request *from the purchaser* to check with particular care for

---

1 [1990] 1 AC 831; [1989] 1 EGLR 169.
2 (1888) 39 ChD 39; see p34.
3 [1990] 1 AC 831 at p 844.
4 *Gurd v A Cobden Soar & Son* (1951) 157 EG 415; see p3.

evidence of dry rot.[1] However, such cases were rare, as the courts would not readily infer that the mortgagee was acting as the mortgagor's agent in commissioning the valuation. Nor, it seems, were the courts prepared to treat the contract which undoubtedly existed between the purchaser and the lending institution as imposing any responsibility on the latter for the contents of the valuer's report.[2]

Following the decision of the House of Lords in *Hedley Byrne & Co Ltd* v *Heller & Partners Ltd*,[3] it was almost inevitable that an attempt would be made to extend the duty of care into this area of activity. In retrospect, the only surprising fact is the length of time (some 18 years) that elapsed before such an attempt was made.

1 Position of valuer
(a) Yianni v Edwin Evans

The case of *Yianni* v *Edwin Evans & Sons*[4] arose out of the purchase in 1975 by the plaintiffs of an end of terrace house in north London, which had been built at the turn of the century. The price paid was £15,000 and the plaintiffs, who were of modest means, applied to the Halifax Building Society for a loan of £12,000 on mortgage. The building society duly commissioned a valuation of the property from the defendant firm of valuers and surveyors (charging the plaintiffs a valuation fee in the process), and the defendants reported to the building society that the house was worth £15,000 and suitable for maximum lending (ie 80% of the valuation). The plaintiffs did not see this report, which they were informed was confidential to the building society; however, they assumed that it must have been satisfactory, since they received the required loan of £12,000 and duly purchased the property. Sadly, within a year the plaintiffs discovered serious structural damage due to subsidence, which the defendant's "grossly incompetent and negligent survey" had failed to detect, and which meant that the house was in truth worth little more than its site value.

When the plaintiffs started proceedings for damages in respect of

---

1 *Wooldridge* v *Stanley Hicks & Son* (1953) 162 EG 513; see p3.
2 See *Odder* v *Westbourne Park Building Society* (1955) 165 EG 261; p55.
3 [1964] AC 465; see p35.
4 [1982] QB 438.

their loss, the defendants admitted that they had been guilty of negligence in their inspection of the property and their subsequent report to the building society. None the less, the defendants denied that they owed any duty of care to the plaintiffs which could result in legal liability. In so arguing, the defendants relied strongly on clear statements in the building society's literature (which the plaintiffs had received) to the effect that no responsibility was accepted for the condition of the property; that the offer of mortgage did not imply any warranty that the purchase price was reasonable; that the plaintiffs should not assume that the property was free from undisclosed defects; and that the plaintiffs were recommended to obtain their own survey before agreeing to purchase.

In denying that these warnings sufficed to exclude the possibility of a duty of care owed by the defendants to the plaintiffs, Park J relied on expert evidence concerning transactions at the lower end of the housing market. This was to the effect that some 90% of purchasers customarily ignored such warnings and in fact relied on the willingness of a building society to lend on mortgage as an indication that the property must have been professionally valued to at least the level of the loan. In the light of this evidence, his lordship stated:[1]

I am sure that the defendants knew that their valuation would be passed on to the plaintiffs and that the defendants knew that the plaintiffs would rely on it when they decided to accept the building society's offer.

And, since the judge had already identified the defendants' knowledge of the plaintiffs' likely reliance as the crucial element in establishing a duty of care, it followed that such a duty was indeed owed.[2]

The *Yianni* case is undoubtedly a landmark in professional liability, and it is thus important and instructive to note the way in which the judge reacted to attempts by defending counsel to describe the undesirable consequences which a decision in favour of the purchaser might produce. This occurred when counsel endeavoured, by painting a nightmarish picture of the overwhelming

---

1 [1982] QB 438 at p 456.
2 As to the defendants' allegation of contributory negligence, see p218.

liability to which professional persons might become subject, to show "considerations which ought to negative, or to reduce or limit the scope of the duty or the class of persons to whom it is owed".[1] Park J's reaction was to stress the perfectly reasonable limits of the decision which he had reached:[2]

[Counsel] also submitted that if the defendants were held liable to the plaintiffs no professional man would be able to limit his liability to a third party, even if he could do so to his own client. He would be at the mercy of a client who might pass on his report to a third party and, as defects in the property he had surveyed might not manifest themselves for many years, he would be likely to remain under a liability for those defects he ought to have detected for a very long period, and at the end of that period, for an unlimited amount by way of damages. In my view, the only person to whom the surveyor is liable is the party named in the building society's 'Instructions to Valuer' addressed to him. That party, as well as the building society, has to be regarded as his client. That does not seem to me to be unreasonable, since, to his knowledge, his fee for the valuation is paid by that party to the building society which hands it over to him. On this submission, it can also be said that the surveyor's report is concerned with the valuation of a dwelling house, the condition of which is important only in so far as it affects its value at that time. It is common knowledge that in the ordinary way, the market value of a dwelling house is not static. Consequently, a valuation made at one time for the purpose of assessing its suitability as security for a loan would be of limited use.

Such reassurance notwithstanding, the surveying profession reacted with some hostility to *Yianni*, which was perceived as the thin end of a very considerable wedge of potential liability to third parties. However, support for the view that a mortgage valuer owed a duty of care to a house purchaser was soon forthcoming from other cases. In some of these *Yianni* was expressly followed;[3] in others it was not even mentioned.[4] The Scottish courts, moreover,

---

1 See *Anns v Merton London Borough Council* [1978] AC 728.
2 [1982] QB 438 at p 456.
3 Eg *Ward v McMaster* [1985] IR 29 (Irish High Court); *Curran v Northern Ireland Co-Ownership Housing Association Ltd* (1986) 8 NIJB 1 (Northern Ireland Court of Appeal); *Westlake v Bracknell District Council* [1987] 1 EGLR 161.
4 Eg *Nash v Evens & Matta* [1988] 1 EGLR 130; the decision of the Court of Appeal in *Smith v Eric S Bush* [1988] QB 743; [1987] 1 EGLR 157 (which was itself followed in *Davies v Idris Parry* [1988] 1 EGLR 147 and *Green v Ipswich Borough Council* [1988] 1 EGLR 239).

appeared to reach a similar conclusion without reliance on *Yianni*.[1]

In spite of this growing support, the decision in *Yianni* seemed open to criticism on purely legal grounds, in that the principles laid down in *Anns v Merton London Borough Council*,[2] on which Park J had placed reliance, had since fallen into increasing disfavour. Indeed, it was judicial recognition of this weakness which led to a redefinition of the requirements for a duty of care in giving advice. According to Nourse LJ in *Harris v Wyre Forest District Council*:[3]

> The circumstances must be such that the maker of the statement ought reasonably to recognise both the importance which will be attached to it by the recipient and his own answerability to the recipient in making it.

Having thus formulated the relevant legal principles, the Court of Appeal in *Harris* held that an effective disclaimer brought to the attention of the purchaser could prevent them from being satisfied. Moreover, in a ruling which appeared inconsistent with the earlier decision of the Court of Appeal in *Smith v Eric S Bush*,[4] it was held that such a disclaimer was not vulnerable to attack under the Unfair Contract Terms Act 1977.[5]

(b) *Smith v Bush*

In 1989 the apparently conflicting decisions in *Smith v Bush* and *Harris v Wyre Forest* were appealed together to the House of Lords where, in addition to resolving the issue of disclaimers, their lordships gave serious consideration to the basic question of a mortgage valuer's duty to house purchasers. The resulting decision[6] is one which deserves careful study, since it naturally represents an authoritative statement of the current legal position. It is moreover of very wide application, in view of the factual range covered by the two cases.

Smith v Bush concerned the purchase in 1980 by the plaintiff of

---

1 See *Hadden v City of Glasgow District Council* 1986 SLT 557; *Martin v Bell-Ingram* 1986 SLT 575.
2 [1978] AC 728.
3 [1988] 1 All ER 691 at p696; [1989] 1 EGLR 132, adopted by Ian Kennedy J in *Roberts v J Hampson & Co* [1989] 2 All ER 504; [1988] 2 EGLR 181.
4 [1988] QB 743; [1987] 1 EGLR 157.
5 See p204.
6 *Smith v Eric S Bush*; *Harris v Wyre Forest District Council* [1990] 1 AC 831; [1989] 1 EGLR 169.

a small terraced house in Norwich. The purchase price was £18,000, of which the plaintiff sought to raise £3,500 by way of a mortgage loan from the Abbey National Building Society. As in *Yianni*, the society commissioned a mortgage valuation from an independent firm of surveyors and charged the plaintiff an inspection fee, having first made clear (by a declaration in the application form which the plaintiff had signed) that neither the building society nor the valuer would accept any responsibility for the contents of the valuer's report. With this caveat, the valuer's report (which valued the house at £16,500 and stated that no essential repairs were needed) was actually passed on to the plaintiff, who relied on it in agreeing to purchase the property. Unfortunately, the valuer who carried out the inspection had failed to notice and report that the chimneys of the house had been left without support following the removal of chimney breasts, an oversight which was only discovered some 18 months later when these chimneys collapsed and fell through the roof and ceilings of the property.

Harris v *Wyre Forest* concerned the purchase in 1978 by the plaintiffs of a small Victorian terraced house in Kidderminster, at a price of £9,000. The plaintiffs, who needed to raise as much as possible of the purchase price by borrowing, applied to the defendant local authority for a loan on mortgage. The application form which the plaintiffs signed made it clear that, while the defendants would obtain a valuation of the property, this would remain confidential to them; moreover, the defendants disclaimed any responsibility for the value or condition of the property. The employee of the defendants who inspected the house valued it at £9,450 (which was its original asking price) and recommended it as suitable security for a loan of 90%, subject to a condition that the purchasers should undertake to carry out certain repairs. The plaintiffs, on being offered a loan of £8,505 subject to this condition, assumed that the property must have been valued at not less than £8,505 and that no serious defects had been found; they thereupon agreed to purchase it. Some three years later, however, when the plaintiffs attempted to sell their house, they discovered that it was subject to settlement, required extensive and expensive under-pinning work and was effectively unsaleable.

In dealing with the claims of these plaintiffs, Lord Templeman identified the three crucial questions which required to be answered:[1]

The first question is whether a valuer instructed by a building society or other mortgagee to value a house, knowing that his valuation will probably be relied on by the prospective purchaser and mortgagor of the house, owes to the purchaser in tort a duty to exercise reasonable skill and care unless the valuer disclaims liability. If so, the second question is whether a disclaimer of liability by or on behalf of the valuer is a notice which purports to exclude liability for negligence within the Unfair Contract Terms Act 1977 and is, therefore, ineffective unless it satisfies the requirement of reasonableness. If so, the third question is whether, in the absence of special circumstances, it is fair and reasonable for the valuer to rely on the notice excluding liability.

A unanimous House of Lords, expressly approving the decision in *Yianni* v *Edwin Evans & Sons*, gave an affirmative answer to each of these questions, with the result that the plaintiffs in both cases were successful. The approach of their lordships to the second and third questions will be considered later;[2] for the moment we may concentrate on their answers to the first question, since it is these which represent the current state of the law on a mortgage valuer's duty of care.

Although the three members of the House of Lords who delivered speeches did not adopt precisely the same words to explain why it was right to impose a duty of care, two factors were clearly regarded as critical. These were the mortgage valuer's knowledge that the purchaser was likely to rely (directly or indirectly) on the valuation, and the fact that the valuer's fee would be paid ultimately by the purchaser. As Lord Templeman stated:[3]

In general, I am of the opinion that in the absence of a disclaimer of liability the valuer who values a house for the purpose of a mortgage, knowing that the mortgagee will rely and the mortgagor will probably rely on the valuation, knowing that the purchaser mortgagor has in effect paid for the valuation, is under a duty to exercise reasonable skill and care and that duty is owed to both parties to the mortgage for which the valuation is made.

Lord Griffiths, having referred to the threefold test of foreseeability,

---

1 [1990] 1 AC 831 at p840; [1989] 1 EGLR 169.
2 See pp205; 207–210.
3 [1990] 1 AC 831 at p 848.

proximity and just and reasonableness,[1] continued:[2]

In the case of a surveyor valuing a small house for a building society or local authority, the application of these three criteria leads to the conclusion that he owes a duty of care to the purchaser. If the valuation is negligent and is relied on damage in the form of economic loss to the purchaser is obviously foreseeable. The necessary proximity arises from the surveyor's knowledge that the overwhelming probability is that the purchaser will rely on his valuation, the evidence was that surveyors knew that approximately 90 per cent of purchasers did so, and the fact that the surveyor only obtains the work because the purchaser is willing to pay his fee. It is just and reasonable that the duty should be imposed for the advice is given in a professional as opposed to a social context and liability for breach of the duty will be limited both as to its extent and amount. The extent of the liability is limited to the purchaser of the house: I would not extend it to subsequent purchasers.[3] The amount of the liability cannot be very great because it relates to a modest house.

Lord Jauncey, while agreeing in the decision, adopted a more cautious approach than his colleagues. For example, while not prepared to dissent from the majority view, his lordship expressed doubts as to whether it was correct to equate the position of a staff valuer employed by the mortgagee with that of an independent professional. More importantly, Lord Jauncey drew attention to the type of property with which both appeals were concerned:[4]

I would not therefore conclude that the mere fact that a mortgagee's valuer knows that his valuation will be shown to an intending mortgagor of itself imposes on him a duty of care to the mortgagor. Knowledge, actual or implied, of the mortgagor's likely reliance on the valuation must be brought home to him. Such knowledge may be fairly readily implied in relation to a potential mortgagor seeking to enter the lower end of the housing market but *non constat* that such ready implication would arise in the case of a purchase of an expensive property whether residential or commercial.

In the light of *Smith* v *Bush*, it now seems undeniable that, at least in respect of "modest" residential property, a mortgage valuer owes

---

[1] See p37.
[2] [1990] 1 AC 831 at p865; [1989] 1 EGLR 169.
[3] On this point see also Lord Jauncey: [1990] 1 AC 831 at p 872.
[4] [1990] 1 AC 831 at p 872.

a duty of care to the purchaser. Furthermore, the existence of this duty of care will not be affected by any of the following factors:

i the status of the mortgagee (whether a bank, building society, local authority or other person or company);
ii the size of the mortgage loan in relation to the purchase price;
iii whether the valuation is carried out by an independent valuer or by an employee of the mortgagee;
iv whether or not the valuer's report is disclosed to the purchaser.

The only limit appears to be that the duty will not extend to anyone other than the particular purchaser whose application for a mortgage has caused the valuer to be instructed.[1]

One point which remains unsettled is the extent to which these decisions can apply to mortgage valuations of property other than small dwellings. According to Lord Jauncey, it could not be assumed that a purchaser of "an expensive property, whether residential or commercial" would place reliance on a mortgage valuer's report in deciding to purchase.[2] Lord Griffiths also emphasised, when considering whether the valuer in *Harris* v *Wyre Forest District Council* owed a duty of care, that the transaction concerned a "modest house". However, his lordship did not in terms suggest that there would be no duty of care in other cases; rather, in his view, the "breathtaking sums of money" involved in purchases of "industrial property, large blocks of flats or very expensive houses" was a factor which might make it reasonable for the valuer to exclude or limit liability for negligence.[3]

Not surprisingly, perhaps, no mortgage valuer has sought since 1989 to challenge the basic principle laid down by these House of Lords decisions, that a duty of care is owed to the purchaser of modest residential property. In the reported cases which have arisen out of mortgage valuations, the existence of such a duty has been either expressly conceded by defendants or simply assumed

---

1 [1990] 1 AC 831 at pp865, 872; [1989] 1 EGLR 169: see also *Yianni* v *Edwin Evans & Sons* [1982] QB 438 at p456.
2 [1990] 1 AC 831 at p872.
3 [1990] 1 AC 831 at pp859–860; these remarks were endorsed by Lord Templeman at p854.

by judges.[1] What is more surprising, however, is that no reported case has explored the limits of the decisions (for example in relation to the type or value of properties to which they apply). Only in the area of disclaimers has any serious attempt been made to restrict the scope of the valuer's liability[2] and, as will be seen, this has met with little success.[3]

Before leaving this topic, there is one further practical point which is worth noting. The duty of care which a mortgage valuer owes to a house purchaser is quite independent of the duty which is owed to the mortgagee, and there is nothing in principle to prevent a valuer who is guilty of negligence from being sued successively by both the lender and the borrower. Moreover, while one such legal action might impact in certain respects upon the other,[4] the mere fact that damages have been paid to one party will provide no defence for the valuer when sued by the other party. In view of this risk, which is especially great where a borrower is known to be in arrears with mortgage repayments, it may be advisable to alert the lender to any proposed settlement of the borrower's action against the valuer. If this is done, then the lender may be able by legal action to restrain the borrower from using the money received for any purpose other than rectifying defects in the property or repaying the mortgage loan in whole or in part. Such action would of course reduce the likelihood of the lender taking action against the valuer.

2 Position of mortgage lender

It is one thing to hold a valuer liable in respect of a negligent mortgage valuation. It is quite another to make the mortgagee, as the one who commissioned that valuation, responsible to the purchaser for it. To do so would come close to creating a legal

---

1 See *Gibbs* v *Arnold Son & Hockley* [1989] 2 EGLR 154; *Bere* v *Slades* [1989] 2 EGLR 160; *Whalley* v *Roberts & Roberts* [1990] 1 EGLR 164; *Lloyd* v *Butler* [1990] 2 EGLR 155; *Henley* v *Cloke & Sons* [1991] 2 EGLR 141; *Peach* v *Iain G Chalmers & Co* [1992] 2 EGLR 135.
2 See *Beaton* v *Nationwide Building Society* [1991] 2 EGLR 145 and the Scottish cases of *Robbie* v *Graham & Sibbald* [1989] 2 EGLR 148 and *Melrose* v *Davidson & Robertson* 1993 SLT 611.
3 See pp196–212.
4 Eg by requiring the mortgagee to take action against the borrower in order to mitigate its losses: see pp174–176.

obligation on a lender, when considering a request for a loan on mortgage, to look after the commercial interests of the borrower, and the courts have repeatedly denied the existence of any such protective duty. As Lord Jauncey pointed out in *Smith* v *Eric S Bush*; *Harris* v *Wyre Forest District Council*:[1]

The fact that A is prepared to lend money to B on the security of property owned by or to be acquired by him cannot per se impose upon A any duty of care to B. Much more is required. Were it otherwise a loan by A to B on the security of property, real or personal, would ipso facto amount to a warranty by A that the property was worth at least the sum lent.

The same point had been made at rather greater length by Kerr LJ when *Harris* v *Wyre Forest District Council* was before the Court of Appeal. Describing the *Yianni* decision as suffering from "inherent jurisprudential weakness", his lordship stated:[2]

Suppose that A approaches B with a request for a loan to be secured on a property or chattel, such as a painting, which A is proposing to acquire. A knows that for the purpose of considering whether or not to make the requested loan, and of its amount, B is bound to make some assessment of the value of the security which is offered, possibly on the basis of some expert inspection and formal valuation. Then assume that B knows that in all probability A will not have had any independent advice or valuation and is also unlikely to commission anything of the kind as a check on B's valuation. B also knows, of course, that any figure which he may then put forward to A by way of a proposed loan on the basis of the offered security will necessarily be seen to reflect B's estimate of the minimum value of the offered security. Suppose that A then accepts B's offer and acquires the property or chattel with the assistance of B's loan and in reliance, at least in part, on B's willingness to advance the amount of the loan as an indication of the value of the property or chattel. Given those facts and no more, I do not think that B can properly be regarded as having assumed, or as being subjected to, any duty of care towards A in his valuation of the security. Even in the absence of any disclaimer of responsibility I do not think that the principles stated in Hedley Byrne & Co Ltd v Heller & Partners Ltd[3] *support the contrary conclusion. B has not been asked for advice or information but merely for a loan. His valuation was carried out for his own commercial*

---

1 [1990] 1 AC 831 at p872; [1989] 1 EGLR 169; similar views were expressed by Lord Templeman at p847 and Lord Griffiths at p865.
2 [1988] QB 835 at p851; [1988] 1 EGLR 132.
3 [1964] AC 465.

purposes. If it was done carelessly, with the result that the valuation and loan were excessive, I do not think that A can have any ground for complaint.[1]

In most of the cases in which the position of the mortgagee has been discussed, the courts have considered whether or not liability for the valuer's negligence might arise in tort. However, it appears that the arguments against imposing a duty of care would still apply if the claim were based on a breach of contract between the parties.[2] In the passage cited above, Kerr LJ continued "and if B made a small service charge for investigating A's request for a loan, I doubt whether the position would be different". Similarly, in a case in the Northern Ireland Court of Appeal,[3] Gibson LJ pointed out that "generally, a mortgage contract in itself imports no obligation on the part of a mortgagee to use care in protecting the interests of a mortgagor". And in the earlier case of *Odder* v *Westbourne Park Building Society*,[4] Harman J pointed out that, if a mortgagee were to owe any duty in its inspection of the property, logic would require it to owe a similar duty in investigating the mortgagor's title.

In the light of such judicial comments, one might assume that a mortgagee could never be held responsible to the mortgagor for a negligent valuation. This, however, is by no means the case, for the courts have identified a number of ways in which such responsibility can be imposed.

(a) In house valuations

In each of the cases quoted above, the court focused its attention upon the mortgagee *as mortgagee* and concluded that there was no justification for imposing a duty of care towards the mortgagor when the latter's application for a loan is under consideration. Such an approach, if correct, renders completely irrelevant the question whether the offending valuation is commissioned by the mortgagee from an independent valuer or is carried out by an employee of the mortgagee. Indeed, in *Odder* v *Westbourne Park Building Society*[5]

---

1 Emphasis supplied.
2 As to whether the contract between mortgagor and mortgagee includes the provision of a valuation, see pp7–10.
3 *Curran* v *Northern Ireland Co-ownership Housing Association Ltd* (1986) 8 NIJB 1.
4 (1955) 165 EG 261.
5 (1955) 165 EG 261.

it was held that the defendant building society could not be made responsible for an allegedly negligent inspection carried out by a surveyor who was also the society's chairman.

There is, however, an alternative approach to the problem, which renders the distinction between independent and in house valuations of crucial importance. This approach focuses on the duty of care which is owed to the house buyer *by the individual valuer*, and simply makes the valuer's employer vicariously liable for that negligence, provided of course that it occurs within the course of the valuer's employment. And, if that employer also happens to be the mortgagee, the arguments noted above are sidestepped.

The House of Lords in *Smith* v *Eric S Bush*; *Harris* v *Wyre Forest District Council*[1] adopted the second approach, albeit in a way which revealed some confusion of thought as to whether it was the valuer's or the mortgagee's duty of care which required examination. Lord Templeman, for example, appeared to be taking the point in stating:[2] "I agree that by obtaining and disclosing a valuation, a mortgagee does not assume responsibility to the purchaser for that valuation. But in my opinion the valuer assumes responsibility". However, his lordship then clouded the issue by suggesting that, "the council accepted the application form and the valuation fee and chose to conduct their duty of valuing the house through [the staff valuer]" and, later, that "the statutory duty of the council to value the house did not in my opinion prevent the council coming under a contractual or tortious duty to [the plaintiffs]".

A similar lack of clarity may be found in the speech of Lord Griffiths who, despite accepting that "the mere fact of a contract between mortgagor and mortgagee will not of itself in all cases be sufficient to found a duty of care", then ruled that "[the staff valuer] was in breach of his duty of care to [the plaintiffs] and the local authority, as his employers, are vicariously liable for that negligence".[3]

Confusion or not, the actual decision in *Smith* v *Bush* makes it clear that, in principle, a mortgagee is responsible for those valuations which are carried out in house. Indeed this basic

---

1 [1990] 1 AC 831; [1989] 1 EGLR 169.
2 [1990] 1 AC 831 at p847.
3 [1990] 1 AC 831 at pp865–866.

principle, which had been generally accepted prior to *Smith* v *Bush*,[1] has not subsequently been challenged in any reported case,[2] although defendants have occasionally sought to rely on disclaimers in this context.[3]

(b) Independent valuations

As a general principle, the client of an independent contractor does not incur vicarious liability in tort for that contractor's negligence. There are various exceptions to this principle;[4] however, it seems that the case of a mortgage valuation is not one of them. As Lord Griffiths stated in *Smith* v *Eric S Bush*; *Harris* v *Wyre Forest District Council*,[5] "the mortgagee will not be held liable for the negligence of the independent valuer who acts as an independent contractor".[6]

Notwithstanding such clear *dicta*, however, there are at least two possible ways in which a mortgagee can incur liability for a mortgage valuation which is carried out by an independent valuer. First, as explained by Lord Griffiths, the mortgagee may owe a duty to exercise care in selecting the valuer concerned:[7]

I do not accept the view of the Court of Appeal in *Curran* v *Northern Ireland Co-ownership Housing Association Ltd*[8] that a mortgagee who accepts a fee to obtain a valuation of a small house owes no duty of care to the mortgagor in the selection of the valuer to whom he entrusts the work. In my opinion, the mortgagee in such a case, knowing that the mortgagor will rely on the valuation, owes a duty to the mortgagor to take reasonable care to employ a reasonably competent valuer.

Although not cited by Lord Griffiths, the earlier Irish case of *Ward* v *McMaster*[9] provides a clear illustration of liability arising in this way. A local authority, on being asked to lend money for the

---

1 *Stevenson* v *Nationwide Building Society* (1984) 272 EG 663; *Hadden* v *City of Glasgow District Council* 1986 SLT 557; *Westlake* v *Bracknell District Council* [1987] 1 EGLR 161.
2 See, for example, *Beaton* v *Nationwide Building Society* [1991] 2 EGLR 145.
3 See pp196–212.
4 See *Alcock* v *Wraith* (1991) 59 BLR 16 at p 23, *per* Neill LJ.
5 [1990] 1 AC 831 at p865: see also at p847, *per* Lord Templeman.
6 See also *Halifax Building Society* v *Edell* [1992] Ch 436 at p454; [1992] 1 EGLR 195, *per* Morritt J.
7 *Smith* v *Eric S Bush*; *Harris* v *Wyre Forest District Council* [1990] 1 AC 831 at p865; [1989] 1 EGLR 169.
8 (1986) 8 NIJB 1.
9 [1985] IR 29.

purchase of a four-year-old house, commissioned a valuation report from a local auctioneer. The latter, who had no professional qualifications relating to house construction but was experienced in market conditions in the area, failed to discover serious defects in the property which affected its roof, foundations, walls and floors. The trial judge somewhat generously[1] refused to find the auctioneer guilty of negligence, on the ground that he had merely been "employed in his capacity as auctioneer to place a market value on the property" and "is not to be blamed for the absence of qualifications which he did not hold himself out as having". However, the local authority did not escape so lightly:

The council had a duty to see that the valuation was carried out with reasonable care, and that implied not only that the person who carried out the inspection would not act carelessly but that the council would ensure that the person carrying out the valuation would be competent to discover readily ascertainable defects which would materially affect its market value.

The second way in which liability in respect of a negligent mortgage valuation might fall upon the mortgagee is rather more controversial and uncertain. In *Beresforde* v *Chesterfield Borough Council*[2] the plaintiffs, who were considering the purchase of a house in the course of construction, applied to a building society (the second defendants) for a loan on mortgage. The building society duly obtained a report on the property from an independent valuer. However, when that report was shown to the plaintiffs, it appeared on the building society's own headed paper and contained a number of references to "the Society's valuer". On these facts the plaintiffs, who complained that the valuer had negligently failed to discover serious defects in the property, argued that the building society had effectively "adopted" the independent valuer's report, had presented it as its own, and should thus be held as liable for that report as if it had been carried out in house.

When the second defendants sought to have the claim against them struck out as disclosing no reasonable cause of action, the Court of Appeal emphasised that there were "formidable difficulties" to be overcome if the plaintiffs were to succeed in their action.

---

1 See p74.
2 [1989] 2 EGLR 149.

Nevertheless, the court held that the claim was at least arguable and that the plaintiffs must accordingly be allowed to pursue it at trial; it could not be struck out at this preliminary stage.

The possibility raised in the *Beresforde* case, that a mortgagee might assume responsibility for the report of an independent valuer, was considered again by the Court of Appeal in *Tipton & Coseley Building Society* v *Collins*.[1] On this occasion the point arose when the building society brought an action to repossess mortgaged property because of the borrowers' default in repayments. The borrowers sought to defend this action by arguing that, since they had a valid claim for damages against the building society (based on its "adoption" of a negligent mortgage valuation carried out by an independent valuer), the damages to which they were entitled would enable them to pay what was due under the mortgage. In order to succeed in this defence, the borrowers were required by section 36 of the Administration of Justice Act 1970 to satisfy the court that they were *likely* to win their case against the building society. As the Court of Appeal pointed out, this was a much more formidable requirement for the defendants than merely having to show an *arguable* case (as in *Beresforde*); accordingly, and without casting any doubt upon the earlier decision, the court on this occasion held that the borrowers' evidence fell a very long way short of what they needed to establish.

E Liability of vendor's surveyor to purchaser

Although relatively unusual, it is by no means unknown (especially in the context of auction sales) for a vendor to commission a survey of the property to be sold, with the intention of making the surveyor's report available to prospective purchasers. The idea was at one time favoured by the Conveyancing Standing Committee of the Law Commission in a consultation paper[2] as part of a general reform of the *caveat emptor* principle, although response to this paper led the committee to reject the idea of vendors' surveys in its final recommendations.[3] The question which this practice raises (albeit one which does not appear to have been directly litigated)

---

1 [1994] EGCS 120.
2 *Caveat Emptor in Sales of Land* (1988).
3 *Let the buyer be well informed* (1989).

is whether, in carrying out such a survey on behalf of a vendor, the surveyor owes any duty of care to the purchaser.

The argument which is most commonly raised against the imposition of a duty of care in such circumstances is that it would create an intolerable conflict of interests for the surveyor concerned. Since the interests of a vendor and a purchaser are (it is said) in direct opposition, it is impossible for the surveyor to have proper regard to both parties. In such a situation, it is the interests of the client which must take precedence.

Proponents of this view also rely for indirect support on cases in which it has been held that, in a normal conveyancing transaction, a vendor's solicitor answering preliminary inquiries owes no duty of care to the purchaser.[1] Those cases, however, are readily distinguishable from the situation involving a surveyor, in that purchasers will normally have instructed their own solicitors, on whose professional expertise they can be expected to rely. It is perhaps significant that the "conflict of interest" argument has not deterred the courts from imposing liability upon a vendor's *estate agent* for negligently misleading a purchaser;[2] here, of course, there is less likelihood that the purchaser's own advisers will afford protection. The estate agent decisions also suggest that the purchaser's claim will not necessarily be defeated by the argument that it is unnecessary to provide a direct right of action against a professional adviser, since the vendor is responsible for misrepresentations made on his or her behalf.

The reported cases which most closely resemble the "vendor's survey" scenario (and which strongly support the view that a vendor's surveyor will owe a duty of care to prospective purchasers) are those concerning specialists in the detection and treatment of dry rot. In *Shankie-Williams* v *Heavey*,[3] for example, a developer who was in the process of converting an old house into flats instructed the defendant, a "dry rot surveying specialist", to inspect the ground-floor flat. The defendant knew that any report or guarantee which he issued was likely to be shown by the client to

---

1 See *Cemp Properties (UK) Ltd* v *Dentsply Research & Development Corporation* [1989] 2 EGLR 192; *Gran Gelato Ltd* v *Richcliff (Group) Ltd* [1992] Ch 560; [1992] 1 EGLR 297.
2 *Computastaff Ltd* v *Ingledew Brown Bennison & Garrett* (1983) 268 EG 906; *McCullagh* v *Lane Fox & Partners Ltd* [1994] 1 EGLR 48.
3 [1986] 2 EGLR 139; see p41.

prospective purchasers, and the Court of Appeal held that this knowledge was sufficient to establish a duty of care on the defendant's part, although the claim failed for other reasons.[1]

A similar duty of care was found to exist in *Bourne v McEvoy Timber Preservation*,[2] where the defendants were instructed by a vendor, as part of the process of "tarting up" a house in preparation for a sale, to report on any fungal infestation and to give an estimate for any necessary work of eradication. The defendants provided a report and estimate on the basis that they would be paid for the work if their estimate was accepted, but would otherwise receive nothing. The work contained in the defendants' estimate was, by agreement with the vendor, paid for by the plaintiff purchaser, and he was named as the client in a guarantee issued by the defendants. On these facts it was held that, whether or not the plaintiff had actually seen the defendants' report prior to purchase, there was sufficient proximity between the parties to give rise to a duty of care (although the evidence failed to establish a breach of that duty). As the defendants knew, their report might well be shown to the prospective mortgagees of the property, in which case it would be likely to affect any purchaser in deciding whether and at what price to purchase.

It is suggested on the basis of these decisions that, where a surveyor instructed by the vendor is actually aware that the report is intended to be shown to prospective purchasers, a duty of care will be owed to any such purchaser who relies on the report in deciding to acquire the property. It is further suggested, albeit with slightly less confidence, that a duty of care will arise in cases where the surveyor merely *ought* to be aware of potential reliance by purchasers on the report.

F Liability to vendor for "down-valuation"

An issue which has fuelled heated debate in recent years, though so far without apparently resulting in litigation, concerns the plight of a vendor who loses a sale, or who is forced to agree to a reduction in price, following an adverse report on his or her property. Such a report might concern the property's condition or

---

1 See p138.
2 (1975) 237 EG 496.

its market value, and might come from a surveyor commissioned by a prospective purchaser or from a valuer appointed by a mortgagee. There is no doubt that, if the misrepresentations contained in such a report were *deliberate*, its author would be liable to the vendor in the tort of malicious falsehood.[1] However, a far more difficult question is whether a valuer or surveyor might incur liability in such circumstances for mere *negligence*.

For such liability to arise, it would be necessary to find a duty of care owed by these professionals to the vendor whose property they are instructed to inspect, and it seems highly unlikely that a court would impose such a duty.[2] While it is no doubt foreseeable to either a purchaser's surveyor or a mortgagee's valuer that any negligence of this kind is likely to have an adverse effect on the vendor, a duty of care requires "proximity" as well as "foreseeability",[3] and it is suggested that neither of the relationships under discussion can be regarded as sufficiently "proximate" in this sense.

The main arguments against imposing a duty of care towards the vendor may be summarised as follows. First, the interests of the vendor are in direct conflict with those of the person (purchaser or mortgagee) who commissions the report and, while such a conflict does not necessarily rule out a duty of care,[4] it militates strongly against it.[5] Second, unlike the case where a survey is commissioned by a vendor for the specific purpose of showing it to purchasers,[6] neither a purchaser's survey nor a mortgage valuation is intended for the use of the vendor; they are designed only to help the client reach a decision. Third, since a vendor who is misled by a purchaser's survey into reducing the price will have an action for misrepresentation against the purchaser (who can presumably

---

1 See *Mayer* v *Pluck* (1971) 223 EG 219.
2 See *Kerridge* v *James Abbott & Partners* [1992] 2 EGLR 162 at p 165, *per* Judge Hordern QC.
3 See p37.
4 As in the duty of a vendor's estate agent to a purchaser: see *Computastaff Ltd* v *Ingledew Brown Bennison & Garrett* (1983) 268 EG 906; *McCullagh* v *Lane Fox & Partners Ltd* [1994] 1 EGLR 48.
5 As in the non-liability of a vendor' solicitor to a purchaser: see *Cemp Properties (UK) Ltd* v *Dentsply Research & Development Corporation* [1989] 2 EGLR 192; *Gran Gelato Ltd* v *Richcliff (Group) Ltd* [1992] Ch 560; [1992] 1 EGLR 297.
6 See p59.

recover then against the surveyor), it might be thought unnecessary to create a direct claim against the surveyor.[1] Fourth, in the case of a mortgage valuer, one of the main reasons for holding this professional liable to a house buyer (that it is the latter who indirectly pays the valuer's fees) is obviously inapplicable where it is the vendor who seeks to complain.

G Liability to mortgagor on sale of repossessed property

It has long been established that a mortgagee, in exercising a power to repossess and sell the mortgaged property on the mortgagor's default, owes some duty to the mortgagor to see that a proper price is obtained. In *Cuckmere Brick Co Ltd* v *Mutual Finance Ltd*[2] the Court of Appeal decided that the mortgagee's duty was not merely to act in good faith and without reckless disregard of the mortgagor's interests, but that it involved taking reasonable care to obtain the true market value of the property. The court also held that, if the reason why a sale took place at an undervalue was that the mortgagee's advisers were negligent, the mortgagee would be responsible for that negligence.[3] The case itself concerned negligent marketing of the property by the auctioneers appointed to handle the sale, but there seems no reason to doubt that the same principles would apply to any other professional advising on a mortgagee's sale; a valuer would be an obvious example of such an adviser.

Although it was not necessary in *Cuckmere Brick* to consider the legal position of the auctioneers, Cross LJ was clearly of the opinion that they would, if sued, have been held personally liable to the mortgagors for their negligence. This view, which was endorsed by the High Court of Australia in *Commercial & General Acceptance Ltd* v *Nixon*,[4] would have resulted in the imposition of liability upon a firm of estate agents in *Garland* v *Ralph Pay & Ransom*;[5] however, in the special circumstances of that case the mortgagor was unable

---

1 This, however, does not solve the problem for the vendor of a purchaser who simply withdraws from the sale.
2 [1971] Ch 949; followed in *Johnson* v *Ribbins* (1975) 235 EG 737.
3 Relying on *Wolff* v *Vanderzee* (1869) 20 LT 350 and *Tomlin* v *Luce* (1888) 41 ChD 573; (1889) 43 ChD 191.
4 (1981) 152 CLR 491.
5 (1984) 271 EG 106.

to establish that a breach by the agents of their admitted duty of care had caused any loss.

While the cases cited above appear to establish an area of potential third-party liability for valuers, a cautionary note may be sounded. It has been held in more recent cases that the liability of a mortgagee to the mortgagor derives, not from the tort of negligence, but from the equitable principles which govern their relationship,[1] and this development has led the courts to take a more restricted view, not only of what the duty entails, but also of the persons to whom it is owed. These include subsequent mortgagees and guarantors[2] but not an individual beneficiary where the mortgagor is the trustee.[3] Although the point has not yet been judicially considered, it seems likely that whatever duties are owed by the mortgagee's professional advisers to the mortgagor or to any other interested party can be no wider than those which are owed by the mortgagee.

H Liability for independent determinations

A valuer may be appointed (as either independent expert or arbitrator) to decide an issue between two parties, such as the rent to be paid under a lease following a rent review. As noted earlier,[4] such an appointment will normally result in a trilateral contract under which the valuer, when acting as expert (though not as arbitrator), will owe a duty of care to each of the other parties. Although there is no direct authority on the point, it appears probable that, in the unlikely event that an appointment creates a contract between the valuer and only one of the disputants, the valuer will nevertheless owe a duty of care in tort to the other party.

I Other cases

Situations which do not fall into any of the categories described

---

1 *China & South Sea Bank Ltd* v *Tan Soon Gin* [1990] 1 AC 536; *Downsview Nominees Ltd* v *First City Corporation Ltd* [1993] AC 295.
2 *Standard Chartered Bank Ltd* v *Walker* [1982] 3 All ER 938; *American Express International Banking Corp* v *Hurley* [1985] 3 All ER 564.
3 *Parker-Tweedale* v *Dunbar Bank plc* [1991] Ch 12.
4 See p14.

above will be decided by the courts on a case by case basis, and the question whether or not a duty of care is owed by a surveyor or valuer to a non-client will be answered by reference to the tests of foreseeability, proximity and what is just and reasonable.[1] There is in general little to be gained by speculating on just how these tests might be applied to various hypothetical relationships, since the earlier parts of this chapter have dealt individually with those relationships out of which legal actions are most likely to arise. However, one specific duty-situation is worthy of comment, if only because it demonstrates how this area of law has developed over the years.

In *Old Gate Estates Ltd* v *Toplis*[2] the promoters of a company, which was about to be formed in order to purchase a block of flats, commissioned a valuation of the property from the defendant firm. The valuation was duly carried out, the company was formed and the property was purchased. When subsequently the valuation was found to be excessive, the company brought an action for negligence against the valuers, but this failed. The trial judge held that the company could have no claim for breach of contract, since the only contract with the valuer had been made by its promoters as individuals and this could not be ratified by the company once it had come into existence.[3] Nor, as the law then stood, could the company claim in the tort of negligence for its losses, since these were of a purely financial kind.

It is instructive to compare the decision in *Old Gate Estates Ltd* v *Toplis* with that in *Miro Properties Ltd* v *J Trevor & Sons*.[4] This later case arose when a married couple, who were seeking to purchase a flat, were advised for tax reasons to make the purchase through an offshore company, which would then permit the couple to reside as licensees in the property. Before committing themselves to this scheme (which involved forming a company for the purpose) the couple commissioned a survey of the flat from the defendants which, it was later alleged, had been negligently carried out. The company duly claimed damages from the defendants, who raised the defence that, since the company had not been incorporated at

---

1 See p37.
2 [1939] 3 All ER 209.
3 *Kelner* v *Baxter* (1866) LR 2 CP 174.
4 [1989] 1 EGLR 151.

the date on which the report had been sent to the couple, it could have no right of action.

This argument, redolent of that which succeeded in the earlier case, was nevertheless roundly rejected by the deputy judge, who described it as "distinguished more by ingenuity than by merit". Having pointed out that the company's cause of action lay in tort rather than in contract, Mr Recorder Bernstein QC stated that the survey reports were intended to be passed to the couple "both as individuals and as agents of the company when the company came into existence". And, since the substance of those reports was communicated before contracts for the purchase of the flat were exchanged, the defendants were "as liable as they would have been if the company had been incorporated immediately before, rather than shortly after, those communications were made".[1]

J Firm's liability for valuer's torts

1 Employee's negligence

The foregoing discussion of potential liability to third parties for professional negligence has assumed that the relevant liability is that of the individual surveyor or valuer who carries out the work in question. In reality, of course, the doctrine of vicarious liability means that action is more likely to be brought against the organisation of which the individual is a part. This does not mean that the individual is free from liability – indeed, unless a tort can be proved against the individual, there is nothing for which the firm can be held liable – but simply that a plaintiff will normally seek a defendant who is likely to be able to pay whatever damages are awarded.

The most highly developed form of vicarious liability in English law is that under which an employer is held responsible for a tort committed by an employee who is acting in the course of his or her employment. This principle is in no way based on the idea of any personal fault on the employer's part, so that liability does not depend upon failure to select competent employees, or failure adequately to supervise their work. If the tortfeasor is an employee,

---

1 For other cases in which the legal distinction between a company and its members failed to assist a negligent surveyor or valuer, see *Freeman v Marshall & Co* (1966) 200 EG 777 and *Kendall Wilson Securities v Barraclough* [1986] 1 NZLR 576.

and the tort is committed in the course of employment, then the employer's liability will automatically follow. It should also be emphasised that, while the vast majority of cases concern an employee's negligence, the principle of vicarious liability is also capable of extending to intentionally committed torts such as deceit.[1]

As to what is regarded as falling within the "course of employment" for this purpose, there is a crucial distinction between *what* a person is employed to do and the *manner* in which he or she is employed to do it. It is sometimes said that the employer cannot be held responsible for acts which are completely unauthorised, but that the employer will be liable for authorised acts which are performed by an employee in an unauthorised way. Thus, for example, a firm would not automatically incur responsibility if an unqualified residential negotiator took it upon himself or herself to carry out a structural survey of factory premises, unless the firm had in some way "held out" the employee as authorised to carry out such work.[2] On the other hand, there would surely be vicarious liability for the negligence (or even the fraud) of a qualified surveyor who failed to follow the firm's standard procedures in carrying out an inspection.

2 Employee's disobedience and fraud

The distinction between an employee's *act* and the *manner* of performing that act explains why the terms of the employment contract, though important, cannot be conclusive in the context of vicarious liability. It also explains how a firm may even be held liable where an employee deliberately contravenes clear instructions; if those instructions merely govern the *way* in which authorised acts are to be performed, they do not operate so as to restrict the "course of employment".

There may of course be circumstances in which an employee's disobedience *does* mean that his or her acts are outside the course of employment, so that the employer cannot be held vicariously liable for them. A good illustration of this is provided by the case of

---

1 *Lloyd* v *Grace, Smith & Co* [1912] AC 716; *Uxbridge Permanent Building Society* v *Pickard* [1939] 2 KB 248: see also *Alliance & Leicester Building Society* v *Edgestop Ltd (No 3)* [1994] 2 EGLR 229; p69.
2 See p69.

Kooragang Investments Pty Ltd v *Richardson & Wrench Ltd*[1] in which the respondents, an Australian firm of valuers, instructed its employees not to carry out any more work for a developer client, from whom substantial fees were overdue. One of the firm's valuers, who had undisclosed business dealings with the client in question, continued in defiance of this instruction to furnish valuations on the firm's notepaper, and the client used these valuations to raise money on mortgage from lending institutions. When two of the valuations were found to have been negligently carried out, the appellant moneylenders which had relied on them took action against the firm. Their claim, however, was rejected by the Privy Council, which refused to infer "authority" from the mere fact that the acts done were within the *class* of acts which the valuer in question was employed to carry out. As Lord Wilberforce emphasised:[2]

> In the present case, the respondents did carry out valuations. Valuations were a class of acts which [the employee] could perform on their behalf. To argue from this that any valuation done by [the employee], without any authority from the respondents, not on behalf of the respondents but in his own interest, without any connection with the respondents' business, is a valuation for which the respondents must assume responsibility is not one which principle or authority can support. To indorse it would strain the doctrine of vicarious responsibility beyond breaking point and in effect introduce into the law of agency a new principle equivalent to one of strict liability.

It is important to appreciate that there was no suggestion in the *Kooragang* case that the disobedient employee might have had "ostensible authority" to act as he did. Such authority depends upon evidence of two things: that the employee has been clothed by the employer with the *appearance of authority*, and that the third party has *relied* upon that appearance. Where this can be established the employer, having held out his employee as authorised to deal with the third party, is in effect estopped from denying the existence of that authority. In *Kooragang*, however, the appellants did not deal with the employee concerned, did not rely on his authority as a valuer and indeed were unaware of his existence.

A major significance of ostensible authority is that it may serve to

---

1 [1982] AC 462.
2 [1982] AC 462 at p475.

render an employer liable for the fraud, as well as the negligence, of an employee. In *Alliance & Leicester Building Society* v *Edgestop Ltd (No 3)*,[1] a dishonest employee of Hamptons Residential perpetrated a series of fraudulent hotel valuations on the firm's headed paper; these valuations apparently bore the signature of a chartered surveyor employed by the firm, but the signatures were in fact forged by the rogue. The valuations were used to induce the plaintiffs and other lending institutions to lend, on the security of the hotels, far more than the properties were in fact worth, as part of a multi-million pound mortgage fraud.

When the plaintiffs sought to hold Hamptons Residential responsible for this fraud, the latter relied on the fact that the employee concerned, who was not a qualified surveyor or valuer, was employed by them only in the capacity of a land buyer, with the main tasks of identifying suitable sites for residential development, securing those sites on behalf of clients and generally advising on their development. In the course of that work the employee had undoubtedly provided appraisals of properties for clients; however, his actual authority from the firm did not extend to work involving hotels, and he was certainly not authorised to carry out valuations for lenders.

Notwithstanding these arguments, Mummery J (after an exhaustive analysis of various transactions which the employee had been permitted to conduct) came to the conclusion that he had been "held out" by the firm as authorised to carry out valuations of commercial property on which lenders might rely. This crucial finding meant that Hamptons incurred vicarious liability for the way in which that ostensible authority was then abused.

3 Partnerships

The above discussion concerns surveyors and valuers operating under a contract of employment. Where a surveying firm operates as a partnership, the position as regards tortious liability incurred by one of the partners is governed by statute. The Partnership Act 1890, section 10 provides:

Where, by any wrongful act or omission of any partner acting in the ordinary course of the business of the firm, or with the authority of his copartners,

---

1 [1994] 2 EGLR 229.

loss or injury is caused to any person not being a partner in the firm, or any penalty is incurred, the firm is liable therefor to the same extent as the partner so acting or omitting to act.

The interpretation which has been placed on this provision by the courts has produced a type of vicarious liability for the firm (and thereby for all the partners) very similar to that incurred by an employer. It is thought therefore that the courts in *Kooragang Investments Pty Ltd* v *Richardson & Wrench Ltd*[1] and *Alliance & Leicester Building Society* v *Edgestop Ltd*[2] would have reached similar decisions if the individual valuers concerned had been members of partnerships rather than employees of companies.

---

1 [1982] AC 462.
2 [1994] 2 EGLR 229.

CHAPTER 3

The meaning of professional negligence

A Introduction

In determining the appropriate standard of care demanded of a professional person, the law does not differentiate between one profession and another. The principles applicable to surveyors and valuers are those which apply to doctors, architects, engineers, solicitors, accountants and other professions (although there is a longstanding suspicion that judges are rather too kind to doctors). The very fact that new professions are being created all the time has had the effect that standards required of the professions are higher now than they used to be 30 to 50 years ago. From society's point of view, this is of course a good thing.

A member of any profession must exercise reasonable skill and care in the carrying out of professional duties. Whether he or she has done so is determined by reference to members of the profession concerned, rather than to the man on top of the proverbial Clapham omnibus. The standard expected of a professional was laid down in *Bolam* v *Friern Hospital Management Committee*.[1] That case was concerned with the duty of a doctor to warn a patient of the risks of a certain course of treatment; nevertheless, it has wide effect and has been cited with approval in many valuation cases.[2] In summing up in *Bolam*, McNair J said:[3]

> Where you get a situation which involves the use of some special skill or competence, then the test whether there has been negligence or not is ... the standard of the ordinary skilled man exercising and professing to have that special skill. A man need not possess the highest expert skill. It is well established law that it is sufficient if he exercises the ordinary skill of an ordinary competent man exercising that particular art.

---

1 [1957] 2 All ER 118.
2 See, for example, *McIntyre* v *Herring Son & Daw* [1988] 1 EGLR 231 and *BNP Mortgages Ltd* v *Goadsby & Harding Ltd* [1994] 2 EGLR 169.
3 [1957] 2 All ER 118 at p 121.

In the recent valuation case of *Banque Bruxelles Lambert SA* v *Eagle Star Insurance Co Ltd*,[1] Phillips J followed the House of Lords decision in *Saif Ali* v *Sidney Mitchell & Co*[2] in holding that:[3]

> No matter what profession it may be, the common law does not impose on those who practise it any liability for damage resulting from what in the result turn out to have been errors of judgment, unless the error was such as no reasonably well-informed and competent member of that profession could have made.

The basis of a contractual relationship between a professional person and the client may be formed by the *Bolam* requirement to exercise "the ordinary skill of the ordinary competent man exercising that particular art". Such a requirement may be an implied term of the contract;[4] however, it has become common practice for professions to publish standard conditions of engagement and to include in these a condition regarding the required standard of care. An example of this is to be found in the RICS and ISVA *Home Buyers' Survey and Valuation*, published in 1994, condition 1.4, which provides:

> In preparing a report the surveyor will exercise the skill and diligence reasonably to be expected from a surveyor and valuer competent to advise on the subject property.

It is worth noting that this condition, by including a requirement of "diligence", imposes a duty on the surveyor to prepare such a report as quickly as is reasonably possible.[5]

In actions against professionals, not every error will amount to negligence. This point was explicitly recognised in *Luxmoore-May* v *Messenger May Baverstock*,[6] which concerned the standard of care owed by a provincial firm of fine art auctioneers and valuers. As Slade LJ there pointed out:[7]

---

1 [1994] 2 EGLR 108.
2 [1980] AC 198.
3 At p137: see also *Nyckeln Finance* v *Stumpbrook Continuation Ltd* [1994] 2 EGLR 143 at p151, *per* Judge Fawcus.
4 Supply of Goods and Services Act 1982, section 13.
5 An implied duty of diligence might in any event arise under the Supply of Goods and Services Act 1982, section 14.
6 [1990] 1 All ER 1067; [1990] 1 EGLR 21.
7 [1990] 1 All ER 1067 at p 1076.

The valuation of pictures of which the artist is unknown, pre-eminently involves an exercise of opinion and judgment, most particularly deciding whether an attribution to any particular artist should be made. Since it is not an exact science, the judgment in the very nature of things may be fallible, and may turn out to be wrong. Accordingly, provided that the valuer has done his job honestly and with due diligence, I think that the court should be cautious before convicting him of professional negligence merely because he has failed to be the first to spot a "sleeper" or the potentiality of a "sleeper".

B Specialists

An inevitable consequence of the emergence of more professions is an increasing degree of specialisation. This may lead to difficulties in assessing the appropriate standard of care and skill. If, for example, a client instructs a firm of surveyors which holds itself out as having specialist skills, it seems right that the firm should be judged by a greater degree of skill, care and perhaps diligence than that which might be required of an ordinary practitioner. No doubt the fee charged by such surveyors would reflect their special skill.

Notwithstanding these considerations, it appears that the courts in such cases have so far tended to judge specialists by the standards of the profession generally.[1] Thus, in *Andrew Master Hones Ltd* v *Cruikshank & Fairweather*,[2] Graham J said:

The degree of knowledge and care to be expected is thus seen to be that degree possessed by a notionally and duly qualified person practising that profession. The test is, therefore, if I may put it that way an objective test referable to the notional member of the profession and not a subjective test referable to the particular professional man employed.

While this "general" test may favour a specialist to the point where it causes injustice to the client, it is undeniably easier to implement. Any other approach would require the courts to undertake the task of distinguishing between different standards of skill, care and perhaps diligence and then deciding how these should vary, allowing for a defendant's age and experience. The courts might be

---

1 See, for example, *Wimpey Construction (UK) Ltd* v *Poole* [1984] 2 Lloyd's Rep 299.
2 [1980] RPC 16.

disposed to adopt a strict liability approach if a more subjective test were to be applied. Such problems were considered by Megarry J in *Duchess of Argyll v Beuselinck*,[1] a case concerning a claim for negligence against a solicitor.

C Inexperienced practitioners

In the same way that the courts are reluctant to impose a higher standard for professionals with a specialist knowledge, they will not reduce the standard for a surveyor or valuer who has no professional qualifications. In *Freeman v Marshall & Co*[2] an action was brought against a surveyor who failed to report on rising damp. In his defence, the surveyor said that he was not qualified; that he had had no organised course of training as a surveyor and had never passed any professional examination in surveying; that he was a member of the Valuers Institution through election, not examination; and that he had only a working knowledge of structures from the point of view of buying and selling. However, the court ruled that, if he held himself out in practice as a surveyor, the defendant must be deemed to have the skills of a surveyor and must be judged upon such skills. The standard of care and skill therefore is determined by the work and not by the particular surveyor who carries it out.

This approach means that it will be no defence to a claim in respect of a negligent valuation for the valuer to maintain that he or she had insufficient experience of the locality in which the property was situated, or insufficient experience in general. In *Baxter v FW Gapp & Co Ltd*,[3] the defendant valuer was experienced generally, but not in valuing properties in the locality of the bungalow he was asked to value. Full and complete enquiries would have revealed that opposite the bungalow there was a similar house for sale and also a smaller house which had been for sale for over a year. It was held that, if the valuer did not know enough about the property market or property values at the place where the bungalow was situated, he should have taken steps to inform himself of such matters.

---

1 [1972] 2 Lloyd's Rep 172.
2 (1966) 200 EG 777.
3 [1938] 4 All ER 457.

A similar decision was reached in *Kenney v Hall, Pain & Foster*,[1] where the plaintiff was advised as to the value of and a suitable asking price for his house by a negotiator employed by the defendant firm. Both the valuation and the asking price proved to be grossly excessive. Prior to giving this advice, the negotiator had very limited experience. He had no formal qualifications, had only six months' experience of working with estate agents in New Zealand and had been working with the defendants for only three months. In holding the defendants liable, Goff J said:

In my judgment, at the material time (the valuer) lacked the skill which could reasonably be expected of a person in his position, to give the valuation. Furthermore, in failing to refer the matter properly back to the office for their opinion, he failed to exercise reasonable care in making the valuation. Lastly, having regard to the nature of the plaintiff's request for a written opinion, he was entitled to assume that the valuation ... had been the subject of full and informal consideration by a partner or a responsible employee of the defendant, and I am satisfied that it was not.

In recent years, the carrying out of valuations outside the locality of which a valuer has knowledge and experience has been a matter of great concern, both to lenders and to valuers' professional indemnity insurers. In the *Mortgage Valuation Guidance for Valuers*, which is published by the RICS and ISVA and which applies to inspections carried out on or after June 1 1992, note 1.1 states that the valuer must have knowledge of and experience in the valuation of the residential property in the particular locality. Failure to comply with this Guidance Note would make it extremely difficult for a valuer to rebut an allegation of professional negligence. Moreover, it might also constitute a disciplinary matter (conduct unbefitting a chartered surveyor) under the byelaws of the RICS, and could constitute a ground for the valuer's professional indemnity insurers to avoid liability on the policy.

D Confirmation of instructions

1 Surveys

By far the most common cause of claims against surveyors and valuers is a misunderstanding as to what was to be included in the

---

1 (1976) 239 EG 355; for the facts of this case see p6.

inspection and report and, more importantly, what was not to be included. It is crucial to define clearly the precise nature of the instructions being undertaken, and failure to do so may well result in a claim for professional negligence. Examples of matters to be included in Conditions of Engagement for a survey are to be found in Chapter 4.[1]

An examination of reported cases shows that it is not always standard practice to confirm instructions. This is sometimes because a report is required urgently, so that there is not time for written confirmation of instructions which have been given orally. To proceed on this basis is dangerous, as it can lead to a misunderstanding as to what was expected of the surveyor or valuer. Wherever possible, a client's instructions which are given by word of mouth should be confirmed in writing.

The property system in Scotland is such that it is fairly unusual for structural surveys to be carried out, largely because of the speed at which a house purchase normally takes place. *Stewart v H A Brechin & Co*[2] is thus one of relatively few reported Scottish decisions involving a surveyor's liability for anything more than a valuation. In this case, solicitors for a prospective purchaser of an 18th-century country property instructed surveyors orally to carry out as a matter of urgency a valuation and to report upon the property's general condition. After the purchaser's offer was accepted by the vendor, parts of the property were found to be infested with woodworm. Lord Cameron was satisfied that this would have been apparent at the time the property was inspected and that the surveyor's unexplained failure to detect it was negligent. As to the surveyor's instructions, Lord Cameron said:

I am of opinion that all the defenders were under contract to do was to make such valuation of the property and to carry out such visual inspection as was reasonably practicable in the circumstances, reporting anything of significance to their client if such should be found.

"Anything of significance" was interpreted as being anything which might have a material effect in deciding what price should be paid for the property or which might make the prospective purchaser

---

1 See pp90–91.
2 1959 SC 306.

reconsider whether to proceed with the transaction.[1]

A similar question of interpretation arose in the English case of *Fisher* v *Knowles*,[2] although it is not clear from the brief report of the case whether there was anything in writing recording a surveyor's instructions. Sir Douglas Frank QC decided that those instructions were:

i to provide a report on the general state of the property;
ii to draw attention to those matters which might give rise to suspicion, such as springing floors or a musty smell which might require further investigation; and
iii to report any matters which might cause the plaintiffs to withdraw or to bargain for a lower price.

The defendant drew attention in his report to some minor defects in the property, but nevertheless valued it at the asking price. Some four years later the plaintiffs complained of many defects in the property, but the judge held the surveyor liable only for failure to report on rot in window frames and defects in ceiling joists and door joinery, expressing doubt as to whether the other items were really defects.

In *Strover* v *Harrington*[3] a clear agreement as to the scope of an inspection enabled a surveyor to avoid liability. The defendant there had reported to his client that a property was served by main drainage through another property, when in fact the drains went into a cesspool. The client alleged that the defendant, who had relied on what he was told by the vendors, was negligent in so doing, but there was no expert evidence before the court to suggest that a careful surveyor would have acted differently. Moreover, the defendant had clearly pointed out in accepting instructions that, if the client so wished, arrangements could be made for specialist tests to be carried out on the drainage system amongst other services, and the client had written back to say that no specialist tests were required.

On these facts Sir Nicolas Browne-Wilkinson V-C refused to hold

---

1 See also *Moss* v *Heckingbottom* (1958) 172 EG 207.
2 (1982) 262 EG 1083.
3 [1988] 1 EGLR 173.

the defendant guilty of negligence:[1]

> That would be my view of the matter if it were for me to decide; but in my judgment it is not for me to apply my yardstick of what is or is not negligent. As a professional man, the surveyor can only be held liable for negligence in the conduct of his profession if he acted in a way which no other surveyor of ordinary skill would be guilty of, if acting with ordinary care. No expert evidence was led as to the practice of careful surveyors, and the burden is on the purchasers [plaintiffs] to prove negligence. Therefore, in my judgment, there is no evidence on which I could hold the surveyor to have been negligent, even if, contrary to my own inclinations, I thought he had been.

In a number of cases, agreed restrictions on what an inspection was to cover have proved insufficient to protect the surveyor. In *Syrett* v *Carr & Neave*,[2] for example, the judge was satisfied that the parties' agreement was accurately reflected by a statement in the surveyor's report that "my survey is restricted to items of major expenditure which would affect your intention to purchase or the price offered". However, the defendant was held negligent in failing to discover a very bad infestation of death-watch beetle, movement in some of the walls and severe damp in some places, since these constituted major defects in the property.

In *Heatley* v *William H Brown Ltd*,[3] the defendants' written conditions of engagement included reference to the inevitable limitations of a report where parts of a property were unexposed or inaccessible. In fact the surveyors were unable to gain access to roof voids but, while pointing this out to the clients, the defendants described the property as "in a reasonable condition for its age" and did not advise the plaintiffs to delay their purchase until access to the roof could be obtained. It was held that, in spite of the limitations expressed, the surveyors had grossly underestimated the defective state of the roof.

In *Matto* v *Rodney Broom Associates*,[4] the defendant's

---

1 See also *Eley* v *King & Chasemore* [1989] 1 EGLR 181 where the surveyor stated that he would have felt happier if he had got up onto the valley gutters of the property so as to inspect the roof covering. This would have required the use of a long ladder which was outside the scope of the surveyor's instructions.
2 [1990] 2 EGLR 161.
3 [1992] 1 EGLR 289.
4 [1994] 2 EGLR 163.

instructions were "to survey the house, to assess the cause of the movement that had been discovered, to determine the structural stability of the house, and to advise what works if any should be carried out at the house for structural purposes". In holding the defendant liable for failing to advise the client that the property would probably require underpinning at some stage, the Court of Appeal expressed some sympathy for a surveyor who "wrote a short report intended to serve his client swiftly and effectively and without a screen of qualifications for his own protection". Nevertheless, it was pointed out that the client "was entitled to receive a report which dealt adequately with the advice required or a report which expressly stated that it was limited in some particular way".

2 Valuations

The standard of care expected of a valuer, like that of a surveyor, will be determined by the instructions given. In *Predeth* v *Castle Phillips Finance Co Ltd*,[1] for example, a valuer received written instructions from a finance company to provide a "crash sale valuation" of a repossessed bungalow. The valuer gave such a valuation and the finance company sold the property at a slightly higher figure, only to be held liable to the mortgagor for failing in its duty to obtain the best available price for the property. The finance company claimed that the valuer was negligent in failing to advise on the property's true market value, but this was rejected by the Court of Appeal on the ground that the job carried out by the valuer was precisely what the client had requested.[2]

In *Sutcliffe* v *Sayer*[3] the defendant, an experienced estate agent with no surveying qualifications, was asked by prospective purchasers whether the asking price of a retirement bungalow was right. He replied that the price was indeed right, but failed to identify that the property was built on a substratum of peat, something which effectively made it impossible to resell. The purchasers' action against the defendant was rejected by the Court of Appeal, which held that they had been given precisely what they had paid for. There was no duty upon the defendant in this particular case to

---

1 [1986] 2 EGLR 144.
2 See also *Tenenbaum* v *Garrod* [1988] 2 EGLR 178, client requesting a "tactically jaundiced" view of a property for negotiating purposes.
3 [1987] 1 EGLR 155.

warn the purchasers as to the potential difficulties of resale.

The dispute which arose in *Beaumont* v *Humberts*[1] concerned the meaning of "reinstatement" in the context of the valuation of a 300-year-old house for insurance purposes. Some policies treat reinstatement as meaning replication (ie an exact copy); others regard this as meaning replacement of the original building with a modern building which is of roughly similar style and general appearance and which offers similar accommodation. The defendants in this case adopted the latter view with the result that, when the property was destroyed by fire, the insurance payout was not enough for the plaintiff to build a perfect replica of his original house.

In holding (by a majority) that the defendants were not guilty of negligence, the Court of Appeal relied on expert evidence to the effect that, when carrying out insurance reinstatement valuations, it is not normal practice for a surveyor to inspect the policy concerned. In consequence, the defendants decision as to the basis of valuation was a reasonable one to have adopted; if the client had wanted a valuation on a different basis, the defendants should have been given specific instructions to this effect.

The decisions described above are in marked contrast with that in *McIntyre* v *Herring Son & Daw*,[2] where the defendant rating valuers were held liable to private clients. The decision has been described as something of a horror story for professionals of all kinds, in that the defendants had carried out an excellent job in negotiating a reduction in the rateable value of the client's property. However, the valuers, in advising the client against taking proceedings to secure a further reduction, had failed to alert the client to the fact that a comparatively slight further redution would give the client a valuable right of enfranchisement under the Leasehold Reform Act 1967. Although the client's instructions to the defendants did not include any suggestion that such implications should be considered, the judge was satisfied that they had fallen below the standard reasonably to be expected of them as competent valuers in accordance with the accepted practice of the profession. They were accordingly held liable for negligence.

---

1 [1990] 2 EGLR 166: see also p4.
2 [1988] 1 EGLR 231.

E Proof of negligence

1 The role of experts

As discussed above, the standard of care and skill required of a professional person is that of a reasonably competent practitioner in the same field. It follows that, in deciding whether or not a defendant has achieved that standard, a court will pay attention to what is said by other suitably qualified practitioners. As Lord Templeman pointed out in *Smith v Eric S Bush*; *Harris v Wyre Forest District Council*:[1]

A valuer will only be liable if other qualified valuers, who cannot be expected to be harsh on their fellow professionals, consider that taking into consideration the nature of the work for which the valuer is paid and the object of that work, nevertheless he has been guilty of an error which an average valuer, in the same circumstances, would not have made.

In deciding whether it may be worthwhile bringing an action for professional negligence, it is therefore sensible practice to instruct an expert, and the sooner the better. If such an expert is then to give evidence in legal proceedings, his or her qualifications should be at least equal to those of the person against whom the claim is made. Moreover, they should be *relevant* qualifications. In *Whalley v Roberts & Roberts*,[2] which concerned an alleged negligent valuation for mortgage purposes, Auld J said:

In my view, it is only the evidence of the surveyors that may be of value on this issue. (The civil engineer and architect), however competent they may be in their respective professions, cannot speak with authority on what is to be expected of the ordinarily competent surveyor: see *Investors in Industry Ltd v South Bedfordshire District Council*.[3]

In consequence, where a claim involves a structural or building survey of a property, the appropriate expert would be a chartered building surveyor rather than a surveyor in general practice. However, where the claim under consideration arises out of what is believed to have been a negligent valuation, the appropriate person

---

1 [1990] 1 AC 831 at p851; [1989] 1 EGLR 169.
2 [1990] 1 EGLR 164.
3 [1986] 1 All ER 787 at pp808–809, *per* Slade LJ.

to instruct is a surveyor in general practice who has extensive experience of valuing property of the kind in question.

The opinion of an expert is commonly sought on one or both of two issues. The first is simply whether the defendant, in carrying out professional work, made an error which no competent practitioner would have made. Thus, in *Peach* v *Iain G Chalmers & Co*,[1] it was the expert evidence which led the court to hold that, in carrying out a mortgage valuation, a surveyor had been negligent in failing to notice that the property was of "Dorran" type construction. Second, the crucial question may be whether the procedures adopted by the defendant reflected those of the profession in general. In *Strover* v *Harrington*,[2] the plaintiff produced no expert evidence to support his allegation that, in the absence of specific instructions to carry out tests upon a property's drainage system, it was negligent for the surveyor to rely upon information given to him by the vendors to the effect that the property enjoyed main drainage. The plaintiff's case accordingly failed, for there was no evidence upon which the judge could hold the surveyor to have been negligent.

In considering the part played by expert witnesses in court proceedings, it is important to remember that an expert's primary duty is to advise the court and not to take a negotiating stance on behalf of his clients. To quote the words of Jeremy Waters, the partner in charge of valuation at Jones Lang Wootton: "his evidence must be entirely uninfluenced by the client's particular line of argument". Judges have often commented adversely on the quality of evidence in cases involving surveyors. For instance, in *Mount Banking Corporation* v *Brian Cooper & Co*,[3] the judge criticised one of the expert witnesses for being "unbending to the point of unreasonableness and somewhat dogmatic". An expert who is prepared to give some ground in seeing the point of an argument being put by the other side is likely to be more plausible so far as the court is concerned.

In *Kerridge* v *James Abbott & Partners*,[4] Judge Hordern QC made the following comments about the plaintiff's expert surveyor:

---

1 [1992] 2 EGLR 135.
2 [1988] 1 EGLR 173.
3 [1992] 2 EGLR 142.
4 [1992] 2 EGLR 162, at p164.

I confess that it is my view that his intimate association with the facts and progress of events is in truth a disadvantage to him in giving expert evidence before me rather than an advantage because I think that, try as he might, and I am sure he tried very hard, he was really unable to exercise that detached judgment which is the most truly vital attribute of an expert.

2 Expert evidence

In *English Exporters (London)* v *Eldonwall*,[1] a distinction was drawn between an expert who gives an opinion of a particular valuation, based upon general experience of similar transactions not necessarily within his or her personal knowledge, and one who gives direct evidence of comparables without having personal knowledge of them. It was said that the expert's evidence would be admissible in the former but not in the latter case. Where comparables in negligence cases against valuers are a matter of concern, it is important that the expert should be in a position to give direct evidence of the comparables to which he refers. Such evidence should ideally be based upon the expert's personal knowledge but, where this is not possible, an alternative is for the comparables to be proved from files in the possession of the expert's firm. If neither of these is available, there is a risk that a court may hold the expert's evidence to be based upon inadmissible facts.

The judgment of Cresswell J in *National Justice Compania Naviera SA* v *Prudential Insurance Co Ltd*, The "Ikarian Reefer"[2] contains valuable guidance for expert witnesses and those who instruct them. His lordship criticised an expert for giving evidence outside his area of expertise. He also criticised another who, having changed his mind on an important issue after writing his report but before giving evidence, neglected to tell the other side and thus caused considerable confusion and an unduly prolonged hearing. The judge accordingly made a number of general points regarding expert evidence, the most important of which were as follows:

i   Expert evidence presented to the court should be the independent product of the expert uninfluenced as to form or content by the exigencies of litigation.[3]

---

1 [1973] Ch 415.
2 [1993] CILL 838: see also *Laserbore Ltd* v *Morrison Biggs Wall Ltd* [1993] CILL 896.
3 A model form of expert's report is published by the Academy of Experts, 116-118 Chancery Lane, London WC2A 1PP.

ii An expert witness should provide independent assistance to the court by way of objective, unbiased opinion in relation to matters within his expertise, and should never assume the role of an advocate.
iii An expert witness should state the facts or assumptions upon which his opinion is based, and should not omit to consider material facts which could detract from his concluded opinion.
iv An expert witness should make it clear when a particular question or issue falls outside his expertise.
v If an expert's opinion is not properly researched because he considers that insufficient data is available, then this must be stated with an indication that the opinion is no more than a provisional one.
vi If, after exchange of reports, an expert witness changes his mind on a material matter, this should be communicated without delay to the other side and, where appropriate, to the court.

Although helpful, such guidance has been subjected to some criticism as placing an expert witness in a difficult if not impossible position. No doubt the expert will have been chosen (and paid) by one of the parties to the claim precisely because his or her opinion supports that party's case. It is now common practice for the parties' experts to attend "without prejudice" meetings, at which they will inevitably endeavour to persuade the opposing experts that their opinion is the correct one. This might well be regarded as an occasion when the expert in effect acts as an advocate on behalf of those instructing him, and there are many who believe that the expert should be entitled to act in precisely this way.

In the surveying and valuation context, consideration of the principles underlying expert evidence was given in the recent case of *Alliance & Leicester Building Society v Edgestop Ltd (No 3)*.[1] A preliminary judgment given by Mummery J[2] dealt with the question whether the whole of a report, made by an expert instructed by the plaintiffs and then served upon the defendants, was admissible in evidence. This report had been prepared in response to amended allegations made by the defendants, that the plaintiff building society knew or ought to have known that the defendant's

---

1 [1994] 2 EGLR 229; see p69.
2 *Alliance & Leicester Building Society v Edgestop Ltd (No 2)* June 28 1993, Chancery Division, unreported.

employee had no authority to value the property for any lending institution. The defendants also claimed that the plaintiff building society had been put on enquiry as to the nature and extent of the employee's authority from his employers, the defendants. In making these assertions, the defendants had relied upon what they said was "standard industry practice", in that valuations of property on the security of which a building society was considering the lending of money should be undertaken by a qualified person. Likewise, the "ordinary business precautions" to be taken by a reasonable lender would include the checking of names in the current RICS handbook and the making of reasonable enquiry to ascertain the nature and extent of authority of a person, such as the valuer in this particular case, to carry out valuations for a lending institution.

When the defendants asserted that the plaintiffs' expert evidence contained much inadmissible and irrelevant material, the judge held that part of the expert's report strayed well outside the area of expert evidence and trespassed into the area of advice on and advocacy of the plaintiffs' case. Moreover, the report included expressions of opinion on factual issues which the court was well able to decide without the benefit of expert evidence. It followed that those parts were inadmissible.

In coming to this conclusion, Mummery J gave general consideration to the issues on which expert evidence might be relevant, and identified the principles which he felt had been overlooked in that particular case and which in his recent experience had been overlooked in other cases. His concern about the undesirable consequences of a failure to observe the proper role of an expert witness echoed criticism made by other judges in other divisions of the High Court.[1]

Nothing said by the judge was intended to underestimate the value of expert evidence. Indeed, his lordship made the point that, when properly used, expert evidence is essential. It can assist the court in arriving at a sound resolution of issues of fact by educating the relevant tribunal in matters which fall outside the knowledge, skill and expertise of the judge. However, when not properly used, expert evidence is at best a waste of effort, time and money; at

---

1 See, for example, *University of Warwick* v *Sir Robert McAlpine* (1988) 42 BLR 11; *National Justice Compania Naviera SA* v *Prudential Assurance Co Ltd*, *"The Ikarian Reefer"* [1993] CILL 838.

worst it carries the risk that the decision-making body, whether judge, jury or other tribunal, may be confused and misled into making unsound findings of fact.

In Mummery J's view, there are two crucial principles which must be borne in mind when dealing with expert evidence. First, when an expert, either in his written report or in oral evidence, expresses to the court opinions which by his skill, specialised knowledge and experience he is qualified to form, then he does so *as a witness*. He does not, and should not, do so as a partisan adviser suggesting possible lines of argument and theories in support of the client's case. He does not, and should not, do so as an advocate, arguing the case for the party who had called him to give evidence. As Lord Wilberforce said in *Whitehouse* v *Jordan*:[1]

While some degree of consultation between experts and legal advisers is entirely proper, it is necessary that expert evidence presented to the court should be, and should be seen to be, the independent product of the expert, uninfluenced as to its form and content, by the exigencies of litigation. To the extent that it is not the evidence is likely to be not only incorrect, but self-defeating.

Second, on matters which do not call for the use of specialised skill, knowledge and experience, an expert witness is no more qualified or entitled to give evidence of opinion on an issue than is an ordinary witness of fact. In general, expressions of opinions in court on issues of fact not requiring expertise for their resolution are inadmissible. They are either: (a) irrelevant or (b) insufficiently relevant to be helpful to the court in the determination of disputed facts. An honest opinion on an honest understanding of all the facts of the case is the requirement of an expert.

An inquiry into the civil justice system is presently being conducted by Lord Woolf. One of his lordship's suggestions is that responsibility for the appointment of expert witnesses should pass from the parties to the court (involving much greater use of the court's existing powers under Order 40 of the Rules of the Supreme Court). The expert's function should be that of assisting the judge to come to the right answer. An expert appointed by the court would be free to talk to all parties before submitting his report and

---

1 [1981] 1 All ER 267 at p276.

would be open to cross-examination by all parties at the trial. It might still be necessary for those parties to seek opinions from others well experienced in the relevant area of business activity; however, it would not be possible for them to call such persons to give evidence at the trial. It is suggested that permitting the court to appoint an expert would enable the court to keep tighter control of the timetable of litigation, which would also benefit other litigants waiting for their cases to come to trial. The expert witness would be the judge's witness, rather than that of any party to the action.

Whether such reforms will in fact be introduced remains to be seen, but it may only be a matter of time before experts are indeed appointed by the court.

3 Applications for summary judgment

In *European Partners In Capital (EPIC) Holdings BV* v *Goddard & Smith*[1] the plaintiffs issued a writ against the defendant valuers, alleging that they had negligently over-valued commercial property on the security of which the plaintiffs had lent money. The plaintiffs then sought summary judgment for the sum claimed under Order 14 of the Rules of the Supreme Court, which requires the plaintiff to establish, on the basis of sworn statements (but without a full trial), that the sum claimed is "indisputably due". By their draft defence, the defendants contended that their valuation was a proper and competent valuation, although expert evidence on behalf of the plaintiffs suggested otherwise. There were thus two rival opinions, being expressions of judgment by professionals who had come to different conclusions.

The Court of Appeal refused to award summary judgment on this claim and instead granted the defendants unconditional leave to defend the action. In coming to this decision, the court said that, where the issue of negligence required a choice to be made between two professional opinions, it would not normally be appropriate to resolve the matter on a summary judgment application. Scott LJ said it would be a very unusual case in which it would be right to deny the defendants the opportunity of standing by and contending for the competence of their valuation at trial. Either the defendants, or the author of the valuation report, could be cross-examined at trial as to the valuation report's competence

---

1 [1992] 2 EGLR 155.

and correctness. Moreover, the defendants would then have the opportunity to challenge the correctness of the views expressed in the rival valuation report which was relied upon by the plaintiffs.

CHAPTER 4

The surveyor's standard of care

Although the standard of skill and care demanded of a surveyor is always the same (that of the reasonably competent member of the profession), what the surveyor must do in order to achieve that standard will vary according to the type of inspection which has been undertaken. In this chapter we consider two particular kinds of inspection and report: the structural survey and the more limited *Home Buyers' Survey and Valuation*.

A Structural survey

The most detailed report is the structural or full building survey. While the surveying profession generally is in favour of the term "structural survey", the RICS and ISVA have proposed that it should no longer be used. This is because of reported misunderstandings with clients when, for example, a structural engineer commissioned to undertake a "structural survey" has concentrated on the structure alone. Such problems serve to emphasise the importance of clearly defined terms of appointment which should wherever possible be confirmed in writing.

The content of a survey report will vary from one surveyor to another. However, it will normally include an inspection of both the condition and the construction of a property, and it is thus especially useful in respect of older properties or those which have been or may be extended. An opinion as to value is not generally included. There is no standard or set format, and the surveyor's report will be prepared to reflect the particular property.

A surveyor instructed to carry out a structural or building survey is under a duty to inspect the property so far as is reasonably practicable. There have been cases where a surveyor has been held negligent for failing to do a specific act. However, it is not clear from the available reports of those cases whether the surveyor in question was under a specific contractual duty to carry out the required act, or whether liability in truth resulted from a breach of the general duty to exercise reasonable care and skill.

In *Sincock* v *Bangs (Reading)*[1] a surveyor was asked to inspect and give "a general opinion" about a farm which his client wished to purchase. It was held that these instructions required the surveyor to warn the client of any defects which might have a material effect on the value of the property. At the time of his initial survey, the surveyor had neither the time nor the opportunity to carry out a detailed examination of the structure. The opinion he expressed was wrong, and was held to amount to negligence.

Likewise, in *Moss* v *Heckingbottom*[2] the defendant architect was instructed to carry out a structural survey of property and to test its services. It was held that this required him to give the property more than a casual inspection, and to report such structural defects or deficiencies in the services as a competent and careful architect would normally draw to the attention of his client. The evidence established that the defendant had failed in a number of respects to comply with this duty.

The second edition of a Guidance Note on structural surveys of residential property was published by the RICS in February 1985.[3] This is being reviewed by the RICS with a view to a third edition being published, together with model terms of appointment. It is not anticipated that amendments to the existing Guidance Note will be substantial.

Model terms of appointment have not previously been published, as it was felt that most surveyors preferred to draft their own terms so as to meet their own individual requirements. Such terms are based upon the service each surveyor is able to provide. As a minimum, these terms should include the following:
- the name and address of the client;
- the address of the property;
- the purpose of the survey (eg for purchase or lease);
- the type of property and its tenure;
- the date when the surveyor hopes to inspect;
- the date when the surveyor hopes to report;
- the fee and any possible increases;
- the size of the property as advised by the client, so that if it is

---

1 (1952) 160 EG 134.
2 (1958) 172 EG 207.
3 This was considered in some detail by Judge Bowsher QC in Watts v *Morrow* [1991] 1 EGLR 150: see p91.

larger the fee can be increased;
- what will be included in the inspection;
- any limitations of the inspection, such as the length of any ladder which may be used and any parts of the property which will not be inspected (eg unexposed parts or outbuildings);
- any assumptions made by the surveyor regarding consents, approvals and searches relating to the property;
- whether or not the survey will include a valuation;
- whether or not specialist tests are to be carried out on such matters as drains, electricity, gas and water supplies;
- a statement the surveyor will not comment upon the existence of contamination as this can only be established by appropriate specialists;
- a restriction on disclosure of the survey report, stating that it is for the sole use of the named client, is confidential to the client and his/her professional advisers, and that any other persons rely on the report at their own risk.

We may now consider a number of specific aspects of surveyors' work which have led in reported cases to a finding of negligence.

1 Method of reporting

Watts v *Morrow*[1] concerned a 1986 survey of a Dorset farm house. Although the case was the subject of a successful appeal on the question of damages,[2] the comments of the trial judge on surveying practice are very important and worthy of separate comment. In his report, the surveyor had pointed out many defects in the roof and made recommendations for repair. However the manner in which those recommendations were made was such as to give a clear impression that these could be dealt with as part of ordinary ongoing maintenance and repair. Nowhere in the report was there any warning that it would be necessary or desirable to undertake an immediate and heavy expenditure on the property. On the evidence, the judge was satisfied that the roof was due for a major overhaul of the coverings including stripping tiles, repairing/replacing the roof structure as required, rebuilding the top courses of brickwork, specialist woodworm treatment, felting, rebattening and retiling. As to the way in which the defendant went

---

1 [1991] 4 All ER 937; [1991] 2 EGLR 152; [1991] 1 EGLR 150.
2 see p149.

about his work, the judge made the following criticism:[1]

The most extraordinary practice adopted by the defendant was not specifically disapproved by the RICS, but the absence of disapproval was, I suspect, due to their failure to realise that some members might adopt the course taken by the defendant. It is the practice of the defendant to dictate his survey as he walks around the property during his inspection. He does not dictate notes into a dictating machine. He dictates his survey report into a dictating machine on site. When he returns to the office, he gives the tapes to his secretary, who types them up and the report is then amended and sent to the client. That was the practice adopted by the defendant on this occasion, so that he had no notes to disclose on discovery of documents. It also led to his report being lengthy and diffuse and to its conclusions being inadequate. That practice is inconsistent with the spirit of the RICS Practice (Guidance) Note "Structural Surveys of Residential Property" which contains the following recommendation:

Site Notes
It is recommended that all details of the property be recorded in writing, together with the date of inspection, the names of individuals present at the time, weather conditions affecting the inspection, sources of information and any other relevant materials. These notes, both typed and handwritten, should be retained for as long as practicable . . .

Apart from what was in the report, the defendant had no notes either written or typed. Moreover, he was unable to give evidence of his first impressions because his first drafts were not retained and were destroyed. While he did not say so in as many words, the expert giving evidence for the defendant surveyor clearly did not approve of this practice.

Many of the departures from the recommended practice adopted by the defendant may not have produced important errors but this departure, in my judgment, was serious. It led to a report which was strong on immediate detail but excessively, and I regretfully have to say, negligently weak on reflective thought.

The judgment of Ralph Gibson LJ in the Court of Appeal in this case contains another important point in relation to the wording of a surveyor's report. This is that, if a surveyor were to warrant explicitly that no repairs other than those indicated in the survey report would be required within some specified period of time, the surveyor could then be held liable for the full cost of repairs. It

---

1 [1991] 1 EGLR 150 at pp 153-154.

follows that a surveyor should be careful to avoid using words which might be interpreted as giving such a warranty.

2 Damp, rot, woodworm and timber defects

From statistics prepared by the insurers to the RICS professional indemnity insurance scheme, it emerges that approximately one-third of claims made on surveys relate to some form of timber defect. Knowledge of such matters takes a considerable time to acquire and comes from experience. Many of the claims have arisen because of inadequate experience on the part of the surveyor concerned and, as already noted, lack of experience is no defence to a claim of professional negligence.

It may seem surprising that there are not more reported decisions of cases involving timber defects. However, the sad fact is that, in many of the claims dealt with by insurers, the timber defects are sufficiently obvious that it is deemed not worth incurring the considerable expense of a trial and so the claim is settled.

One reported case in which a surveyor was held liable for failing to comment upon the existence of dry rot in a property is *Hardy* v *Wamsley-Lewis*.[1] In evidence, the surveyor concerned admitted that there had been dry rot in a Dorset property, but said that he had come to the conclusion that it was dormant. He was able to put his fingers behind it and lift it up carefully. He said that it was dry rot but that for one reason or another it had ceased to spread, and that it was dead in the sense that the little insects which eat away at the wood were no longer alive. However, the judge was satisfied that there were places in the property where a careful examination would have found waviness in the skirting and other evidence of active dry rot.

The surveyor's written report stated:

I looked where possible for either dry rot or beetle, but found none.

When asked why his report had not contained an appropriate warning, the surveyor gave an interesting response but, no doubt, a truthful one:

If I put anything concerning dry rot in a report my client probably would not

---

[1] (1967) 203 EG 1039.

buy the building, or, probably, if one uses another expression, they get the wind up.

Paull J was not impressed with this response and held the surveyor liable. His lordship ruled that the client should have been given a warning that dormant dry rot had been found and that it might be advisable to have the house further examined.

Fryer v *Bunney*[1] is a decision which brings anguish to many surveyors. The defendant, in a 1979 survey report on an Essex property, indicated that it had been checked for damp with a Protimeter and that no reading of dampness had been registered. While the property was being redecorated soon after purchase, it was found that water was being lost from the central heating tank and, when part of the hall floor was taken up, leaks were discovered in defective piping. More extensive use of the Protimeter would have revealed the existence of dampness, which was not apparent to the human eye or by placing hands against walls.

In holding the defendant liable for negligence, the Official Referee made some interesting comments regarding the surveyor's general standard of competence. He felt that, while there was no deliberate intention by the surveyor to "skimp" his work, it was perhaps a case of a man doing a job of standard type too frequently:

Everyone makes mistakes, everyone forgets and can be guilty of carelessness and I think that is what happened to Mr Bunney in this case. I think it was a non-deliberate omission, but I am sure that he did omit to check properly. It may be that Mr Bunney as a result of this experience will be a better surveyor in future. I think he is probably a very good one now, but having had the experience of having made a mistake, I am fairly confident that he will be even more careful in the future.

The moral of this decision must be for surveyors to prepare a very simple sketch plan of a property as it is surveyed, marking roughly where a Protimeter has been applied. It may be a long time after the survey before a complaint is received, and many other surveys may have been carried out on other properties in the meantime. It cannot be easy to remember each property clearly without some form of sketch to rely upon. Indeed, many surveyors take photographs as an aid to memory.

---

1 (1982) 263 EG 158.

In *Syrett* v *Carr & Neave*,[1] although the surveyor's instructions referred only to "the main walls and roof of the property", an attendance note of the surveyor concerned confirmed that he was to consider damp. On the first day of the trial admissions were made to the effect that the surveyor had failed to carry out an adequate inspection and to see evidence of death-watch beetle and its effects on the timber in various parts of the property, in particular the roof void, the attic bedrooms and the first-floor bedrooms. In addition, the surveyor failed in his written report to report upon the evidence of death-watch beetle in the property and to warn that the full extent could not be determined by a survey such as he had carried out, that extensive remedial work might be required and that it would be prudent to obtain a specialist's inspection.

In the light of these decisions it is hardly surprising that, where it is clear that a surveyor should have given some warning in his report or should have recommended some further investigation, a claim involving timber defects is usually settled. Nevertheless, two recently reported cases may give some encouragement to surveyors, although it must be stressed that each of them turns upon its own particular facts and creates no binding precedent for the future.

Hacker v *Thomas Deal & Co*[2] arose out of the 1987 purchase of a house in Belgravia. Having paid £1.625m for the property, an American investment banker discovered "an extremely virulent, extensive and concentrated attack of dry rot" in an area above the basement and below the kitchen. A claim was duly made against the firm of surveyors which had carried out a building survey prior to the purchase. It was alleged upon behalf of the plaintiff that at the time of the surveyor's inspection, the signs of dry rot were there for any competent surveyor to see or indeed to smell. As Judge Fawcus QC remarked, dry rot has a very distinctive smell "which one would expect a surveyor, even of limited experience, to be familiar with". Various aspects of the inspection and report were considered by the court, in particular the fact that the surveyor had not investigated or even spotted a small trapdoor in the ceiling of the basement sauna and had not used a torch and mirror to inspect the small gap at the back of the kitchen sink unit.

---

1 [1990] 2 EGLR 161; see p78.
2 [1991] 2 EGLR 161.

In rejecting all the specific allegations of negligence, the judge pointed out that, although a "mirror" inspection three months later had discovered the dreaded mycelium of serpula lacrymans, the rate at which the fungus can spread is such that it was impossible to conclude that it could have been seen by the surveyor. There were limits to the investigations which a surveyor could reasonably be expected to carry out. Having acknowledged that "the expert is to be taken to be able to recognise the signs which could give rise to the suspicion of hidden defects", he went on to say:

Although one is acting as a detective one does not start going into all the little crevices in the hopes of finding something unless there is some tell-tale sign which indicates that it would be advisable to do so.

The plaintiffs in *Kerridge* v *James Abbot & Partners*[1] were similarly unsuccessful, despite making a large number of allegations of negligence in respect of a surveyor's report. The judge held that it was not necessary for a surveyor to give a warning about dry rot or timber decay merely because an Ipswich property had a valley/parapet gutter, or because staining had been seen on the rafters and there were holes in the roof. Moreover, evidence of the existence of a defective pipe was not such as to cause a surveyor to give a warning about dry rot. In relation to a parapet wall, a surveyor did not have to remove stonework in the course of a structural survey.

The only complaint which was upheld by the judge related to the surveyor's failure to mention either the presence or the absence of a damp proof course in his report (despite having noted the existence of a damp area). However, since the plaintiffs had on moving into the property discovered a damp proof course and supplemented it with a chemical one, the judge concluded that they had not been disadvantaged in any way by not being told of the existence of a damp proof course.

By contrast with the two cases discussed above, another recent decision makes rather less pleasant reading for surveyors. This is the case of *Oswald* v *Countrywide Surveyors Ltd*,[2] in which a surveyor was held negligent for failing to warn clients of the severe

---

1 [1992] 2 EGLR 162.
2 [1994] EGCS 150.

structural damage that death-watch beetle was capable of causing to a timber framed farmhouse. At the time of his inspection, the surveyor identified the presence of death-watch beetle, but referred to this in his report as woodworm infestation. In giving evidence, the surveyor said that he did not distinguish in his report between common furniture beetle and death-watch beetle because he always tried to be as practical as possible and to give a report that clients could understand, avoiding jargon in order to make the report more readable. It had always been his practice to refer to either species of beetle as woodworm, although he intended to change this practice in future.

The surveyor had concluded that infestation was inactive because the flight holes did not appear to be fresh, the survey inspection having taken place in December when death-watch beetle would not have been in evidence. Moreover, the surveyor was told by the vendor that woodworm treatment had been carried out in the course of renovation. However, the surveyor did not inspect the schedule of works on which the guarantee was based, but merely recommended in his report that a further inspection be carried out after a period of approximately five years, a recommendation which the judge regarded as "giving the green light to purchase".

The judge accepted evidence from the plaintiffs that, while they had budgeted for extensive roof repairs as recommended in the report, they would not have proceeded with the purchase if the report had mentioned an infestation of death-watch beetle without stating whether it was active or not. The plaintiffs would not have touched the property "for love or money". The defendants were accordingly liable for negligence.

3 Roof defects

The second largest group of negligent survey claims, amounting to some 13% of the total, are those in which it is alleged that the roof of a property is defective. In many of these cases the basic problem results from a lack of appropriate knowledge on the surveyor's part.

In *Hooberman* v *Salter Rex*,[1] for example, the point at issue was the extent of a surveyor's knowledge in 1977 of ventilation problems associated with flat roofs. The surveyor there carried out an

---

1 [1985] 1 EGLR 144.

inspection of an upper maisonette formed by the conversion of a five-storey Victorian house in North London. The property had a flat roof terrace of timber construction, which the plaintiff turned into a roof garden. The construction of this terrace was defective in a number of respects (none of which was mentioned in the survey report): the felt upstands at the walls of the terrace were inadequate; there were neither zinc nor lead wall flashings; the edge of the felt was turned into a groove in the perimeter walls and bonded; and there were no timber angled fillets at the junction of the perimeter walls and at the decking.

As a result of these defects, water leaked from the terrace into space above the plaintiff's bedroom ceiling, leading to an outbreak of dry rot. The client thereupon claimed damages from the surveyor, arguing that a warning should have been given. To this the surveyor replied that it was desirable not to alarm a client who was keen to purchase a property; the surveyor's job, it was maintained, was limited to warning of those defects which might make the client change his or her mind about a purchase.

In holding the defendant liable, Judge Smout QC rejected this limited view of his responsibilities:

The surveyor was there to inspect the property so far as reasonably practicable, so as to report candidly upon its condition. No doubt he has to be selective and determine what aspects are important and what are unimportant but whether his conclusions are comfortable or uncomfortable to the client is immaterial.

In *Cross* v *David Martin & Mortimer*[1] it was alleged that a surveyor carrying out what was then known as a *House Buyers' Report and Valuation* failed to comment fully on a loft conversion in a roof and, in particular, had failed to consider whether it was structurally strong enough to sustain live loading if used as a room. Phillips J envisaged the possibility of a vigorous party taking place in the loft room while the roof was laden with snow and a gale was howling outside. The survey report contained a comment to the effect that the construction was sound but that further enquiries should be made with regard to planning permission or building regulations for the conversion, but this was held to be insufficient. The judge said

---

1 [1989] 1 EGLR 154: see pp102–103.

the plaintiffs should have been informed that unless building regulation approval had been obtained for the conversion, it would not necessarily be safe to use the loft as other than a light storage space.

One of the unsuccessful allegations made against the surveyor in *Eley* v *King & Chasemore*[1] related to defects in a slate roof. The surveyor stated in his report that the roof had at some point (possibly because of war damage) been completely stripped and refelted, and noted that this had been done in a most unusual way, the felt having been laid over rather than under the battens. However, while the surveyor admitted that he would have felt happier if he had got up on to the valley gutters so as to inspect them, this would have required the use of a long ladder, something beyond the scope of his instructions.[2] Moreover, the surveyor's general impression was that the roof covering was proving to be effective.

It was suggested by the plaintiffs that the surveyor should have pointed out that lack of ventilation could be a problem, but the Court of Appeal disagreed. Furthermore, in the absence of any sign of water penetration, the court was satisfied that there was no need for the surveyor to go up on to the roof. A crucial finding was that none of the independent evidence produced by the unsuccessful plaintiffs reached any substantially different conclusions to those of the defendant surveyor. Indeed, in another survey of the same property carried out only some six weeks previously, there had been no mention at all of any problem with the roof.

In *Allen* v *Ellis & Co*[3] the plaintiff, relying on a structural survey from the defendants, purchased a house in Mill Hill. The defendants' report, which was generally favourable, stated specifically that the garage (which was used as a utility room) was brick-built and in satisfactory condition. In truth, as the judge held, what the report *ought* to have stated was that the garage was constructed of breeze blocks and that its asbestos sheet roof was "brittle or fragile, likely to split or crack, scantily supported, much repaired and right at the end of its useful life". In holding that the surveyor's failure to draw attention to the true state of affairs amounted to negligence,

---

1 [1989] 1 EGLR 181.
2 See p91.
3 [1990] 1 EGLR 170.

Garland J held him liable for the injuries suffered by the plaintiff who, in attempting to investigate the source of a leak from the roof and to inspect its general condition, stood on the roof and fell through.[1]

In *Bigg* v *Howard Son & Gooch*,[2] a surveyor was accused of negligence in failing to detect inadequacies in the design of a house roof. As a result of these deficiencies the roof had spread, forcing apart the front and rear walls to such an extent that the outward movement of the rear wall near the top amounted to as much as 36mm. Shortly after the trial began, the defence conceded that the surveyor's failure to observe and report on the defects did indeed constitute negligence.

4 Subsidence

It may come as something of a surprise that claims in respect of subsidence damage normally amount in total to less than 10% of those notified under the RICS insurance scheme. However, the overall figure disguises considerable variations, for extreme weather conditions inevitably have a marked effect upon the structure of properties and claims figures can thus increase significantly following, for example, the kind of drought conditions experienced in 1976.

Household insurers pay out many millions of pounds to cover the cost of structural repairs, including underpinning. Those insurers sometimes suggest that surveyors have over-reacted to movement cracks in properties, some of which could well have been of a thermal nature. However, when a case of subsidence is established and it is found that a survey was carried out prior to purchase, the same insurers may well seek to pursue a claim against the surveyor by exercising a right of subrogation.

A particular problem in negligence actions involving subsidence is that many years may have passed between the carrying out of the survey and the intimation of the claim. Whether or not the surveyor will be held negligent will largely depend upon expert evidence as to what should have been observed at the time of the survey inspection, and care must be taken to ensure that such evidence is not unduly coloured by hindsight. An example of this

---

1 See p163.
2 [1990] 1 EGLR 173.

problem may be found in *Leigh* v *Unsworth*,[1] where the trial took place more than seven years after the survey was carried out.[2] It was alleged that the surveyor was negligent for failing to detect indications of serious settlement, following upon the initial settlement which can effect newly built properties. In holding that there were only indications of such initial settlement, and that the surveyor was accordingly not liable, Judge Everett QC said:

The mere fact that one professional man might suffer from an excessive caution does not mean that another man, exercising his judgment to the best of his skill and ability and taking perhaps a somewhat more optimistic view, is guilty of a departure from the appropriate standard of professional care and skill.

Surveyors must have regard to local ground conditions and the effect these might have upon a structure as a result of certain types of tree growing in the vicinity. If a surveyor is not familiar with ground conditions for the area where he is undertaking a survey inspection, then study of a geological survey map may be appropriate. That said, however, it it is worth noting that the RICS Guidance Note on structural surveys of residential property makes no reference to such a procedure.

In *Daisley* v *BS Hall & Co*,[3] a row of trees along one boundary of the property included poplars, some of which were 40 ft in height and the nearest of which was within 25 ft of the corner of the house. The court accepted expert evidence to the effect that it was well known that where poplar, willow or elm trees were growing on clay soil, the very high transpiration through the leaves of these trees would tend to dry out the clay round their root systems and thus cause the clay to shrink. It was said to be part of a surveyor's training to be familiar with this. Moreover, *Building Research Station Digest 63* was available at the time of the survey in 1968. It was held that the surveyor was negligent in failing to appreciate and report on the risk created by the trees.

A surveyor is expected to have detective powers. Many prospective vendors, anxious to dispose of their properties, make

---

1 (1972) 230 EG 501.
2 Such delays are not necessarily fatal to a claim: see for example *Gurd* v *A Cobden Soar & Son* (1951) 157 EG 415; *Lawrence* v *Hampton & Sons* (1964) 190 EG 107.
3 (1972) 225 EG 1553.

deliberate efforts to conceal possible defects by means of redecoration or cosmetic repairs. In *Hingorani* v *Blower*,[1] where the surveyor's terms of employment were to report on observable defects, it was argued that there were no such defects, even though the property had suffered from subsidence to the point where it required underpinning. The defendant claimed that, like any other competent surveyor carrying out a proper and thorough survey, he was deceived by the fact that the vendor had fixed the property up so successfully that defects which were undoubtedly there were not observable.

In holding the surveyor guilty of negligence, the court pointed out that the property had a large crack on the rear elevation which had been filled in. It was noted that although persons "faking" a property can colour the mortar so as to make it more difficult to see, anyone looking at the whole length of the wall can still detect a wide band of filling. Moreover, the house (which was empty at the time of survey) had been redecorated internally throughout. It was held that the surveyor should have been put on suspicion that there might have been reasons for this redecoration, such as the disguising of defects in the property.

A similar decision was reached in *Morgan* v *Perry*,[2] where repointing, infilling and overpapering had the same effect as "a deliberate cover-up job". The surveyor was held negligent in failing to observe clear signs of subsidence.

A surveyor's failure to warn of the possibility of subsidence was considered in great detail by Phillips J in *Cross* v *David Martin & Mortimer*.[3] In carrying out a *House Buyers' Report and Valuation* (HBRV) on the standard RICS form, the surveyor reported that there was no evidence of structural faults or significant disrepair. However, when the plaintiffs moved in a professional carpet layer noted that the lounge floor was irregular and that the hall floor revealed a noticeable "hump". Having reinspected, the defendants advised that these irregularities were due to past occurrences and that no action was necessary. However, independent advice obtained by the plaintiffs revealed that the concrete floor had subsided and that there were misalignments of doors on the first floor.

---

1 (1975) 238 EG 883.
2 (1973) 229 EG 1737.
3 [1989] 1 EGLR 154: see also pp98–99.

On the question of subsidence, the judge held that the defendants should have discovered evidence of the movement of the concrete slab and should have been alerted to the possibility of subsidence by certain features, namely that the property was built on clay soil, that there were poplar trees in the vicinity and, most significantly, that the property was built on a nine degree slope which would require an unusually large amount of fill under the floor slab. His lordship made detailed reference to *BRE Digest 251* of July 1981, which tabulates visible damage caused by ground-floor slab settlement according to five different degrees of severity from negligible through to severe.

In holding that the defendants were guilty of negligence, the judge stated that, even if they considered that any subsidence was stable and not progressive, it was their duty to draw the plaintiff's attention to a feature which involved uncertainty as to the condition of the property. A house purchaser could expect to be informed of any feature of a property that involved uncertainty as to its condition, present or future, even if the surveyor's opinion as to its significance was reassuring. Furthermore, his lordship drew attention to the defendants' failure to follow their own usual good practice of opening and closing doors, which had led them to miss evidence of subsidence (one of the first-floor doors was misaligned to the point where it would not close at all).

Nevertheless, while the defendants were held to have fallen below the standard of care expected of them, the judge stressed that this was not a case where a slapdash survey had been carried out. The surveyor's notes showed that a great deal of care had been taken. The surveyor had inspected many other properties on the same development and had inspected the same property at the time of its previous sale. It was perhaps a case in which familiarity had lulled the surveyor into a slight sense of false security.

Where a surveyor believes that there may be a structural problem and gives practical advice as to how this may be overcome, it is unlikely that the surveyor will be found liable. This is exactly what happened in *Eley* v *King & Chasemore*,[1] where the defendants inspected a West Sussex property built in the mid-19th century but with more recent additions. The defendants' report drew attention to cracks both in the rendering on the walls and in other features

---

1 [1989] 1 EGLR 181.

of the property. It stated that the property (like many in the area) stood on a shrinkable clay subsoil, which would be liable to be affected by seasonal changes in its moisture content. It also commented in detail upon a very tall fir tree close to the property, as a result of which the tree was removed by the plaintiffs.

In relation to the construction generally, the report gave the following advice:

All houses on clay are more at risk than those constructed on a more stable subsoil. It would be a good idea to see if you could obtain insurance protection against subsidence, ground heave, settlement and landslip although with so many present and previous cracks in the walls, such cover might not be easy to obtain.

The plaintiff took this advice, obtaining insurance from a company which did not call for further investigations before taking on the risk. When, within a year of purchase, structural engineers reported that the property had suffered structural movement because of the soil substance and recommended underpinning, the cost of the necessary works was largely met by the insurers. Nevertheless, the plaintiffs brought an action for negligence against the defendants, arguing that they should have been alerted specifically to the possibility that underpinning would be necessary.

In rejecting this claim, the court held that, far from suffering loss as a result of the surveyor's advice, the purchasers had benefited financially from it. This was because, if they had simply negotiated with the vendor for a reduction in price, to take account of the possibility that underpinning would in future be required, they would almost certainly have received less than they actually obtained from the insurers.

It is not suggested, on the basis of this case, that advice as to the obtaining of specific insurance cover will be an effective answer in all cases. Nevertheless, it should be considered carefully when circumstances so warrant. For a survey to lead to liability in negligence the question is not just "what was missed?" but also "what was the client told?"

Reference has been made already to the time which can elapse between the survey inspection being carried out and the matter coming to trial.[1] There is no doubt that in recent years many judges have been influenced by the statement of Ian Kennedy J in *Roberts v J Hampson & Co*[2] that, if an inspection revealed indications which gave grounds for suspicion, the surveyor should take reasonable steps to follow the trail of suspicion. This line was adopted by Scott Baker J in *Hipkins v Jack Cotton Partnership*[3] where neither a valuation nor a survey report gave any hint of a structural problem affecting a Kidderminster property. Negative answers were given to questions as to subsidence or landslip. The surveyor's site notes gave no indication that he had seen any cracks or other evidence of settlement. Although the trial took place more than seven years after the surveyor's inspection, the judge was satisfied, from evidence as to the condition of the property before, at the time of and after the plaintiff's purchase of the property, that cracks would have been visible at the time of the survey and should have been noted.

In *Pepler v Roger Stevens & Chance*[4] an investigation of burst water pipes, some two years after purchase, revealed serious structural cracks in a property. Mr Barry Green QC held that if the cracks had been found the surveyor should have advised that wallpaper be stripped. If the vendor of the property would not agree to this, the judge was satisfied that the sale would have fallen through. It was common ground that, if the stripping off of the wallpaper revealed the cracks, the surveyor should then have advised further investigation by an engineer.

In one of the few recently reported cases involving liability for surveys, the Court of Appeal has given some guidance as to what is expected of a survey report as to the consequences of possible future movement in a property. In *Matto v Rodney Broom Associates*,[5] the defendant engineer's report stated that the property was generally structurally stable, and recommended minor remedial works in order to ensure that it continued to be so. Future movement was considered to be minimal.

In holding that this report fell below the standard required, and

---

1 See pp100–101.
2 [1989] 2 All ER 504; [1988] 2 EGLR 181; see p125.
3 [1989] 2 EGLR 157.
4 October 6 1989, Queen's Bench, unreported.
5 [1994] 41 EG 152: see also pp78–79.

that the defendant was therefore liable to pay £18,000 damages, the court stressed that the result might seem hard on the defendant and that it was probably rather more than the plaintiff deserved. The basic skill and experience of the defendant had not been shown to be lacking. He had been caught in an unfortunate set of circumstances in which he wrote a short report intended to serve his client swiftly and effectively and without a screen of qualifications for his own protection. Nevertheless, Ralph Gibson LJ said:

His client was entitled to receive a report which dealt adequately with the advice required or a report which expressly stated that it was limited in some particular way. The report, for example, might have added words to the effect that having regard to the nature of the subsoil and the nature of the foundations likely to have been constructed for this house there was a risk of more than minimal movement in the future because such a house can be stable for a number of years and then suddenly move; but that the cost of removing that risk by underpinning would be very large. The plaintiff would then have been faced with the risk of having his application for a mortgage rejected but he would have been able to try to negotiate a reduction in the price of the house to a fair value having regard to that risk of future movement as described.

In my judgment the plaintiff was wrongly deprived of that opportunity.

5 Defects in services

Between 11 and 12% of claims against surveyors which are notified to insurers arise out of alleged defects in the services of a property. Many of these claims are successfully defended by showing that the surveyor's terms of appointment have specifically excluded or restricted the requirement to inspect the particular service or services. In *Strover* v *Harrington*,[1] for example, where the surveyor's terms of appointment stated specifically that an inspection of the property's drainage system was excluded unless specifically requested by the purchasers, no such request was made, and the surveyor was accordingly under no duty to make such an inspection. Similarly, the *Conditions of Engagement for a Home Buyers' Survey and Valuation* (formerly the *House Buyers' Report and Valuation*), make it clear that the surveyor will only inspect services visually where they are accessible, and will not carry out tests.

---

1 [1988] 1 EGLR 173.

In *Pfeiffer* v *E & E Installations*,[1] which concerned the purchase of a South London house in 1987, the plaintiffs had commissioned a full inspection by a firm of surveyors. However, so far as the property's gas-fired central heating system was concerned, the surveyors recommended that this should be checked by a specialist firm. This firm reported that there was nothing wrong with the heating system but, shortly after the plaintiffs purchased the property, a second inspection revealed that there was a crack in the heat exchanger.

The Court of Appeal held that the defendants were instructed to carry out a "full working test and inspection" of the system. They should have examined the heat exchanger using a torch and mirror and, had they done so, the crack in the heat exchanger would have been discovered. It followed that the defendants were guilty of negligence.

B Home Buyers' Survey and Valuation

An intermediate form of survey report, called the *Home Buyers' Survey and Valuation* – HBSV, replaces the former *House Buyers' and Flat Buyers' Reports* – HBRV. Guidance is laid down by the RICS and ISVA in joint documentation, published in August 1993.

The extent of the HBSV inspection is described in the Standard Conditions of Engagement, which are split into six paragraphs. These are in much the same form as the Guidance Notes for Mortgage Valuations, which are discussed in Chapter 5.[2]

The standard form of report is also split into six paragraphs, covering information, general description of the property, external condition, internal condition, common parts and services and further advice and valuation. It is intended to be a concise report that comments specifically on significant but not minor defects and those likely to affect materially the value of the property. It will highlight defects obvious from a visual inspection and will give the value of the property in the open market and also the estimated reinstatement cost for insurance purposes.

The surveyor, who may be either a chartered surveyor or an incorporated valuer, will not be expected, for instance, to lift carpets

---

1 [1991] 1 EGLR 162.
2 See p117.

or to look into unexposed or inaccessible areas. As such, the report is a limited one which should provide most of the information that a typical purchaser requires when buying a fairly modern and standard property. The surveyor will advise if the age or condition of the property is such that a more detailed report is required.

Although the *Home Buyers' Survey and Valuation* envisages an inspection more limited in *scope* than a structural survey, this does not mean that a surveyor carrying out such an inspection will be judged by a lower standard of care and skill. This point was specifically accepted by Phillips J in *Cross* v *David Martin & Mortimer*.[1] The judge there noted the view expressed in July 1984 by a Joint General Practice and Building Surveyors Division Working Party of the RICS on structural surveys that:

We are convinced that the same level of expertise is required from the surveyor in carrying out an HBRV as that for a structural survey.

A particular limitation of the *Home Buyers' Report and Valuation* is that the surveyor will only inspect services visually where they are accessible and will not carry out tests of those services. The standard report form specifically points out that the standard and adequacy of installations can only be ascertained as a result of a test by an appropriate specialist. Despite this limitation, however, the defendant surveyor was held liable in *Howard* v *Horne & Sons*[2] for errors in relation to a property's electrical supply. The surveyor's report stated that "electrical wiring is in PVC cable" which, in the opinion of the judge, implied that the wiring was modern and that there was no cause for concern about it. In reality, while the wiring in the kitchen was PVC covered, much of the rest was not and, indeed, was dangerous. The most important part of the evidence given concerned a board on which several junction boxes were mounted. Some of these had PVC cables on one side but not on the other. Although this board was not easy to examine, the judge held that the surveyor should have been able to overcome the difficulties of bad light, and could have commented more adequately upon the condition of the electrical wiring.

---

1 [1989] 1 EGLR 154.
2 [1990] 1 EGLR 272.

CHAPTER 5

The valuer's standard of care

With valuers as with surveyors (and indeed all professional persons), the question whether reasonable care and skill has been displayed can only be properly answered in the light of the instructions under which that person acts. To take a simple example, it seems obvious that a valuer who overlooks structural defects in the course of a mortgage valuation *may* escape a finding of negligence in circumstances where a structural surveyor would undoubtedly have incurred liability. Nevertheless, the idea of a variable duty depending upon instructions received is sometimes obscured by suggestions that a "valuation" can mean only one thing, irrespective of the use to which it is to be put. Thus, in *Singer & Friedlander Ltd* v *John D Wood & Co*, Watkins J said:[1]

Whatever conclusion is reached, it must be without consideration for the purpose for which it is required. By this I mean that a valuation must reflect the honest opinion of the valuer of the true market value of the land at the relevant time, no matter why or by whom it is required, be it by merchant bank, developer or prospective builder. So the expression, for example, 'for loan purposes' used in a letter setting out a valuation should be descriptive only of the reason why the valuation is required and not as an indication that were the valuation required for some other purpose a different value would be provided by the valuer to he who seeks the valuation.

It may be true to say that a "valuation" as such should reflect the valuer's honest estimation of a property's worth,[2] but it is suggested that the judge in this passage goes too far. While we would not subscribe to the view expressed in *Corisand Investments Ltd* v *Druce & Co*,[3] that a "mortgage valuation" is an open market valuation discounted by 20% to allow for the possibility of a forced sale, there is no doubt that different types of valuation require the valuer to make different assumptions, and indeed this is recognised

---

1 (1977) 243 EG 212 at p213.
2 See *Axa Equity & Law Home Loans Ltd* v *Hirani Watson* [1994] EGCS 90.
3 (1978) 248 EG 315.

in the Guidance Notes which are issued by the RICS and the ISVA. Moreover, a client will in many cases want more from a professional adviser than a mere statement of value; if the valuer is specifically required to advise on how much may safely be lent on the security of a particular property, or what level of insurance cover should be taken out, the question whether or not the valuer is guilty of negligence will fall to be judged against the background of that requirement.

We may now turn to consider a number of specific matters bearing on the general standard of care which a valuer is expected to demonstrate in carrying out professional work.

A Accuracy

1 The nature of valuation

While most, if not all, of the valuations which lead to professional negligence actions may be described as "wrong", the courts are usually at pains to point out that an error in itself does not amount to negligence. The judicial view of the valuation process was clearly expressed by Goddard LJ in *Baxter v F W Gapp & Co Ltd*:[1]

Valuation is very much a matter of opinion. We are all liable to make mistakes, and a valuer is certainly not to be found guilty of negligence merely because his valuation turns out to be wrong. He may have taken too optimistic or too pessimistic a view of a particular property. One has to bear in mind that, in matters of valuation, matters of opinion must come very largely into account.

Similar sentiments, and a clear recognition that valuation is inherently imprecise, can be seen in the judgment of Watkins J in *Singer & Friedlander Ltd v John D Wood & Co*:[2]

The valuation of land by trained, competent and careful professional men is a task which rarely, if ever, admits of precise conclusion. Often beyond certain well-founded facts so many imponderables confront the valuer that he is obliged to proceed on the basis of assumptions. Therefore, he cannot be faulted for achieving a result which does not admit of some degree of

---

1 [1938] 4 All ER 457 at p459.
2 (1977) 243 EG 212 at pp213–214: see also *Corisand Investments Ltd v Druce & Co* [1978] 248 EG 315 at p321, *per* Gibson J.

error. Thus, two able and experienced men, each confronted with the same task, might come to different conclusions without anyone being justified in saying that either of them has lacked competence and reasonable care, still less integrity, in doing his work.

This acceptance that, for any property, there is a range of values which competent practitioners might give, means that a defendant whose valuation falls within that range is effectively safe from a negligence claim. Even if the valuer has arrived at a conclusion by a wholly erroneous route, the client cannot claim to have suffered from this negligence if a reasonably competent valuer could have produced the same result.[1] As was stated by the Court of Appeal in *Matto* v *Rodney Broom Associates*:[2] "A professional man is entitled to be lucky."

As for the converse proposition, there is no legal rule stating that a valuation which falls outside the permitted range must by definition have been arrived at through negligence. Nevertheless, common sense suggests that most judges will in such circumstances agree with what was said by Watkins J in *Singer* v *Friedlander Ltd* v *John D Wood & Co*:[3] "Any valuation falling outside what I shall call the 'bracket' brings into question the competence of the valuer and the sort of care he gave to the task of valuation."

2 The "bracket"

The "margin of error" or "bracket" approach appears to have originated in *Singer* v *Friedlander Ltd* v *John D Wood & Co*.[4] In developing his argument that all valuations are imprecise, Watkins J stated:

Valuation is an art, not a science. Pinpoint accuracy in the result is not, therefore, to be expected by he who requests the valuation. There is, as I have said, the permissible margin of error, the "bracket" as I have called it. What can properly be expected from a competent valuer using reasonable skill and care is that his valuation falls within this bracket.

---

[1] *Mount Banking Corporation Ltd* v *Brian Cooper & Co* [1992] 2 EGLR 142; *Private Bank & Trust Co Ltd* v *Salmans (UK) Ltd* [1993] 1 EGLR 144. Cf *Henley* v *Cloke & Sons* [1991] 2 EGLR 141.
[2] [1994] 2 EGLR 163.
[3] (1977) 243 EG 212.
[4] (1977) 243 EG 212.

Although this approach is now routinely adopted in valuation cases, it should be appreciated that it appears in two different versions. Originally, the court would fix the appropriate "bracket" for any particular case by identifying (with the aid of expert evidence) the "right figure" or true value of the property, and then deciding what "margin of error" would be permissible. Thus, in *Singer & Friedlander* itself, the parties' expert witnesses agreed that the permitted margin would normally be 10% in either direction, rising to 15% in the case of a very unusual property or an exceptionally volatile market. However, in some later cases judges have argued that there is no such thing as the "right figure"; all that can be identified is a range of values which might have been attributed to the property at the relevant date by reasonably competent members of the valuation profession. The question is then simply whether or not the defendant's valuation falls within that range.

A "broad brush" description of the way in which a court should deal with valuation cases was given by a deputy judge in *Mount Banking Corporation Ltd* v *Brian Cooper & Co*,[1] where it was said that a judge:

must look at the component figures properly to be taken into account by the competent surveyor using proper skill and care; from there he must reach a conclusion as to whether in total the valuer complained of erred, and he must then stand back and ask whether that is, by the standards of the profession, a margin of error which can be tolerated or which can only be sensibly stigmatised as negligence.

In the *Mount Banking* case it was clear that, while the defendant valuer's case notes showed that he had taken into consideration all the correct matters in carrying out his valuation, part of that valuation was reached by "a fault in the process of calculation". This was the valuer's failure to realise and take into account the possibility that an owner-occupier of a site might choose not to develop it immediately and would thus incur financing costs. However, since the resultant valuation was within the acceptable range of figures that a competent valuer using due skill and care could reach (albeit towards the upper end of that range), there was no finding of negligence.

---

1 [1992] 2 EGLR 142.

Deciding upon the size of the bracket, or the permissible margin of error, is obviously an important part of any negligent valuation case. Unfortunately, perhaps, it is a matter on which judicial opinions may differ considerably. In *Beaumont* v *Humberts*,[1] for example, Staughton LJ felt that the conventional bracket of 10 or 15% imposed a high (perhaps an unduly high) standard upon valuers.[2] On the other hand, the judge in *Nyckeln Finance* v *Stumpbrook Continuation Ltd*[3] was prepared to permit no more than a 10% margin in a case where, as he acknowledged, "it is common ground that there could be a wide variation".

The courts do not expect valuers to be blessed with the benefit of hindsight.[4] In *Private Bank & Trust Co Ltd* v *Sallmans (UK) Ltd*,[5] an office development was valued at the end of 1988 at £1.7m. In June 1990 the defendants revalued the property at between £1.35m and £1.45m, whereupon the plaintiff bank lent the developer £780,000. When the borrower defaulted, the plaintiff bank was left with a property which it claimed was worth no more than £500,000, but its action against the defendants failed. It was held that the June 1990 valuation was held to have been within 15% of "the right figure",[6] since nobody could have foreseen the depth of the forthcoming recession, nor the speed and extent of the decline in the property market during the second half of 1990.

In a number of recent cases, the "right figure" theory has been applied to valuations of residential property. In *Axa Equity & Law Home Loans Ltd* v *Goldsack & Freeman*,[7] for example, the defendants were instructed to value a leasehold flat in Brighton, for which very few comparables were available. The court held that the correct approach was to ask where the proper bracket of valuation lay and whether the impugned valuation lay within a permissible limit of that bracket ("the right figure"). Having done so, the judge

---

1 [1990] 2 EGLR 166; see pp4, 40, 80.
2 In *Banque Bruxelles Lambert SA* v *Eagle Star Insurance Co Ltd* [1994] 2 EGLR 108 at p118, the experts were said to have agreed that, when valuations are based on comparables, one competent valuation might differ from another by as much as 20%.
3 [1994] 2 EGLR 143.
4 See *Macey* v *Debenham Tewson & Chinnocks* [1993] 1 EGLR 149; *Perry* v *Wilson* October 20 1993, Queen's Bench Division, unreported.
5 [1993] 1 EGLR 144.
6 See also *Muldoon* v *Mays of Lilliput* [1993] 1 EGLR 43.
7 [1994] 1 EGLR 175.

concluded that, although the valuation was at the very top of the bracket, it nevertheless fell within it, and so the defendants were not liable in accordance with the *Mount Banking* principle.[1]

In *BNP Mortgages Ltd* v *Barton Cook & Sams*,[2] the property concerned was part of what was Charles Darwin's stately home in Nottingham. The court decided that, since the property was unique, a 15% margin of error from "the right figure" was appropriate. Interestingly, the court accepted in passing that, for houses on a uniform estate, even a 10% margin would be too wide, and that the acceptable margin on a standard estate house might be as low as 5%.

B Valuation methods

1 General

The courts have in general resisted the temptation to demand that a valuer should use any optimum method of valuation, confining themselves instead to pointing out just where a particular defendant went astray. Indeed, the courts have been careful to stress that there *is* no single "correct" method. As Kekewich J put it in *Love* v *Mack*:[3]

The law does not say that in any breach of intelligent operation, intelligent skill, there is necessarily one defined path which must be strictly followed, and that if one departs by an inch from that defined path one were necessarily at fault . . . There is no absolute rule as regards the proper method of ascertaining the value in this case, and [the defendant] adopted methods which, if they are not perfect, if they are not the best, if they might have been improved upon, still are methods which a man of position, endeavouring to do his duty, might fairly adopt without its being said he was wanting in reasonable care and skill.

Not only is there no optimum method; there have even been suggestions that a valuer need not use any "method" at all! True, it has been described as "not very helpful" for a valuer whose work is challenged simply to say: "The only thing I did was to go and look

---

1 *Mount Banking Corporation Ltd* v *Brian Cooper & Co* [1992] 2 EGLR 142.
2 February 18 1994, Official Referees' Business, unreported.
3 (1905) 92 LT 345, at p349.

at the place"[1] So too, in *Johnson v Ribbins*,[2] a judge was highly critical of an expert witness who simply stated a figure without any evidence or reasoning to support it. However, in *Corisand Investments Ltd v Druce & Co*,[3] after considering various ways of calculating the value of an hotel, Gibson J made it quite clear that a valuer might legitimately base conclusions simply upon comparables (without further calculation), or even upon experienced instinct; in the latter case, of course, such comparables as there were would be indirect ones, which could not therefore be produced for checking.

Although a valuer has comparative freedom in how to use the data which he or she possesses, the courts are more ready to find negligence where no reasonable steps are taken to collect suitable data in the first place. It was suggested in *Old Gate Estates Ltd v Toplis*[4] that, in a normal case, "it would be negligent for a valuer to value a property without himself collecting the material upon which the valuation is made, such as the income and the outgoings". This view formed the basis of the decision in *Singer & Friedlander Ltd v John D Wood & Co*,[5] where an employee of the defendants valued a development site in Gloucestershire at £2,200,000, without either visiting the site or speaking on the telephone to the planning department of the county council. Not surprisingly, negligence was established and the defendants were held liable.

Notwithstanding the above discussion, judges in a number of recent cases have paid very close attention to the precise way in which a valuation was arrived at, and some useful guidance has emerged as to what matters should be taken into account by a competent valuer. In *Mount Banking Corporation Ltd v Brian Cooper & Co*,[6] for example, where an action of negligence failed, it was specifically held (following an examination of the valuer's case notes) that he had considered all the correct matters. These were:
- the size, condition, tenure and location of the property;
- planning permission and permitted user;
- the value and use of adjoining and neighbouring properties;

---

1 *Baxter v F W Gapp & Co Ltd* [1938] 4 All ER 457 at p462, *per* Goddard LJ.
2 (1975) 235 EG 757.
3 (1978) 248 EG 315.
4 [1939] 3 All ER 209.
5 (1977) 243 EG 212.
6 [1992] 2 EGLR 142.

- the value, particularly as to rent and capital, of other offices in the locality and their comparability and any consequent adjustments to be made when applying that information to the property in question;
- the state of the property market;
- the effect of increases in bank interest rates; and
- the realism of the projected development and its costing.

Moreover, the valuer had quite properly carried out a number of cross-check valuations to verify his answers before making his valuation report.

Similar views were expressed by the judge in *Axa Equity & Law Home Loans Ltd v Hirani Watson*,[1] where once again a negligence claim was successfully defended. It was said that, while the list was not intended to be exhaustive, a reasonably competent valuer would normally be expected to consider the following matters:

- the prices at which similar properties in the same area exchange hands at the relevant time – the comparables;
- any features peculiar to the property distinguishing it from the comparables;
- the valuer's own experience and knowledge of the area. (So far as valuation is concerned, location is a very important matter – one witness said that there were three guiding factors affecting valuation, namely, position and position and position!);
- valuations, if any, placed upon the property by other competent valuers in the recent past; and
- the general state of the market.

One particular aspect of the valuer's "method" which has received judicial scrutiny in a number of cases concerns the significance which should be attached to a recent transaction involving the property in question. As long ago as 1891, a defendant whose valuation departed widely from the price at which the property had recently changed hands was held guilty of negligence.[2] More recently, when the defendants in *Banque Bruxelles Lambert SA v Eagle Star Insurance Co Ltd*[3] attempted to justify their valuation (which exceeded by some 40% the price at which the property had

---

1 [1994] EGCS 90.
2 *Scholes* v *Brook* (1891) 63 LT 837: see also *Baxter* v *F W Gapp & Co Ltd* [1938] 4 All ER 457.
3 [1994] 2 EGLR 108.

just been acquired) on the basis of comparables, Phillips J was not convinced:[1]

> The complexity of the task of producing a valuation by a process of comparison tends to conceal a simple fact. A valuation is no more than the opinion of the valuer of the price that the property is likely to realise if sold on the open market ... where a property has just been sold, the sale price is potentially the most cogent evidence of the open market value of that property.

The judge acknowledged that a valuer should of course consider whether the property had been properly and competently marketed prior to sale, and whether the vendor might have had a special reason for selling at an undervalue. However, his view was that, outside such special circumstances:

> Absent such express instructions [ie to disregard a recent sale price and to base a valuation exclusively on comparables], a valuer who gives an open market valuation without considering the implications of a recent sale in the market of the property being valued is ... negligent.[2]

2 RICS/ISVA Guidance Notes
(a) Current relevance

The governing bodies of many professions publish Guidance Notes or Practice Statements as an indication to their members of what is regarded as good practice. Once published, such documents are frequently relied on by the courts as evidence of the kind of procedure which, if not adopted, may justify a finding of negligence against a practitioner. They are not conclusive on this issue, but will be given considerable weight in a professional negligence action.

In the valuation context, one of the most important documents of this kind is the RICS/ISVA *Mortgage Valuation: Guidance for Valuers*. As originally published, this related to inspections carried out on or after July 1 1990; it was revised in May 1992 in respect of inspections carried out on or after June 1 1992.[3] The notes are in

---

1 [1994] 2 EGLR 108 at p118.
2 Similar views have been expressed by judges in *Nyckeln Finance* v *Stumpbrook Continuation Ltd* [1994] 33 EG 93 and *BNP Mortgages Ltd* v *Goadsby & Harding Ltd* [1994] 2 EGLR 169.
3 Relating to residential property.

six sections covering the valuer's roles; the valuer's inspection; the valuer's report; the valuation; valuation for insurance purposes; and the valuer's record of inspection and valuation. The notes also contain model conditions of engagement between the lender and the valuer, which stress the purpose for which the report and valuation are required. Importantly, the notes further impose a duty upon the lender to take all reasonable steps to inform the borrower as to the limitations of the inspection report and valuation, and to suggest that the borrower commissions a more detailed inspection and report before entering into a legal commitment.

In a number of recent cases, scrutiny of the relevant Guidance Notes has resulted in a court ruling that a valuer has not been guilty of professional negligence. In *Predeth* v *Castle Phillips Finance Co Ltd*,[1] for example, a valuer was instructed to carry out a "crash sale valuation" of a repossessed property on behalf of a finance company. The "Guidance Notes on the Valuation of Assets" which applied at the time made no mention of "crash sale valuations"; however, the Court of Appeal, having considered the definitions of "open market value" and "forced sale value", decided that the valuer had complied with his instructions and was accordingly not liable for negligence.

The point at issue in *PK Finans International (UK) Ltd* v *Andrew Downs & Co Ltd*[2] was the extent of a valuer's duty to verify planning consents. The valuer's report on a nursing and residential home stated:

We have made verbal enquiries but have not undertaken any official searches and for the purpose of this valuation we have assumed that full planning consents were obtained for the development of the property as a nursing home, that consents are also in existence for additional nursing home facilities in the stable block and that consent has been given for sheltered housing on plot No 426.

When it transpired that these planning assumptions were completely false (due to fraud on the part of the borrower), the lender client brought an action for negligence, alleging that the valuer should have stressed the need for verification of the planning

---

1 [1986] 2 EGLR 144.
2 [1992] 1 EGLR 172.

position. However, the valuer relied upon the RICS *Guidance Notes on the Valuation of Assets* (2nd ed), which states:[1]

Town planning
The valuer should state if he has made written or oral enquiries of planning authorities as to zoning and possible presence of any adverse planning proposals. The valuer should state if he has inspected the statutory register and the information noted; he should also give details of planning consents made available to him and note any conditions which adversely affect value.

Sir Michael Ogden QC was satisfied that the valuer had observed good valuation practice. The judge said:

. . . these Guidance Notes are not to be regarded as a statute. I suspect they are as much for the protection of surveyors as anything else, in that they set out various recommendations which, if followed, it is hoped will protect the surveyor from the unpleasantness of being sued. In any event, mere failure to comply with the Guidance Notes does not necessary constitute negligence . . .

Reference was made to the RICS Statement of Asset Valuation Practice No 1 (July 1992) in *Allied Trust Bank Ltd* v *Edward Symmons & Partners*.[2] This concerned a mortgage valuation of a Georgian country house in Norfolk. In arriving at his conclusions, the valuer included an element of "hope value" to reflect the prospect of planning permission for conversion of the property. Although the RICS Statement had not been published at the time of the valuation in question, it was held that a valuer who acted in accordance with its contents could not justifiably be criticised, at least where the client had given no specific instructions to the contrary. Thus, since the Statement refers to "hope value" and provides confirmation that it was reasonable to include hope value in valuing the property, the valuer was held not to have been negligent.

In relation to the valuation of residential property for mortgage purposes, a matter which has given rise to considerable controversy

---

1 Guidance Note 6, para 7 – the verification of information supplied to or adopted by a valuer.
2 [1994] 1 EGLR 165: see also *Craneheath Securities Ltd* v *York Montague Ltd* [1994] 1 EGLR 159; *Perry* v *Wilson* October 20 1993, Queen's Bench, unreported.

concerns the need for an internal inspection of the roof. When the first edition of *Mortgage Valuations Guidance Notes for Valuers* was published (in December 1985), these stated that an inspection of the main roof void was included, where reasonably accessible and to the extent visible from the roof access, for the purpose of identifying readily apparent fundamental defects only. This became known as a "head and shoulders" inspection of the roof space.

In *Gibbs* v *Arnold Son & Hockley*,[1] Stephen Desch QC was satisfied that the defendants had complied with this guidance when inspecting a Norwich property for mortgage valuation purposes. The chimney within the roof space was defective, but the judge was not convinced that cracks in the chimney would have been reasonably noticeable from the hatch, even with a torch, in the course of such an inspection.

The same Guidance Note received further judicial scrutiny from Judge Bowsher QC in *Ezekiel* v *McDade*.[2] In his valuation report, the valuer accurately described the property as being of "non-traditional construction". However, he went on to say the following:

There is no evidence of any serious defect in the examined areas of the premises and it has been modernised and improved to a good standard throughout.

It transpired that the property was constructed of the "Bison Unit System" and that a concrete purlin in the roof was not balanced. The experts instructed by each of the parties could not agree as to whether a "head and shoulders" inspection of the roof would have revealed the defect. The judge accordingly inspected the property personally and concluded that such an inspection should have revealed the defect, emphasising that there was no evidence to suggest that there was anything stored in the roof space at the time of the original inspection which might have obstructed the valuer's view. The judge made it clear that, wherever a mortgage valuer finds a trapdoor into a roof, he should at least put his head and shoulders through the trapdoor and make a visual inspection.

The judgment in *Ezekiel* v *McDade* also refers specifically to Guidance Note 2(d) of the same notes. This states:

---

1 [1989] 2 EGLR 154; see p126.
2 [1994] 1 EGLR 255.

If the valuer suspects that hidden defects exist, he may, if he thinks it necessary, recommend that further investigation be carried out.

While useful, this note should not be regarded as an automatic escape route for practitioners. A valuer who makes such a recommendation must have reasonable grounds for doing so. It is not a recommendation which can be made as a matter of course following every inspection.

(b) The future

In April 1994, the General Council of the RICS accepted a proposal that the former Practice Notes (the "Red Book") and Guidance Notes (the "White Book") should be merged into a single document. This followed consideration of a Report of the RICS President's Working Party on Commercial Property Valuations (the *Mallinson Report*). The proposed new manual is to be called *The RICS Statements of Valuation of Appraisal Practice Guidance Notes*, and will be divided into three sections: statements of practice; guidance notes on good valuation practice and methods; and appendices. The statements of practice in section one are to have mandatory status, with disciplinary powers for non-compliance under the RICS byelaws. Any departure from the mandatory requirements would have to be justified. As before, the Guidance Notes forming section two will be advisory only, but will undoubtedly continue to have very persuasive effect in the context of negligence actions.

The proposed mandatory requirements in section one are as follows:
1 Application of the statements and Guidance notes
2 Clarification and agreement of conditions of engagement
3 Purposes of valuations and their bases
4 Definitions of bases of valuation; assumptions
5 Qualifications of valuers
6 Inspections and investigations
7 Reports and published references to them
8 Review of previous valuations, further inspections and associated reporting
9, 10 etc Valuations for specific purposes

In an attempt to avoid the kinds of conflict which followed the 1980s property crash, the *Mallinson Report* recommended that clients should agree in advance with valuers the basis on which the valuation was being made and that a memorandum of instructions should form part of any valuation certificate.

The RICS has published a consultation document, inviting comments from its members as well as from statutory and regulatory bodies and bodies representing elements of the client base. Once such comments have been received and considered, it is proposed that a revised draft of the merger document should be considered in the early months of 1995 with a final text being prepared for endorsement by the RICS General Council in July 1995. Subject to this, the new manual will become operational on October 1 1995.

3 Legal knowledge

It is well established that the "reasonable care and skill" which is demanded of a valuer includes a certain degree of legal knowledge. This is hardly surprising; no practitioner could even begin to contemplate valuing property for the purposes of compulsory purchase or a rent review without a sound working knowledge of at least the general principles of law on which these procedures are based. However, this is not to say that a valuer's grasp of the law should necessarily equal that of a solicitor or other specialist legal adviser; it is rather that the valuer should understand the general rules sufficiently to avoid basic errors, and also sufficiently to recognise when more expert advice is required.

That a valuer must know something of the law has long been settled. In *Jenkins* v *Betham*,[1] for example, a clergyman who had been presented to a certain living instructed the defendants to make a valuation of the dilapidations of the rectory. The defendants, who had some experience of ecclesiastical valuations, none the less based their valuation upon an erroneous view of the law, in that they allowed only for rendering the premises habitable (as in the case of normal tenants) and not for putting them into good and substantial repair. The trial judge told the jury that the defendants were under no duty to supply any skill in, or knowledge of, the law, where upon the jury found them not liable. On appeal to the Court of Common Pleas, a new trial was ordered, and Jervis CJ said:

The defendants could not be expected to supply minute and accurate

---

1 (1855) 15 CB 167.

knowledge of the law; but we think that, under the circumstances, they might properly be required to know the general rules applicable to the valuation of ecclesiastical property, and the broad distinction which exists between the cases of an incoming and an outgoing tenant, and an incoming and outgoing incumbent.

Furthermore, this legal knowledge must be kept up to date, a point well illustrated by the case of *Weedon* v *Hindwood, Clarke & Esplin*.[1] The defendants there were retained to act for a client in compulsory purchase negotiations. Shortly before these negotiations began, a well-publicised decision of the Court of Appeal[2] altered the law as to the date on which property should be valued for this purpose, and this new rule was confirmed by the House of Lords before the defendants agreed a figure on behalf of their clients.[3] Despite this change, which would have been very favourable to their client, the defendants allowed themselves to be persuaded by the district valuer to agree upon a figure which was clearly based on the old law. For this they were held liable in negligence. Similarly, in *Corisand Investments Ltd* v *Druce & Co*,[4] one of the reasons for holding the defendants liable in negligence for their valuation of an hotel was that they failed to take into account the provisions of the Fire Precautions Act 1971 relating to the need for obtaining a fire certificate.

C Types of valuation

1 Mortgage valuations of residential property

As we have aiready noted,[5] the decision in *Yianni* v *Edwin Evans & Sons*[6] opened the way for a mortgage valuer to be liable, not only to the lender client but also to a borrower. Moreover, such liability could arise even where the lender did not disclose the content of the mortgage valuation report to the borrower. The courts, aware perhaps of the burden which this type of claim could impose upon

---

1 (1974) 234 EG 121.
2 *West Midland Baptist Trust Association (Incorporated)* v *Birmingham Corporation* [1968] 2 QB 188.
3 [1970] AC 874.
4 (1978) 248 EG 315.
5 See pp45–48.
6 [1982] 1 QB 438.

valuers, attempted in a number of later cases to ensure the duty of care created by *Yianni* was kept within its proper context. In *Nash v Evens & Matta*,[1] for example, a chartered surveyor carrying out a mortgage valuation inspection and report on a flat did not report wall tie failure. However, it was held that the valuer had not been negligent; he had been asked only to carry out a limited inspection of the property and had properly fulfilled this request. On the evidence, there was nothing visible at the time of inspection to alert the valuer as to potential problems which might arise.

A similar decision was reached in *Green* v *Ipswich Borough Council*,[2] where a mortgage valuation report noted that the property was in an area where some settlement had taken place. The report contained no recommendation for further investigation, on the basis that the matter was discussed with the building control officer and the necessary remedial works carried out. This report was held not to be negligent.

One of the most significant judgments dealing with the standard of care required in carrying out an inspection and report for mortgage purposes is that of Ian Kennedy J in *Roberts* v *J Hampson & Co*.[3] In reply to the defendants' point that such an inspection is very different from a survey, the judge had the following to say:

What is the extent of the service that a surveyor must provide in performing a building society valuation? The service is, in fact, described in the Halifax's brochure. It is a valuation and not a survey but any valuation is necessarily governed by condition. The inspection is, of necessity, a limited one. Both the expert surveyors who gave evidence before me agreed that with a house of this size they would allow about half an hour for their inspection on site. That time does not admit of moving furniture, nor of lifting carpets, especially where they are nailed down. In my judgment, it must be accepted that where a surveyor undertakes a scheme 1 valuation it is understood that he is making a limited appraisal only. It is, however, an appraisal by a skilled professional man. It is inherent in any standard fee work that some cases will colloquially be "winners" and others "losers", from the professional man's point of view. The fact that in an individual case he may need to spend two

---

1 [1988] 1 EGLR 130.
2 [1988] 1 EGLR 138.
3 [1989] 2 All ER 504 at p510; [1988] 2 EGLR 181.

or three times as long as he would have expected, or as the fee structure would have contemplated, is something that he must accept. His duty to take reasonable care in providing a valuation remains the root of his obligation. In an extreme case ... a surveyor might refuse to value on the agreed fee basis, though any surveyor who too often refused to take the rough with the smooth would not improve his reputation. If, in a particular case, the proper valuation of a £19,000 house needs two hours work that is what surveyor must devote to it.

This passage was cited in *Smith* v *Bush*[1] by Lord Templeman, who described the *Roberts* case as being "one of general application". A crucial part of the reasoning behind the judgment in *Smith* v *Bush* is that the professional person who carries out the original valuation knows that there is a high probability that his valuation will be relied upon by the prospective borrower in deciding whether or not to proceed with the purchase. To a very large extent, there is an understandable judicial predisposition to hold that a borrower who has paid for a report is entitled to have its contents passed on to him.

A more specific aspect of mortgage valuations, one which also concerned Ian Kennedy J in *Roberts* v *J Hampson & Co*,[2] was the extent to which a mortgage valuer may be expected to move furniture and lift carpets. As to this, the judge said:

As it seems to me, the position that the law adopts is simple. If the surveyor misses a defect because its signs are hidden, that is a risk that his client must accept. But if there is specific ground for suspicion and the trail of suspicion leads behind furniture or under carpets, the surveyor must take reasonable steps to follow the trail until he has all the information which it is reasonable for him to have before making his valuation.

This passage, which has caused immense concern among valuers and surveyors, was also approved by Lord Templeman in *Smith* v *Bush*.[3] Nevertheless, his lordship emphasised that the duty of care imposed upon valuers was not unduly harsh or onerous. As he pointed out:[4]

---

1 *Smith* v *Eric S Bush*; *Harris* v *Wyre Forest District Council* [1990] 1 AC 831 at p850; [1989] 1 EGLR 169.
2 [1989] 2 All ER 504 at p510; [1988] 2 EGLR 181.
3 [1990] 1 AC 831 at p851.
4 At p851.

A valuer will only be liable if other qualified valuers, who cannot be expected to be harsh on their fellow professionals, consider that, taking into consideration the nature of the work for which the valuer is paid and the object of that work, nevertheless he has been guilty of an error which an average valuer in the same circumstances would not have made.

The lead thus given was followed almost immediately by judges in a number of other cases against valuers. In *Gibbs* v *Arnold Son & Hockley*,[1] for example, it was alleged that a mortgage valuer had carried out a negligently inadequate "head and shoulders" inspection of the roof space. In rejecting this claim, the judge stressed that there was a world of a difference between a valuation and a structural survey and said:

I formed a high opinion of the defendants as professional men of thoroughness and integrity. This firm is a credit to the surveyors' profession. I hope the firm will suffer no discredit through this unfortunate and ill-advised young couple bringing this action.

In *Whalley* v *Roberts & Roberts*,[2] failure by a valuer carrying out a mortgage valuation to detect that the property had been built out of level was held on the facts not to be negligent. The judge, applying the test in *Roberts* v *J Hampson & Co*,[3] emphasised that the valuer had not been instructed to undertake either a structural survey or a *House Buyers' Report* (as it was then known). He concluded that a mortgage valuation inspection did not normally involve the use of a spirit level unless lack of level in the property was evident on a visual inspection so as to call for further inspection. On the evidence in the particular case, the defect in question had been camouflaged to such an extent that it had not even been noticed by the previous owner of the property who had lived there for some years.

In *Bere* v *Slades*[4] a house buyer's claim that a mortgage valuer should have "followed the trail" failed, since the expert evidence which was accepted by the judge indicated that there was no "trail" to follow. The defect in question was caused by the fact that some

---

1 [1989] 1 EGLR 154.
2 [1990] 1 EGLR 164.
3 [1989] 2 All ER 504; [1988] 2 EGLR 181.
4 [1989] 2 EGLR 160.

of the cement used in the building of cellar walls was unstable, but it appeared that the construction was such that this would not have been discovered, even on a full survey.

In giving evidence in this case, the valuer conceded that he had no recollection of his visit to the property to carry out the mortgage valuation inspection, other than from his notes. The decision emphasises how important it is to make and retain careful site notes, for the judge was clearly impressed by the notes made by this particular valuer. So far as the valuation report itself was concerned, the judge described it as thoroughly competent, carefully done and masterly succinct.

Since every negligence action turns on its own particular facts, it is hardly surprising that some mortgage valuers have been held in recent years to have fallen below the requisite standard of care.[1] In *Lloyd* v *Butler*,[2] for example, the plaintiff relied on a mortgage valuation of the property carried out by the defendant, on the instructions of a building society, in deciding to purchase a house. The defendant's report indicated that no serious repairs were needed. However, it transpired that there were some serious defects which, it was held, a reasonably competent valuer should have brought to the plaintiff's attention. In commenting upon the nature of an inspection for mortgage valuation purposes, Henry J said:

It is taken on a basis of inspection which, on average, should not take longer than 20-30 minutes. It is effectively a walking inspection by someone with a knowledgeable eye, experienced in practice, who knows where to look – I take the cupboard under the stairs as an example – to detect either trouble or the potential form of trouble. He does not necessarily have to follow up every trail to discover whether there is trouble or the extent of any such trouble. But where such an inspection can reasonable show a potential trouble or the risk of potential trouble, it seems to me it is necessary ... to alert the purchaser to that risk, because the purchaser will be relying on that valuation form.

In *Henley* v *Cloke & Son*,[3] the judge had no hesitation in finding negligence where a valuer in his mortgage valuation report to have described the main structure of the property as "satisfactory". Within

---

1 See, in addition to the cases cited below, *Davies* v *Idris Parry* [1988] 1 EGLR 147.
2 [1990] 1 EGLR 155.
3 [1991] 2 EGLR 141.

a few months of moving into the property, the plaintiffs noticed that the front bay was seriously distorted, and it was held that the valuer should have seen this. All that the valuer need have done was to step over the front flowerbed and to look at the property from the end of the lawn.

In the Jersey case of *Duquemin v Reynolds*,[1] a valuer inspecting a house for mortgage purposes failed to note defects in the roof, in that nails holding slates were rotted and roof battens were decayed. It was held by the Jersey Royal Court that the valuer should have recommended a full investigation of the roof. The evidence showed that the defects would have been clear, even on an external visual inspection, with the use of binoculars.

In the Scottish case of *Smith v Carter*,[2] a mortgage valuer was held negligent for failing to observe and report on the fact that load-bearing walls in a flat had been removed without building warrant, and that the flat acordingly did not comply with the relevant building regulations. Moreover, another Scottish case serves as a useful reminder that, as well as being alert to the possibility of defects, mortgage valuers should be aware that certain properties may not be of traditional construction. In *Peach v Iain G Chalmers & Co*,[3] a valuer failed to recognise that a property was of a "Dorran" type construction, the walls having been constructed of a series of thin concrete panels bolted together. Should these corrode, extensive and expensive repairs would be necessary. It was held that, by valuing the property as if it was of traditional construction, the valuer was guilty of negligence.

Finally, it is perhaps worth making the point that, where mortgage valuations are concerned, the standard required of "in-house" valuers is exactly the same as that of those in private practice. Thus, in *Beaton v Nationwide Building Society*,[4] for example, a valuer employed by the defendant building society believed that cracks found in the property showed signs only of past subsidence, and that there was no future risk of subsidence. It was held, however, that the valuer had been negligent, since the expert evidence showed that soil conditions, foundation depth and nearby

---

1 (1987) JLR 259.
2 1994 SCLR 539.
3 [1992] 2 EGLR 135.
4 [1991] 2 EGLR 145.

oak trees growing at a distance of less than their own height from the property should have put the valuer on notice that further investigation was required. The building society thereupon conceded that it was vicariously liable for the negligence of its employee.

Similarly, in *Jowitt v Woolwich Equitable Building Society*[1] a valuer employed by the defendant building society stated in his report that "as far as I am aware" there was no subsidence. However, some five years later when a negligence action came to court, the valuer admitted that, if faced with the same situation again, he would call for a structural engineer's report. The building society was held to be liable for its employee's report.

2 Valuations by independent experts

We have already noted the view of the courts that, in carrying out a valuation as an independent expert, a valuer will owe a duty of care and skill to each of the parties.[2] Thus, for example, an independent expert who is instructed to decide a rent review will owe a duty to both the landlord and tenant. While this is naturally a matter of concern to professional valuers, it is to be noted that there is as yet no reported case in which such a claim for negligence has succeeded. The courts, while acknowledging the existence of the valuer's duty, have not yet heard a case in which that duty has been breached.

The case of *Wallshire Ltd v Aarons*[3] gives an indication of the kind of complaints which may be made against an independent expert. The defendant there was sued by the landlord following a rent review of a shop with a maisonette over it. The landlord's allegations were:

- that the defendant, in dealing with one particular comparable, had wrongly made a deduction for goodwill;
- that the defendant had wrongly dismissed another comparable on the ground that the user of the premises was different;
- that the defendant had not made sufficient enquiries as to further comparables, beyond those submitted to him by the parties.

Although all these allegations were ultimately rejected by the

---

1 December 14 1987, Official Referees' Business, unreported.
2 See pp19–20.
3 [1989] 1 EGLR 147.

judge, the case demonstrates clearly that, when a valuer is appointed as an independent expert, he cannot simply rely upon the submissions put to him, but must carry out his own thorough and careful independent valuation.

3 Other valuations

No matter what type of valuation is undertaken, a valuer owes the same duty, namely to act with reasonable care and skill. Precisely what constitutes a breach of that duty may of course differ in relation to different types of valuation, and some examples may be taken from reported cases.

In *Bell Hotels (1935) Ltd* v *Motion*,[1] the defendants advised their vendor clients as to an appropriate price at which to sell their hotel. The clients relied on this advice, which was subsequently held to have been negligently given, since the defendants had failed to appreciate the fact that there would be a strong demand from brewery companies for the property.

In *Beaumont* v *Humberts*,[2] it was held (on the basis of evidence from expert witnesses) that it is not negligent for a valuer to place a "reinstatement value" on property for insurance purposes without inspecting the policy in question, even though it is known that different policies define "reinstatement" in different ways.

Finally, in *Perry* v *Wilson*[3] the defendant was instructed in 1983 to value certain property in Cheshire for the purpose of matrimonial proceedings. The defendant gave a valuation of £45,000 (updated a few months later to approximately £50,000) and stated that the land had no commercial value; the question of any development potential or "hope value" was not mentioned. The land was transferred by the plaintiff husband to his wife at a notional value of £50,000 as part of the divorce settlement; some six years later, following the grant of planning permission for the erection of 31 houses, it was sold for £1m.

When the plaintiff brought an action for negligence against the valuer, Swinton Thomas J stressed that it was important not to be too heavily influenced by the knowledge of what had actually happened in planning terms to the land. The expert evidence called

---

1 (1952) 159 EG 496.
2 [1990] 2 EGLR 166; see p80.
3 October 20 1993, Queen's Bench, unreported.

on behalf of the defendant suggested that few valuers in 1983 would have regarded the site as having any potential other than in the very long term, and then only if massive expansion in the area were to be permitted. Accepting this evidence, the judge held that, on the evidence which the defendant had at the time of his valuation, the conclusion at which he had arrived was a perfectly reasonable one. The husband's action accordingly failed.

CHAPTER 6

Damages – general principles

Where a client sues a surveyor or valuer in contract, proof that the contract has been breached (ie that the survey or valuation has been negligently carried out) is sufficient in itself to entitle the client to an award of nominal damages, whether or not any loss has resulted. By contrast, where an action is based in tort, proof of a breach of duty by the surveyor or valuer in itself entitles the plaintiff to nothing, since the tort of negligence is not complete unless and until damage is caused. In either case, a plaintiff who seeks *substantial* damages will have to satisfy the court that reliance on the defendant's negligent advice has caused some injury, loss or damage and, furthermore, that this is not too remote a consequence of the negligence in question.

A The causing of loss

1 Causation in fact and law

"The court, before making any award in a plaintiff's favour, must be satisfied, albeit upon the narrowest balance of probabilities, that the breach of duty caused or contributed to the loss."[1] It must accordingly be proved that the loss in respect of which damages are sought results from the defendant's negligence and not solely from some other extraneous factor. Of course, it may be that the plaintiff's loss is the product of more than one cause, in which case the damages payable by the defendant may fall to be reduced (if the other cause is the plaintiff's own contributory negligence),[2] or the defendant may obtain a contribution towards the damages payable (if the other cause is the negligence of a third party).[3]

In matters of causation, as in other elements of a claim, the onus

---

1 *Thomas Miller & Co* v *Richard Saunders & Partners* [1989] 1 EGLR 267 at p272, *per* Rougier J.
2 See pp213–227.
3 See pp228–231.

of proof is firmly on the plaintiff.[1] In *Mount Banking Corporation Ltd v Brian Cooper & Co*,[2] for example, where the plaintiff lending institution sued in respect of an allegedly negligent valuation, a dispute arose as to whether, if the plaintiffs had been aware of the true value of the property offered as security, any mortgage loan would have been made. It was held that, since it was the plaintiffs who were claiming to have suffered damage, the onus lay on them to establish that they would not have entered into the transaction had they known the truth.

In approaching the issue of causation, courts in negligence cases frequently ask whether the plaintiff would have suffered the damage under discussion "but for" the negligence of the defendant. If the answer to this question is that the damage would have been suffered in any event (ie whether or not the defendant had been negligent) then it follows that the defendant's negligence has not "caused" that damage and that the defendant cannot therefore be held liable for it. Thus, in *Thomas Miller & Co v Richard Saunders & Partners*,[3] for example, the defendants, who were acting for tenants on a rent review, failed to place certain evidence before an arbitrator. This failure was held to be negligent, but the defendants nevertheless avoided liability, since the court was convinced that the arbitrator's decision would have been the same, even if the relevant evidence had been presented to him.

While the "but for" test of causation appears quite acceptable in cases of negligent professional advice, two cautionary notes may be sounded. First, as will be seen, the factual questions which arise in this area usually revolve around the issue of "reliance", and it is clearly not necessary for the plaintiff to have relied *exclusively* upon the defendant's advice in order for liability to arise.[4] There is undoubtedly a distinction in principle between cases where the defendant's advice is one of a number of factors contributing to the plaintiff's decision, and cases where the other factors would themselves have justified that decision. However, the courts have shown no great readiness to exonerate a negligent defendant on this ground, finding it sufficient for the plaintiff to establish "that the

---

1 *Thomas Miller & Co v Richard Saunders & Partners* [1989] 1 EGLR 267.
2 [1992] 2 EGLR 142.
3 [1989] 1 EGLR 267.
4 See pp135–138.

breach of duty caused *or contributed* to the loss".[1]

The second point worth making is that, even where it is proved that the plaintiff's loss would not have been suffered "but for" the defendant's negligence, this does not mean that the defendant *must* be held responsible for that loss, but only that he or she *may* be so liable. Satisfaction of the "but for" test means that something is a *factual* cause; whether it is a *legal* cause (and thus carries liability) is dependent upon the weight given by the judge to a range of other less tangible factors, such as whether the loss was foreseeable and whether there are any reasons of policy for not imposing liability. In effect, therefore, conduct which fails the "but for" test *cannot* result in legal liability; conduct which passes that test can lead to liability but will not always do so.

This point may be illustrated by reference to the common case of a purchaser who sues a surveyor for negligence and alleges that, had the true condition of the property been known, he or she would never have purchased it. If this allegation is established, it might well be said that, "but for" the surveyor's negligence, the purchaser would not have incurred the cost of repairing that property. And yet, as we shall see,[2] the purchaser will not be entitled to damages on a "cost of repair" basis. Similarly, it has been held in a number of recent cases that a negligent mortgage valuer is not responsible to the lender for increased losses resulting from a fall in the property market, despite proof that, if an accurate valuation had been provided, no loan would have been made.[3]

Two decided cases give some idea of the range of judicial approaches to questions of causation. In *Kenney* v *Hall, Pain & Foster*[4] the defendants were found guilty of negligence for overvaluing the plaintiff's house and thus encouraging the plaintiff to embark on a financially disastrous venture (the purchase and refurbishment of an old property). As a result of this negligence, the defendants were in principle liable for all the losses suffered by the plaintiff, who was brought close to insolvency. However, it was held that their liability did not exceed such expenditure on repairs and

---

1 *Thomas Miller & Co* v *Richard Saunders & Partners* [1989] 1 EGLR 267 at p272, per Rougier J (emphasis supplied).
2 See p146.
3 See pp167–168.
4 (1976) 239 EG 355.

redecoration as it was reasonable for the plaintiff to have incurred in the circumstances; beyond that point, the plaintiff had to be regarded as the cause of his own loss.

The second case, *PK Finans International (UK) Ltd v Andrew Downs & Co Ltd*,[1] arose out of a claim that the defendant valuers had negligently failed to warn their client (a licensed deposit-taker, which was a subidiary of one of the largest banks in Sweden) of the need to verify certain planning assumptions on which a development valuation was based. The judge decided that there had been no negligence, since the plaintiffs were experienced enough not to need such a warning. Had he reached the opposite conclusion, the judge stated that he would not have regarded the plaintiff's failure to show the valuation to their solicitors as a *novus actus interveniens* sufficient to "break the chain of causation" linking the defendants' negligence to the plaintiffs' loss; he would, however, have regarded it as a matter of contributory negligence by the plaintiffs sufficient to deprive them of no less than 80% of their damages!

2 Reliance

In most, though not all, cases involving surveyors or valuers where causation is in issue, the dispute turns essentially on the question of whether or not the plaintiff *relied* on the defendant's negligent advice in deciding to enter into the relevant transaction. If there has been no such reliance, then the defendant's negligence cannot be said to have caused the plaintiff's loss and the claim accordingly fails. If the plaintiff has in fact relied on the defendant's advice, but that reliance was unreasonable, the defence of contributory negligence may come into play.[2]

In considering the issue of reliance, it is important to appreciate that it is not necessary for the plaintiff to have relied upon the defendant's advice to the exclusion of all other factors. It is sufficient that the plaintiff's judgment was affected to a material degree. As Stephenson LJ put it in *JEB Fasteners Ltd v Marks Bloom & Co*, a case where an action was brought by a takeover bidder in respect of the target company's negligently audited accounts:[3]

---

1 [1992] 1 EGLR 172.
2 See pp213–227.
3 [1983] 1 All ER 583 at p589.

As long as a misrepresentation plays a real and substantial part, though not by itself a decisive part, in inducing a plaintiff to act, it is a cause of his loss and he relies on it, no matter how strong or how many are the other matters which play their part in inducing him to act.

Indeed, exclusive reliance is the exception rather than the rule, a point recognised by the New Zealand Court of Appeal in *Kendall Wilson Securities* v *Barraclough*:[1] "The valuer was entitled to expect that considerations additional to his advice would be influential in the decision as to whether or not a loan would be made." Thus, in *Banque Bruxelles Lambert SA* v *Eagle Star Insurance Co Ltd*,[2] for example, it was held that a lending institution had sufficiently relied on a negligent valuation of the mortgaged property, even though it would not have agreed to lend without first obtaining a mortgage indemnity guarantee policy from an insurance company.

The negligent valuation case most frequently cited in this context is *Kenney* v *Hall, Pain & Foster*.[3] The plaintiff there, having received assurances from the defendants that his current house was worth at least £100,000, put it on the market at that price and, leaving what he believed to be an adequate safety margin, committed himself to the purchase of another property. By the time that he took this step, the plaintiff had clearly come to realise that the defendant's valuation of his house was too high; moreover, his belief was supported by warnings given to the plaintiff by a local estate agent and by his bank manager. Nevertheless, Goff J held that the plaintiff had continued to rely, at least in part, on the defendants' valuation:[4]

Certainly . . . he had come to suspect that [the defendants'] valuation was rather high; he was also exercising his own judgment, in the light of all the factors known to him, but one of those factors remained [the defendants'] advice, and I am satisfied that the plaintiff was still relying substantially on that advice, in the sense that, even allowing for the fact that he suspected [the defendants'] figure to have been rather high, still the valuation made him feel that he could safely commit himself to spending £65,000 on Wickham Lodge and cover his commitments by achieving a quick sale of Culverlands

---

1 [1986] 1 NZLR 576 at p601, *per* Somers J.
2 [1994] 2 EGLR 108.
3 (1976) 239 EG 355.
4 (1976) 239 EG 355 at p433.

House by a dramatic reduction of 25 per cent in the asking price. He felt that, in the light of the advice that he had received from [the defendants], even allowing that his valuation might have been rather high, this was a risk that he could safely take.

It seems clear from the above that, where a person enters into a loss-making transaction after having received negligent professional advice, the inference that he or she relied on that advice will be difficult to displace. In *Allen* v *Ellis & Co*,[1] for example, where a house purchaser stood on his garage roof with disastrous results, Garland J found sufficient "reliance" on a surveyor's report, despite the plaintiff's admission that he did not have that report in mind at the time. So too, in the commercial lending case of *HIT Finance Ltd* v *Lewis & Tucker Ltd*,[2] Wright J pointed out:[3]

One of the elements of the scheme of protection that a lender sets up when negotiating an advance of this kind, in order to protect himself against loss should the borrower default, is an assurance as to the value of his security. It would only be in a most exceptional set of circumstances that the negligent valuer would not be at least in part responsible for the consequential loss suffered by the lender upon the failure of the borrower to honour his obligations.[4]

Notwithstanding such *dicta*, however, there remain cases in which, despite proof that a survey or valuation has been negligently carried out, the necessary element of reliance is lacking. In *Rona* v *Pearce*,[5] for example, the purchaser of a bungalow failed in his action for negligence against the defendant who surveyed the property for him. The defendant was held to have been negligent in his inspection, but the judge "could not believe ... that the report was a factor which influenced [the plaintiff] in buying the bungalow". The cause of the judge's disbelief is not clear from the report, but it is to be noted that the defendant had told the plaintiff that in his opinion the bungalow was overpriced.

In other cases, the question of reliance has been subjected to

---

1 [1990] 1 EGLR 170.
2 [1993] 2 EGLR 231.
3 At p234.
4 See also *Nyckeln Finance Co Ltd* v *Stumpbrook Continuation Ltd* [1994] 2 EGLR 143 at p148, *per* Judge Fawcus.
5 (1953) 162 EG 380.

somewhat closer analysis. In *Shankie-Williams* v *Heavey*,[1] where the vendor of newly converted flats obtained a report from a "dry rot surveying specialist" which negligently gave the property a clean bill of health, the specialist was held not liable to the purchasers of one of those flats, since the Court of Appeal could find no evidence to show that the purchasers had been shown his report before deciding to purchase. In *Banque Bruxelles Lambert SA* v *Eagle Star Insurance Co Ltd*,[2] on the other hand, the plaintiffs were undoubtedly aware, when agreeing to lend £72m on the security of a commercial property, that John D Wood & Co had valued it at £82m (thus providing some confirmation for an earlier valuation of £83.95m from another firm). However, the evidence satisfied Phillips J that the plaintiffs were in fact highly sceptical about both valuations and that their decision to go ahead with the loan transaction was based on commercial considerations which had nothing to do with those valuations. In these circumstances, the plaintiffs could not be said to have "relied" on the valuation so as to hold the valuers responsible for it.

3 Remoteness of damage

Even where the (overlapping) elements of causation and reliance are present, a plaintiff can still not recover damages from a negligent surveyor or valuer for any consequences of that negligence which are too "remote". In the context of a claim in contract, loss is not too remote if it was at the time of the contract reasonably foreseeable as liable to result from the breach.[3] Where a claim is based in tort, loss is not too remote if it was at the time of the defendant's breach of duty reasonably foreseeable as a consequence of that breach.[4]

Remoteness in this sense is seldom a live issue in cases involving surveyors or valuers, since the kinds of loss in respect of which claims are made are normally just what would be expected to result. However, where a plaintiff seeks damages for more unusual consequences, a defendant may seek to argue that these were

---

1 [1986] 2 EGLR 139.
2 [1994] 2 EGLR 108.
3 *Victoria Laundry (Windsor) Ltd* v *Newman Industries Ltd* [1949] 2 KB 528.
4 *Overseas Tankship (UK) Ltd* v *Morts Dock and Engineering Co Ltd, The Wagon Mound* [1961] AC 388.

unforeseeable. In *Allen* v *Ellis & Co*[1] it was held, in the face of strenuous arguments by the defendant surveyors, that they should have foreseen the possibility that a house purchaser might rely on their report as justifying his decision to stand on the asbestos roof of his garage. In *Drinnan* v *CW Ingram & Sons*,[2] on the other hand, a Scottish judge expressed the "gravest doubts" as to whether it could reasonably be foreseen that a purchaser would suffer hypertension, leading to the loss of her job, as a consequence of a negligent survey report.

Where a person enters into a transaction on the basis of negligent advice from a surveyor or valuer, the resulting loss may be amplified due to movements in the property market. In *Morgan* v *Perry*[3] it was held on the facts that an unprecedented rise in house prices in the early 1970s was not something which could have been foreseen by a surveyor in 1968. In later cases involving commercial lenders, however, the courts have treated the question whether or not a negligent valuer should be liable for losses caused by a falling market as being a matter of policy rather than of foreseeability.[4]

B Limits on liability

1 Mitigation

It is a well established principle of English law, applicable to claims in both contract and tort, that no damages can be recovered in respect of losses which the plaintiff ought reasonably to have avoided. This principle is often expressed as the plaintiff's duty to mitigate his or her losses, although such a description is in truth not quite accurate, since the plaintiff is not under any "duty" in the sense of an obligation which can be enforced. The true legal position is simply that the plaintiff will not be awarded any damages in respect of losses which could have been prevented by the taking of reasonable steps.

In the context of claims against surveyors and valuers, the doctrine of mitigation has surfaced in two main areas. First, where a house purchaser claims damages for "inconvenience and

---

1 [1990] 1 EGLR 170.
2 1967 SLT 205.
3 (1973) 229 EG 1737.
4 See p167.

discomfort" resulting from living in a defective dwelling, those damages will reflect only the period up to the time when the plaintiff ought reasonably to have removed the source of the discomfort by putting in hand the necessary repairs.[1] In deciding when that time arises, however, the courts have refused to penalise purchasers who cannot afford such repairs, especially where the surveyor concerned continues to deny liability, and thus leaves the purchaser with no guarantee that the cost will ultimately be recouped.[2]

The second situation in which the question of mitigation has arisen is where a lending institution sues in respect of a negligent over-valuation of the security, and the mortgage valuer claims that the lender should have taken action to reduce its losses, for example by enforcing its security at an earlier date or by taking action against the borrower on the latter's personal covenant to repay the loan. Such an argument proved successful in *Nyckeln Finance Co Ltd* v *Stumpbrook Continuation Ltd*,[3] where the court agreed that, against the background of a rapidly falling commercial property market, the lender had delayed unreasonably in repossessing and selling the security following the mortgagor's default. However, a different decision was reached in *Nykredit Mortgage Bank plc* v *Edward Erdman Group Ltd*,[4] on the straightforward basis that the borrower was "engulfed in debt with no significant assets" and was thus not worth suing. More controversially, a plea that a lender had unreasonably failed to mitigate its losses also failed in *London & South of England Building Society* v *Stone*,[5] where the building society took a positive decision to release the borrower from all liability, partly as a gesture of goodwill and partly because "the lender felt morally responsible for the loss of the borrowers' home and ... enforcement of the covenant to pay would injure the lender's public relations". It is at least possible that a court today might take a different view of similar facts, given that the borrower's right to recover damages from the negligent mortgage valuer is well established.[6]

---

1 *Cross* v *David Martin & Mortimer* [1989] 1 EGLR 154: see p161.
2 *Perry* v *Sidney Phillips & Son* [1982] 3 All ER 705: see p162.
3 [1994] 2 EGLR 143.
4 October 1 1993, Mayors and City of London Court, unreported.
5 (1983) 267 EG 69: see p174.
6 See p44.

2 Collateral benefits

A particularly difficult aspect of the law governing the assessment of damages is the extent, if any, to which the court will take into account benefits which accrue to the plaintiff from independent sources and which might be seen as reducing the impact of the defendant's negligence. On one view, failure to take account of such a benefit will result in the plaintiff being over-compensated for his or her losses. On another view, however, it would be quite wrong to allow something which flows from a relationship between the plaintiff and a third party to operate as a "windfall" benefit to the defendant, who has no connection whatsoever with that relationship.

On balance, the English courts have tended to favour the second of these views, albeit by treating each case on its merits rather than by seeking to lay down some readily ascertainable governing principle. The approach commonly adopted by the courts is to ask whether the benefit in question should be regarded as *res inter alios acta* ("something between other people"), although it should be acknowledged that this is in truth merely another way of asking whether that benefit should be taken into account. The legal position was summarised by Phillips J in *Banque Bruxelles Lambert SA v Eagle Star Insurance Co Ltd*:[1]

> Whatever circumstances *res inter alios acta* embraces, they have, I believe, one thing in common. They are circumstances in which a third party, or an extraneous event, intervenes to provide a plaintiff with some form of indemnity, in whole or in part, for the loss which the defendant has caused. The law ignores the intervention so that the plaintiff remains entitled to recover from the defendant the full amount of the loss or damage initially suffered.

One of the most important applications of the doctrine of *res inter alios acta* is the well established principle that, in assessing the damages to be awarded to a plaintiff, no deduction is to be made in respect of any benefits which that plaintiff has received by virtue of an insurance policy. Here the true beneficiary is frequently the insurance company which, having paid the plaintiff in accordance with the policy, then brings legal proceedings in the plaintiff's name

---

1 [1994] 2 EGLR 108 at p130.

under the doctrine of subrogation. It is obvious that, if the damages fell to be reduced by virtue of the insurance payout, the insurer would be unable to recoup its losses in this way.

In the context of claims against surveyors and valuers, the question of insurance benefits arises most commonly in the context of actions brought by house purchasers. However, it is no less applicable where a mortgage lender sues a negligent valuer in respect of losses which are in fact covered by a mortgage indemnity guarantee policy.[1]

Apart from insurance, it appears that the principle of ignoring extraneous benefits to the plaintiff also applies to statutory grants, at least where the award of these is a matter for the discretion of the public authority concerned. In *Treml* v *Ernest W Gibson and Partners*[2] the plaintiff, having purchased a house in reliance on the defendants' negligent report, subsequently received a grant from the local authority towards the cost of repairing the serious defects which the defendants' survey had failed to detect. When the defendants claimed that the amount of this grant should be deducted from the plaintiff's damages, the plaintiffs countered that, since the damages in such a case were based on difference in value,[3] money spent on repairs was irrelevant. Popplewell J had no doubt that the plaintiffs' view was correct:

I am clearly of the view that the sum does not fall to be deducted. First, because it is irrelevant to a claim where the difference in value is the measure of damage and, secondly, because, to use legal shorthand, it is a collateral benefit which does not have to be taken into account.

The "collateral benefit" which was in issue in *Marder* v *Sautelle & Hicks*[4] was of a very different kind. The plaintiffs, having purchased a house in reliance on the defendants' survey report, subsequently discovered that (unnoticed by the defendants) it was of inferior construction and was unlikely to remain inhabitable for very long. The plaintiffs recovered damages from the defendants which reflected the difference between what they had paid for the property

---

1 *Banque Bruxelles Lambert SA* v *Eagle Star Insurance Co Ltd* [1994] 2 EGLR 108.
2 (1984) 272 EG 68.
3 See p146.
4 [1988] 2 EGLR 187.

(£33,000) and what it was actually worth (£13,500, that being its site value less the cost of demolition). In effect, therefore, the court had declared the property to be worthless, so it was perhaps not surprising that the defendants, on learning that the plaintiffs had sold the property for £70,000, sought to appeal. In the event, however, this appeal proved unsuccessful. As Staughton LJ pointed out, there were various possible explanations for the price obtained by the plaintiffs, such as the hope of increased development value due to a change in the local planning climate, or merely a rise in property values generally. Moreover, if the truth was that the new purchasers had simply paid too much, "that would be a collateral matter for which the defendants could claim no credit".

The limits of the doctrine of *res inter alios acta* were explored in *Banque Bruxelles Lambert SA v Eagle Star Insurance Co Ltd*[1] where the plaintiff bank, having agreed to make very substantial mortgage loans on the security of commercial properties valued by John D Wood & Co, then syndicated those loans to a group of other banks. When the plaintiffs brought an action for negligence against the valuers, a question which arose was whether the plaintiffs' damages should reflect the total loss on any given loan, or whether the share of that loss which was borne by the other banks was to be disregarded.

Phillips J was in no doubt:[2]

The principle of *res inter alios acta* requires the court to disregard an indemnity received by the plaintiff from a third party in respect of the loss caused by the defendant. It does not require or permit the court to assess damages on the basis of a fiction; to treat losses sustained by third parties as if they had been sustained by the plaintiff. The intervention of the syndicate banks did not indemnify BBL (the plaintiffs) in respect of consequences of entering into the loan transactions. It resulted in the syndicate banks suffering those consequences in place of BBL. The loss claimed by BBL is not loss suffered by BBL prior to syndication, but loss suffered by all the syndicate banks after syndication. The principle of *res inter alios acta* does not permit BBL to recover damages in respect of the losses sustained by the syndicate banks.

The syndication point reached its logical conclusion in the later

---

1 [1994] 2 EGLR 108.
2 At p130.

Ltd,[1] where mortgage loans arranged by the plaintiffs were syndicated in full among a number of client companies. It was held that, in instructing the defendant mortgage valuers, the plaintiffs had acted purely as agents for the other companies; it was accordingly to those companies *and not to the plaintiffs* that the valuers' duty of care was owed.

C Interest on damages

Whenever a court makes an award of damages to a plaintiff, the sum awarded constitutes a judgment debt and consequently bears interest from the date of judgment until it is paid. The applicable rate of interest, which is laid down from time to time by statutory instrument made under the Judgments Act 1838, is set at a level designed to coerce defendants into paying what is due, and is thus almost invariably higher than current commercial lending rates.

Apart from this type of interest, a court which awards damages for negligence against a surveyor or valuer has a statutory power to rule that the basic sum shall bear simple interest from the date of the plaintiff's loss to the date of judgment.[2] The court's discretion will normally be exercised in the plaintiff's favour, unless there is some compelling reason why this should not be so. Such a reason was found in *Morgan v Perry*,[3] for example, where house purchasers were awarded damages against a negligent surveyor equivalent to the full price which they had paid for the property. The basis of this award was that the house was in truth worth nothing, but the plaintiffs were nevertheless still living in it at the date of trial. The judge accordingly refused to award interest on the principal sum, in recognition that the plaintiffs had received some value at least from their "worthless" investment.

Where a court decides to award interest in this way, the choice of an appropriate rate is a matter within the discretion of the judge.[4] It would seem in principle that, if the interest is intended to compensate the plaintiff for being deprived of a capital sum until

---

1 June 15 1994, Official Referees' Business, unreported.
2 Supreme Court Act 1981, section 35A(1).
3 (1973) 229 EG 1737.
4 Interest on damages for "inconvenience" (see p157) will almost invariably be at 2%, by analogy with awards of general damages in personal injury cases.

judgment, a reasonable commercial borrowing rate should be selected, and this view has indeed been taken in cases involving both house purchasers[1] and commercial lenders.[2] However, the courts in some recent cases[3] have instead applied the rate laid down under the Judgments Act 1838 for interest on judgment debts, which will almost invariably be higher and which seems unduly harsh upon defendants.[4]

It is suggested that the use of this latter rate in professional negligence actions is misguided, for the reasons given by Bingham LJ in *Watts* v *Morrow*:[5]

Since the award of interest on damages is intended to compensate a plaintiff for being kept out of money lawfully due to him, there is much to be said for applying a rate of interest which reflects the cost or value of money over the relevant period rather than a flat rate fixed under the Judgments Act which has remained fixed over a number of years despite fluctuations in interest rates during that time.

Notwithstanding these views, however, Bingham LJ regarded himself as bound by the decision of the Court of Appeal in *Pinnock* v *Wilkins*[6] to rule that the trial judge's choice of the Judgments Act rate was an exercise of his discretion which could not be challenged. In this his lordship was supported by Ralph Gibson LJ, who had delivered a dissenting judgment in *Pinnock* v *Wilkins* for precisely the reasons given above!

---

1 Eg, *Treml* v *Ernest W Gibson and Partners* (1984) 272 EG 68; *Wilson* v *Baxter Payne & Lepper* [1985] 1 EGLR 141.
2 Eg *Corisand Investments Ltd* v *Druce & Co* (1978) 248 EG 315; *Swingcastle Ltd* v *Alastair Gibson* [1991] 2 AC 223; [1991] 1 EGLR 157; *HIT Finance Ltd* v *Lewis & Tucker Ltd* [1993] 2 EGLR 231; *Nykredit Mortgage Bank plc* v *Edward Erdman Group Ltd* October 1 1993, Mayors and City of London Court, unreported, where the plaintiffs themselves suggested that such a rate would be fair.
3 Eg, *Bigg* v *Howard Son & Gooch* [1990] 1 EGLR 173; *Heatley* v *William H Brown Ltd* [1992] 1 EGLR 289.
4 In *Oswald* v *Countrywide Surveyors Ltd* [1994] ECGS 150, the £60,000 awarded to purchasers for "difference in value" was almost matched by the interest on that sum.
5 [1991] 4 All ER 937 at p960; [1991] 2 EGLR 152.
6 Times, January 29 1990.

CHAPTER 7

The assessment of damages

A Purchaser

1 The basic measure

In the vast majority of cases in which the purchaser of a property sues a surveyor or valuer, the purchaser's main complaint is that he or she has been induced by a negligent report to pay more for the property than it is worth. In such circumstances, the purchaser's basic loss consists of the difference between two figures: the price which has been paid in reliance on the survey or valuation, and the true value of the property.[1] It is for the purchaser to prove such overpayment by leading evidence as to the property's true value; if no such evidence is before the court, then no damages for "difference in value" should be awarded.[2]

This "basic loss" is normally assessed at the date of purchase,[3] and the sum awarded bears interest until the date of judgment.[4] In addition, the purchaser may be entitled to recover for certain incidental losses and expenses,[5] and may also be awarded a sum to reflect any inconvenience suffered.[6]

The above analysis of a purchaser's basic loss appears very difficult to criticise in cases which arise out of a pure valuation of property (whether that valuation is commissioned by the purchaser or by a mortgagee). However, where the alleged negligence occurs in the course of a survey of the property's physical condition, it has from time to time been suggested that a different approach to the question of damages may be justified. It is said that a purchaser relies on a surveyor's report, not only as a guide to the property's value, but also for reassurance that there are no hidden defects

---

1 See p153.
2 *Duncan* v *Gumleys* [1987] 2 EGLR 263.
3 Note however the views of Bingham MR in *Reeves* v *Thrings & Long* [1993] NPC 159.
4 See p144.
5 See p154.
6 See p157.

which will require expensive repair work. Hence, it is argued by some, a purchaser who would not have purchased at all without such reassurance should be entitled, on discovering defects which a competent survey would have revealed, to be compensated for all losses which flow from the decision to purchase. Such losses will include, in particular, the full cost of repairing the relevant defects, even where this exceeds the difference between the property's values in its assumed and its actual condition.

(a) The cases

Until some 40 years ago, the weight of judicial authority in cases of negligent surveys undoubtedly favoured "cost of repair" as the appropriate measure of damages. However, since that time the Court of Appeal has ruled on three occasions that the damages payable by a negligent surveyor are normally to be assessed on the basis of "difference" or "diminution" in value. The court has moreover insisted that this is so even where, if properly advised, the purchaser would not have acquired the property in question.

The first of the cases in which the Court of Appeal rejected "cost of repair" as an appropriate measure of damages for a purchaser was *Philips* v *Ward*.[1] The plaintiff there purchased a house for £25,000 on the basis of a survey carred out by the defendant which negligently failed to discover the ravages of death watch beetle and woodworm. The evidence before the court indicated that, although the necessary repair work would have cost £7000 at the time of purchase, the property was actually worth £21,000 at that date. The Court of Appeal duly upheld the decision of the trial judge to award the plaintiff £4,000 and not £7000 as damages for the negligent survey. Their lordships' reasons were clearly stated by Denning LJ:[2]

I take it to be clear law that the proper measure of damages is the amount of money which will put the plaintiff into as good a position as if the surveying contract had been properly fulfilled . . . Now if the defendant had carried out his contract, he would have reported the bad state of the timbers. On receiving that report, the plaintiff either would have refused to have anything to do with the house, in which case he would have suffered no damage, or he would have bought it for a sum which represented its fair

---

1 [1956] 1 All ER 874.
2 At pp 875-876.

value in its bad condition, in which case he would pay so much less on that account. The proper measure of damages is therefore the difference between the value in its assumed condition and the value in the bad condition which should have been reported to the client . . . In this action, if the plaintiff were to recover from the surveyor £7,000, it would mean that the plaintiff would get for £18,000 (£25,000 paid less £7,000 received) a house and land which were worth £21,000. That cannot be right. The proper amount for him to recover is £4,000.

Morris LJ was likewise aware of the difference between compensation and over-compensation:

The plaintiff must not be placed in a better position by the award of damages than he would have been in had the defendant given a proper report. If the plaintiff had received £7,000 damages in 1952 on the basis of what it would then cost him to do the repair work, and if the plaintiff instead of doing the work had sold the property for £21,000, which was its value, he would have profited to the extent of £3,000.

Philips v *Ward* was followed in *Perry* v *Sidney Phillips & Son*,[1] where the plaintiff paid £27,000 for a house which was stated by the defendant surveyors, in the course of their report, to be worth £28,500. The defendants had negligently overlooked a number of serious structural defects in the property, and the trial judge[2] awarded damages against them based on what it would cost at the date of judgment to repair those defects. When the defendant appealed the plaintiff, who had meanwhile sold the property for £43,000, did not attempt to justify an assessment based on the cost of repair, but claimed instead that the appropriate measure of damages was the difference *at the date of judgment* between the value of the property in its assumed and its actual condition. This argument was unanimously rejected by the Court of Appeal, which treated *Philips* v *Ward* as authority for awarding the difference between the price paid for the property and its true value at the date of purchase. As Oliver LJ pointed out: "The position ... is simply this, that the plaintiff has been misled by a negligent survey report into paying more for the property than that property was actually worth."

---

1 [1982] 3 All ER 705.
2 [1982] 1 All ER 1005.

Notwithstanding these clear rulings by the Court of Appeal, there remains a school of thought which regards "cost of repair" as a more realistic description of the loss which a purchaser suffers at the hands of a negligent surveyor. Such a belief led the judge at first instance in *Watts* v *Morrow*[1] to award the purchasers of a substantial farmhouse, which they intended to make their second home, the cost of repairing defects overlooked by their surveyor (some £34,000) rather than the £15,000 by which the purchase price of £177,500 exceeded the property's value. Judge Bowsher QC relied on certain *dicta* of Bingham LJ[2] to the effect that "difference in value" is not the invariable measure of damages against a negligent surveyor and held that, since the plaintiffs' decision to retain the property and to repair it was a reasonable one, they were entitled to recover all their ensuing costs.

On appeal to the Court of Appeal, this departure from the principles laid down in *Philips* v *Ward* and *Perry* v *Sidney Phillips & Son* was roundly condemned, and the judge's award of damages replaced by one which would reflect merely the excessive amount which the plaintiffs had been led to pay for the property. Once again, the need to avoid over-compensating the plaintiff was stressed, this time by Bingham LJ:[3]

The plaintiffs paid £177,500, the value of the house as it was represented to be. The value of the house in its actual condition was £162,500, a difference of £15,000. The actual cost of repairs was (in rounded-up figures) £34,000. If the plaintiff were to end up with the house and an award of £34,000 damages he would have obtained the house for £143,500. But even if the defendant had properly performed his contract this bargain was never on offer. The effect of the award is to put the plaintiffs not in the same position as if the defendant had properly performed but in a much better one.

In delivering the leading judgment in *Watts* v *Morrow*, Ralph Gibson LJ exposed what he regarded as the underlying fallacy in the argument for "cost of repair" damages, namely that it does not accurately reflect what a surveyor undertakes to do for the client. As his lordship pointed out, "the task of the court is to award to the

---

1 [1991] 1 EGLR 150.
2 *County Personnel (Employment Agency) Ltd* v *Alan R Pulver* [1987] 1 All ER 289 at p297; [1986] 2 EGLR 146.
3 [1991] 4 All ER 937 at p959; [1991] 2 EGLR 152.

plaintiffs that sum of money which will, so far as possible, put the plaintiffs into as good a position as if the contract for the survey had been properly fulfilled". Given that task, it is obviously critical to identify what is included in "the contract for the survey", and this is where the "cost of repair" argument goes astray:[1]

From his [ie the plaintiff's] point of view, it would indeed be better if the surveyor could be treated as having warranted that no repairs, beyond those described as indicated in the survey report, would be required within some period of time. No such warranty, however, was given in this case, or said to have been given, and, in the absence of such a warranty, there is no basis for awarding the cost of repairs.

In the light of these three cases[2] it now appears (subject, of course to any appeal to the House of Lords), that the basis of assessment is undeniably "difference in value". Indeed, the only reported decisions since 1956 in which a surveyor has been held liable to a purchaser for the cost of repairing undiscovered defects[3] have all been specifically declared wrong by the Court of Appeal in *Watts* v *Morrow*.

However, this is not to say that the cost of repair is entirely irrelevant in negligent survey cases; on the contrary, it may well play an important part in arriving at the value of the property in its defective condition, so as to assess "difference in value". As Purchas LJ put it in *Steward* v *Rapley*:[4]

There is no objection to a person who wishes to present a professional assessment of a market value from arriving at that market value by taking a value based on a good state of condition in the house and then deducting from it, either fully or appropriately discounted, the cost of putting it into an acceptable marketable condition.

Although reliance on "cost of repair" evidence for this purpose seems wholly unobjectionable in principle, it might perhaps be felt

---

1 [1991] 4 All ER 937 at p954; [1991] 2 EGLR 152.
2 *Philips* v *Ward* [1956] 1 All ER 874, *Perry* v *Sidney Phillips & Son* [1982] 3 All ER 705 and *Watts* v *Morrow* [1991] 4 All ER 939; [1991] 2 EGLR 152.
3 *Hipkins* v *Jack Cotton Partnership* [1989] 2 EGLR 157; *Syrett* v *Carr & Neave* [1990] 2 EGLR 161; and the first instance decision in *Watts* v *Morrow* itself (reported at [1991] 1 EGLR 150).
4 [1989] 1 EGLR 159 at p161.

that the court in *Steward* v *Rapley* itself exceeded the permissible limits. That case concerned an old house which was purchased by the plaintiffs for £58,500, after the defendants valued the property at £60,000 and stated that there were no signs of dry rot. A year later, when outbreaks of dry rot had been discovered, an expert instructed by the plaintiffs opined that the defendant should have recognised the problem in the first place and ought accordingly to have valued the property at £50,000. However, when the remedial work was begun and the damaged areas opened up, it became apparent that the dry rot was far more extensive than had been anticipated and that to eradicate it would cost £26,800. The plaintiffs' expert thereupon altered his "backdated valuation" from £50,000 to £33,200 (ie the value of the property in apparent good order less the cost of repair), and stated that the plaintiffs should have been advised not to purchase the house at all.

The trial judge, refusing to be diverted by hindsight from basic principles, awarded the plaintiffs damages of £8500, this being the difference between what they had paid for the property and what it was actually worth at that time. However, the Court of Appeal held that the cost of the necessary repairs, although completely unknown at the time of purchase, nevertheless represented the best available evidence of the extent to which the dry rot diminished the property's "value". With all due respect to their lordships, this seems incorrect; it is difficult to see how the value of a property in the market can be affected by the cost of any repairs other than those which the market believes to be necessary *at the time of valuation*.

(b) The implications

Although the principle of assessing damages by reference to "difference in value" seems logical enough, it carries with it some implications which may not appear quite so self-evident. The first of these is that where the valuation evidence before a court establishes that, defects notwithstanding, the property in question has been purchased for no more than its market value, an action for breach of contract should result in an award of nominal damages and an action in tort should fail altogether (because the tort of negligence is not complete unless and until damage is suffered). The principle established in *Philips* v *Ward* was applied in this way in the Scottish case of *Upstone* v *GDW Carnegie & Co*,[1] so as to restrict the liability of the defendant surveyors to the payment of nominal damages only. True, this ruling might appear to conflict with the later decision in *Howard* v *Horne & Sons*,[2] where a purchaser who bought a house for what the expert witnesses agreed was its true market value was nevertheless awarded £1,500 for "loss of the opportunity to negotiate a reduction in price". However, it is suggested that the judgment in the *Howard* case contains an inherent contradiction, since, if such a reduction in price could indeed have been negotiated on the basis of an accurate surveyor's report, it is the reduced price which in truth represented the market value of the property. It may be that this is what the experts actually said, but that their opinion was misinterpreted in the judgment; or it may be that the judge rejected the experts' evidence. In the absence of such an explanation, however, the decision in this case appears impossible to justify.

A further implication of *Philips* v *Ward* may be seen in cases where a property is subject to a progressive defect such as dry rot. If a surveyor negligently fails to discover such a defect, with the result that it becomes far more expensive to remedy, there appears to be no way in which the surveyor can be held liable for the purchaser's increased loss.[3] In *Hooberman* v *Salter Rex*,[4] where the cost of remedying dry rot had increased fourfold by the time the purchaser discovered it, the judge held that this additional cost was undoubtedly caused by the negligence of the defendant surveyor, but that the purchaser was restricted to recovering the "difference in value" at the date of purchase, with interest on that sum.

The *Philips* v *Ward* principle is capable, albeit in rather unusual cases, of operating to the benefit of purchasers as well as to their detriment. In *Daisley* v *BS Hall & Co*,[5] for example, the plaintiff paid £1750 more than the true market value of a property, in reliance on a survey carried out by the defendants which failed to report on damage caused by soil shrinkage. By the time the case came to trial it was clear that the risk of further damage to the property had

---

1 1978 SLT 4.
2 [1990] 1 EGLR 272.
3 See *Morgan* v *Perry* (1973) 229 EG 1737.
4 [1985] 1 EGLR 144.
5 (1972) 225 EG 1553.

receded, and that the problem could be permanently solved by works costing no more than £250. It was nevertheless held by Bristow J that "what is sauce for the goose is sauce for the gander", and that the plaintiff was entitled to damages of £1,750.

(c) The meaning of "difference in value"

It remains for us to examine a little more closely the concept of "difference in value" as it applies to a purchaser's damages against a negligent surveyor or valuer. This has been described in a number of cases as the difference between the value of the property as stated or implied in the surveyor's report and its value in its actual condition at the date of purchase.[1] It is suggested, however, that a better description of the measure of damages laid down in *Philips* v *Ward* is "the difference between the price actually paid for the property on the basis that the advice was good, and the price at which it would be bought as it was in fact".[2] This formulation was endorsed in *Watts* v *Morrow*[3] by Ralph Gibson LJ, who stated that "the diminution in value rule is more accurately to be expressed as the difference between the price paid and the value in its true description".

In the majority of negligent survey or valuation cases, the price paid and the assumed value have been identical, so that the court's attention has not been drawn to the question of which of these figures should be used in the assessment of damages. Where this is not so, and the purchaser has managed to acquire the property for less than its stated value, it is suggested that damages must reflect the price actually paid; if they do not, then the purchaser will receive compensation for a "loss" which has not in fact been suffered, and the surveyor will be treated as if his or her report amounts to a warranty of the property's value.

In the converse case, that of a purchaser who agrees to pay *more* for the property than the value placed on it by the surveyor or valuer, it is suggested that the damages to be awarded should reflect the lower figure (ie the stated value rather than the purchase

---

1 See, for example, *Philips* v *Ward* [1956] 1 All ER 874 at p876, *per* Denning LJ; at p878, *per* Morris LJ.
2 *Simple Simon Catering Ltd* v *Binstock Miller & Co* (1973) 228 EG 527 at p529, *per* Lord Denning MR.
3 [1991] 4 All ER 937 at p945; [1991] 2 EGLR 152: see also *Ford* v *White & Co* [1964] 2 All ER 755 at p758, *per* Pennycuick J.

price), since the purchaser can hardly claim to have relied on the surveyors' report in deciding to pay more than the value given therein. Thus, in *Hardy* v *Wamsley-Lewis*,[1] where the plaintiff paid £4,600 for a house which the defendant surveyor had valued at £4,300 (and which was in reality worth only £3,500), it was held that the appropriate measure of damages was £800 (ie £4,300 – £3,500).

Notwithstanding the logical attraction of this approach, it must be conceded that it has not always been followed by the courts. In *Oswald* v *Countrywide Surveyors Ltd*,[2] for example, where the plaintiffs purchased a house for £225,000 after the defendant surveyors had valued it at £215,000, the judge decided that damages for "diminution in value" should be based upon the purchase price rather than the valuation. The judge was satisfied "that the excess of £10,000 which the price paid represents over [the defendants'] valuation cannot reasonably be said not to be attributable to [the defendants'] default. In short, I am satisfied that by reason of the report [the plaintiffs] were caused to pay £225,000 for Bell Farm."

If this decision appears somewhat difficult to justify, the same may be said of *Shaw* v *Halifax (SW) Ltd*.[3] In that case a mortgage valuer negligently valued a house at £37,000 when it was worth only £32,000. The plaintiff purchased the property two months later for £42,000, by which time it was worth actually £37,000. Damages of £5,000 were awarded.

2 Incidental items of loss

Although it is seldom explicitly stated, an underlying assumption which helps to explain and rationalise the assessment of damages in this area is that a purchaser's basic entitlement is to be extricated free of charge from the transaction into which he or she has entered in reliance on a negligent survey or valuation. Thus, where a purchaser exchanges contracts but then discovers the truth in time to withdraw from completion of the transaction, the surveyor or valuer is *prima facie* liable for the purchaser's abortive legal costs.[4]

---

1 (1967) 203 EG 1039: see also *Morgan* v *Perry* (1973) 229 EG 1737; *Hingorani* v *Blower* (1975) 238 EG 883.
2 [1994] EGCS 150.
3 [1994] 2 EGLR 95.
4 *Buckland* v *Watts* (1968) 208 EG 969.

This liability should in principle extend to other wasted expenditure; the court's refusal in *Parsons* v *Way and Waller Ltd*[1] to award the purchaser the fees paid to a building society for inspecting the property (following which it refused to lend) seems incorrect.

In addition to the "conveyancing" costs of the purchase, it has been held that the purchaser is entitled to recover the amount of any deposit which has been forfeited to the vendor.[2] Moreover, although there appears to be no authority on the point, the defendant's liability would presumably extend to any damages for breach of contract which the purchaser is forced to pay to the vendor. In any event, the surveyor or valuer may be held liable for any expense which the purchaser incurs in investigating the defects overlooked, before taking the decision to withdraw.

In the majority of reported cases in which purchasers have sued surveyors or valuers for negligence, the purchase has in fact been completed. If, on then discovering the true condition of the property, the purchaser moves out of it, the "underlying assumption" described above means that the damages should comprise the property's diminution in value, all the legal costs and other expenses incurred in moving both into and out of the property, together with the costs of reselling it. This is indeed how damages in such cases have normally been assessed, both where the plaintiff chooses to leave[3] and where there is no choice (for example because the property is repossessed by a mortgagee[4]); the decision in *Hardy* v *Wamsley-Lewis*,[5] where the plaintiff was awarded his solicitors' costs on resale but not on purchase, appears wholly unjustifiable.

The situation which has provoked the greatest debate is that of the purchaser who decides to remain in the property, and to take on the responsibility of rectifying those defects which have been negligently overlooked by the surveyor or valuer concerned. As we have already noted, the purchaser in such circumstances is

---

1 (1952) 159 EG 524.
2 *Parsons* v *Way and Waller Ltd* (1952) 159 EG 524; *Buckland* v *Watts* (1968) 208 EG 969.
3 See *Philips* v *Ward* [1956] 1 All ER 874 at p879, *per* Romer LJ; *Watts* v *Morrow* [1991] 4 All ER 937 at p948, *per* Ralph Gibson LJ; at p959, *per* Bingham LJ; *Heatley* v *William H Brown Ltd* [1992] 1 EGLR 289.
4 See *Ezekiel* v *McDade* [1994] EGCS 194.
5 (1967) 203 EG 1039.

certainly not entitled to recover the cost of carrying out the necessary remedial work, but is limited to a basic award reflecting the "overpayment" or "diminution in value". Indeed, an attempt to argue that at least part of the cost of repair might be recovered as a substitute for the cost of resale was specifically rejected by the Court of Appeal in *Watts* v *Morrow*.[1] Nevertheless, while higher authority is so far lacking,[2] judges at first instance have for the most part been prepared to award damages to cover certain *incidental* expenses incurred by the purchaser in taking reasonable action to deal with defects, while recognising that such an award may not be entirely logical.[3]

The items for which damages have been awarded on this basis include costs incurred[4] and "management time" wasted[5] in investigating the defects and in carrying out temporary works of an emergency nature in order to render the property safe.[6] In *Martin* v *Bell-Ingram*[7] the plaintiffs recovered the cost of certain unsuccessful attempts at repair which were undertaken at the defendants' suggestion. In connection with the actual job of repairing the property, plaintiffs have been held entitled to recover the cost of alternative accommodation for themselves[8] or for their children[9] (although accommodation for a 19 year old son was held too remote);[10] the expense of removing and storing furniture[11]

---

1 [1991] 4 All ER 937.
2 In *Watts* v *Morrow* [1991] 4 All ER 937, Ralph Gibson LJ in the Court of Appeal noted the point but declined to express an opinion upon it.
3 See, for example, *Cross* v *David Martin & Mortimer* [1989] 1 EGLR 154 at p159, per Phillips J.
4 *Morgan* v *Perry* (1973) 229 EG 1737.
5 *Broadoak Properties Ltd* v *Young & White* [1989] 1 EGLR 263.
6 *Treml* v *Ernest W Gibson and Partners* (1984) 272 EG 68; *Broadoak Properties Ltd* v *Young & White* [1989] 1 EGLR 263; *Heatley* v *William H Brown Ltd* [1992] 1 EGLR 289.
7 1986 SLT 575.
8 *Hood* v *Shaw* (1960) 176 EG 1291; *Collard* v *Saunders* (1972) 221 EG 797; *Treml* v *Ernest W Gibson & Partners* (1984) 272 EG 68; *Cross* v *David Martin & Mortimer* [1989] 1 EGLR 154; cf *Gibbs* v *Arnold Son & Hockley* [1989] 2 EGLR 154.
9 *Hunter* v *J & E Shepherd* 1992 SLT 1096.
10 *Cross* v *David Martin & Mortimer* [1989] 1 EGLR 154.
11 *Hill* v *Debenham Tewson and Chinnocks* (1958) 171 EG 835; *Treml* v *Ernest W Gibson & Partners* (1984) 272 EG 68; *Cross* v *David Martin & Mortimer* [1989] 1 EGLR 154.

(including the damage suffered by carpets through shrinkage);[1] and the cost of removing and reinstalling a burglar alarm.[2] Other successful claims linked to the reasonable carrying out of the necessary works of repair have included loss of rent[3] and a general award for loss of use of the plaintiffs' home.[4] Finally, where a surveyor negligently failed to warn purchasers to postpone works of decoration until a problem of damp had been rectified, the plaintiffs recovered their wasted expenditure on plastering and decorations.[5]

It should be noted that, even if the principle on which these decisions have proceeded is a correct one, it is none the less subject to two important qualifications. First, as was pointed out in *Shaw* v *Halifax (SW) Ltd*,[6] a purchaser is clearly not entitled to recover under this heading for any items which ought properly to be regarded as part of the cost of repair, since that cost does not form the basis for the assessment of damages. Second, in order to avoid any element of "double counting" in the award of damages, it is necessary to exclude any items which are already reflected in the diminution in value of the property. As was stated by Judge Hicks QC in *Bigg* v *Howard Son & Gooch*:[7]

If such an award [ie for the cost of accommodation during the period of repairs] is ever appropriate it is not so when the likely need for and probable cost of vacating the premises during repair, as foreseeable by a purchaser buying at the relevant date with knowledge of the defects, has been taken into account in assessing what price he would have been prepared to pay.

3 Damages for "inconvenience"

In recent years it has become common for plaintiffs in negligence actions against surveyors and valuers to include a claim for compensation for what judges have variously referred to as "distress, worry, inconvenience and trouble";[8] "vexation and

---

1 *Fryer* v *Bunney* (1982) 263 EG 158.
2 *Syrett* v *Carr & Neave* [1990] 2 EGLR 161.
3 *Tremayne* v *T Mortimer Burrows and Partners* (1954) 165 EG 232; *Freeman* v *Marshall & Co* (1966) 200 EG 777.
4 *Gibbs* v *Arnold Son & Hockley* [1989] 2 EGLR 154.
5 *Hill* v *Debenham Tewson and Chinnocks* (1958) 171 EG 835.
6 [1994] 2 EGLR 95.
7 [1990] 1 EGLR 173 at p175.
8 *Perry* v *Sidney Phillips & Son* [1982] 3 All ER 705 at p709, *per* Lord Denning MR.

discomfort";[1] "disturbance and disruption";[2] "heartache and upheaval";[3] and "bother".[4] Subject to certain limitations described below, such claims are in principle acceptable. Following early cases such as *Moss* v *Heckingbottom*[5] and *Sinclair* v *Bowden Son and Partners*,[6] it was held by the Court of Appeal in *Perry* v *Sidney Phillips & Son*[7] that, where a client sued a surveyor for breach of contract, for negligence in carrying out a structural survey of a dwelling, the damages awarded might legitimately include a modest amount under this head. This ruling has been endorsed in numerous subsequent cases concerning both structural surveys[8] and a *House Buyer's Report and Valuation*.[9] Moreover, it has been held on numerous occasions that a negligent mortgage valuer may also be liable for such damages,[10] although courts have seldom considered whether the fact that the action is based in tort rather than in contract could or should make any difference to the legal position. The point was addressed in *Shaw* v *Halifax (SW) Ltd*,[11] where it was held that the nature of the action was irrelevant.

Of the limitations mentioned above, the most important lies in the definition of "inconvenience" for this purpose. As a general rule,[12]

---

1 *Ibid* at p710, *per* Oliver LJ.
2 *Roberts* v *J Hampson & Co* [1989] 2 All ER 504 at p514; [1988] 2 EGLR 181, *per* Ian Kennedy J.
3 *Westlake* v *Bracknell District Council* [1987] 1 EGLR 161 at p 163, *per* PJ Cox QC.
4 *Fryer* v *Bunney* (1982) 263 EG 158 at p 164, *per* Judge Newey QC.
5 (1958) 172 EG 207 (£250 for physical inconvenience).
6 (1962) 183 EG 95 (£100 for "inconvenience and discomfort for a family man").
7 [1982] 3 All ER 705.
8 By the Court of Appeal in *Watts* v *Morrow* [1991] 4 All ER 937; [1991] 2 EGLR 152, and at first instance in *Fryer* v *Bunney* (1982) 263 EG 158; *Treml* v *Ernest W Gibson & Partners* (1984) 272 EG 68; *Wilson* v *Baxter Payne & Lepper* [1985] 1 EGLR 141; *Hooberman* v *Salter Rex* [1985] 1 EGLR 144; *Broadoak Properties Ltd* v *Young & White* [1989] 1 EGLR 263; *Hipkins* v *Jack Cotton Partnership* [1989] 2 EGLR 157; *Syrett* v *Carr & Neave* [1990] 2 EGLR 161; *Hacker* v *Thomas Deal & Co* [1991] 2 EGLR 161 and *Heatley* v *William H Brown Ltd* [1992] 1 EGLR 289.
9 *Cross* v *David Martin & Mortimer* [1989] 1 EGLR 154.
10 *Martin* v *Bell-Ingram* 1986 SLT 575; *Westlake* v *Bracknell District Council* [1987] 1 EGLR 161; *Roberts* v *J Hampson & Co* [1989] 2 All ER 504; [1988] 2 EGLR 181; *Whalley* v *Roberts & Roberts* [1990] 1 EGLR 164; *Henley* v *Cloke & Sons* [1991] 2 EGLR 141; *Shaw* v *Halifax (SW) Ltd* [1994] 2 EGLR 95; *Ezekiel* v *McDade* [1994] EGCS 194.
11 [1994] 2 EGLR 95.
12 Based on *Addis* v *Gramophone Co* [1909] AC 488.

damages for breach of contract cannot include compensation for purely mental distress, frustration, anxiety, displeasure, vexation, tension or aggravation on the part of the plaintiff.[1] However, there are certain exceptions to this general rule, notably where the contract in question has as a specific object the provision of pleasure (as in the "defective package holiday" cases[2]) or the removal of displeasure (as where a solicitor should have obtained an injunction to protect a client from being molested).[3] The crucial question therefore is whether contracts for surveys or valuations fall into one of these exceptional categories, or whether the "inconvenience" for which a surveyor or valuer may be held liable bears a more limited meaning.

In *Perry v Sidney Phillips & Son*,[4] Lord Denning MR appeared to lend support to the former view. His lordship there, having cited the "exceptional" cases mentioned above as providing a basis for the plaintiff's claim, then emphasised that a purchaser who discovered that a house was in a deplorable condition would naturally be "most upset", especially if he could not afford to repair it. A similar line is taken by a small number of subsequent cases in which the plaintiff's "distress" appears unrelated to any physical inconvenience suffered,[5] while in *Drinnan v CW Ingram & Sons*[6] a Scottish judge refused to strike out the claim of a flat purchaser to have suffered hypertension resulting from the local authority's decision to condemn the entire tenement building, thus requiring the purchaser to move out. More recently, in *Ezekiel v McDade*,[7] the plaintiff's considerable inconvenience and distress appears to have resulted from the plaintiffs' loss of their home through repossession, rather than from any physical discomfort inherent in its defective condition, but damages of the type now under discussion were nevertheless awarded.

The great weight of authority, however, favours a narrower definition of "inconvenience". Thus in *Perry v Sidney Phillips & Son*

---

1 *Watts v Morrow* [1991] 4 All ER 937 at p959; [1991] 2 EGLR 152, *per* Bingham LJ.
2 See *Jarvis v Swan Tours Ltd* [1973] 1 QB 233.
3 See *Heywood v Wellers* [1976] QB 446.
4 [1982] 3 All ER 705 at p709.
5 See *Bolton v Puley* (1982) 267 EG 1160; *Whalley v Roberts & Roberts* [1990] 1 EGLR 164; *Hacker v Thomas Deal & Co* [1991] 2 EGLR 161.
6 1967 SLT 205.
7 [1994] EGCS 194.

itself, Oliver LJ referred to the plaintiff's "vexation, that is the discomfort and so on suffered by the plaintiff as a result of having to live for a lengthy period in a defective house".[1] Kerr LJ was even more specific:[2]

So far as the question of damages for vexation and inconvenience is concerned, it should be noted that the deputy judge awarded these not for the tension or frustration of a person who is involved in a legal dispute in which the other party refuses to meet its liabilities ... He awarded these damages because of the physical consequences of the breach, which were all foreseeable at the time.

The views of the majority in *Perry v Sidney Phillips & Son* were unequivocally endorsed by the Court of Appeal in *Watts v Morrow*.[3] Ralph Gibson LJ, having stated his opinion that contracts for surveys do not fall into the "exceptional" categories described above, concluded that "in the case of the ordinary surveyor's contract, damages are recoverable only for distress caused by physical consequences of the breach of contract".[4] A similar view was adopted by Bingham LJ, whose judgment contains a clear summary of the present legal position:[5]

Where the very object of a contract is to provide pleasure, relaxation, peace of mind or freedom from molestation, damages will be awarded if the fruit of the contract is not provided or if the contrary result is procured instead . . . A contract to survey the condition of a house for a prospective purchaser does not, however, fall within this exceptional category. In cases not falling within this exceptional category, damages are, in my view, recoverable for physical inconvenience and discomfort caused by the breach and mental suffering directly related to that inconvenience and discomfort. If those effects are foreseeably suffered during the period when defects are repaired I am prepared to accept that they sound in damages even though the cost of the repairs is not recoverable as such.

One particular consequence of defining "inconvenience" in physical terms is that a plaintiff whose interest in property is commercial will not be entitled to damages under this head. The

---

1 [1982] 3 All ER 705 at p710.
2 *Ibid* at p712.
3 [1991] 4 All ER 937; [1991] 2 EGLR 152.
4 *Ibid* at p159.
5 [1991] 4 All ER 937 at p960; [1991] 2 EGLR 152.

courts have taken this line in actions brought against solicitors,[1] architects[2] and builders,[3] and it would presumably be followed in relation to a valuer or surveyor, although there is as yet no direct authority on the point.

One situation in which a purchaser should not be awarded damages for inconvenience is where this factor has already been taken into account in assessing the reduced value of the house, with the result that it forms part of the basic measure of damages payable by the negligent surveyor or valuer. This was accepted in principle in *Bigg* v *Howard Son & Gooch*,[4] where the judge referred to an earlier case involving solicitors' negligence[5] in which the point had been applied. However, while undoubtedly correct in principle, it may be that this issue will seldom arise in practice; when counsel in *Perry* v *Sidney Phillips & Son*[6] put forward a similar argument, Oliver LJ retorted: "I do not think that that is a realistic view at all, and I should be extremely surprised to find any valuer who is prepared to say that that is a factor which he took into account in making his valuation".[7]

The courts' insistence that a purchaser's distress is only compensable in damages in so far as it results from physical discomfort and inconvenience means that damages under this head can only relate to the period until the source of discomfort is removed by the repair of the property. This in itself might appear fairly obvious, but it leads to the further conclusion that, where the plaintiff ought reasonably to have remedied the defect at an earlier date, his or her damages for inconvenience may fall to be reduced. This application of the doctrine of mitigation of damage (which requires a plaintiff to take all reasonable steps to minimise the loss suffered) was recognised in *Cross* v *David Martin & Mortimer*,[8] where the plaintiffs were denied compensation for the inconvenience resulting from a hole in their hall floor caused by subsidence of the floor slab. The court held that they had acted

---

1 *Hayes* v *Dodd* [1990] 2 All ER 815.
2 *Hutchinson* v *Harris* (1978) 10 BLR 19.
3 *Michael* v *Ensoncraft Ltd* [1990] EGCS 156.
4 [1990] 1 EGLR 173.
5 *Walker* v *Giffen Couch & Archer* [1988] EGCS 64.
6 [1982] 3 All ER 705.
7 [1982] 3 All ER 705 at p710.
8 [1989] 1 EGLR 154.

unreasonably in leaving this defect unremedied for four years.

It should not be assumed, on the basis of this decision, that the doctrine of mitigation will be readily invoked against a plaintiff purchaser, whose predicament is after all due to the negligence of the defendant. In particular, it seems that a modern court is unlikely to apply this principle in cases where the plaintiff's failure to repair is due to lack of the necessary financial resources, notwithstanding the House of Lords' ruling in *Liesbosch* v *Edison*[1] that the plaintiff's lack of funds is to be ignored. This judicial generosity towards plaintiffs is especially noticeable where the defendant has persisted in denying liability (thus leaving the plaintiff with no assurance that the expense involved will ultimately be recouped).[2]

The final "limitation" on awards of damages for inconvenience relates simply to their size. The courts, while not laying down any arbitrary limit or "conventional" amount, have stated repeatedly that such awards should be "modest". As to what sum is appropriate in any particular case, it may be remembered that the plaintiff is normally receiving compensation either for discomfort caused by defects in the property or for inconvenience suffered over the period when they are repaired (including the disruption involved in moving out temporarily into what may be unsuitable accommodation). It seems logical, therefore, that the precise award should depend on both the severity of the inconvenience and its duration or likely duration.[3] In what appears to be the largest award so far reported under this heading, a diabetic husband and wheelchair-bound wife received £12,500 for the extreme physical inconvenience suffered by them for two and a half years in a seriously defective house, followed by four more years in unsuitable alternative accommodation (a mobile home).[4]

In general, however, damages for inconvenience have tended to fall within a fairly narrow band, with few plaintiffs receiving more than £1,000.[5] Of those awards which have been set at a higher

---

1 [1933] AC 449.
2 See *Perry* v *Sidney Phillips & Son* [1982] 3 All ER 705 at 711, *per* Oliver LJ; at p712, *per* Kerr LJ.
3 For useful summaries of awards in this area, see "Damages for Heartache" (1988) 4 Const L 264 and "More Heartache" (1992) 8 Const LJ 318, by Kim Franklin.
4 *Goodwin* v *Phillips* June 17 1994, Official Referees' Business, unreported.
5 However, in *Oswald* v *Countrywide Surveyors Ltd*, [1994] ECGS 150, a husband and wife were each awarded £2,000 under this head.

level, a number have come from Judge Bowsher QC, whose award of £4,000 to each of the plaintiffs in *Watts* v *Morrow*[1] was reduced by the Court of Appeal to £750 each. Nothing daunted, Judge Bowsher has since awarded £1,500 to a husband and £3,000 to a wife in a case where dangerous defects in their house deprived them of normal toilet and washing facilities for a year,[2] and £6,000 to a married couple for what was arguably purely mental distress.[3]

4 Personal injury

In addition to the normal heads of loss for which a purchaser may seek damages, it appears that there may in certain circumstances be a claim for personal injuries. In *Allen* v *Ellis & Co*[4] the plaintiff purchased a house in reliance on a structural survey from the defendants. The report, which was generally favourable, stated specifically that the garage was in satisfactory condition. A year after moving into the property, the plaintiff, in seeking to investigate a leak, placed a piece of wooden board on the roof, stepped on to it and fell through, sustaining fairly severe injuries.

Garland J, having first ruled that the defendants were guilty of negligence, acknowledged that "a structural survey is not a safety audit", but pointed out that "if the roof had been accurately described ... the plaintiff would never have been in peril of suffering the injuries which he did in fact suffer". His lordship accordingly found that the necessary elements of causation and remoteness were present,[5] rejected the defendants' allegations of contributory negligence[6] and held them liable for the plaintiff's injuries.

A further sense in which "personal injury" may arise in the context of a negligent survey or valuation is where the discomfort and inconvenience suffered are sufficiently great to affect the plaintiff's health. Medical evidence to this effect may certainly result in a larger award of general damages for "inconvenience";[7] whether a

---

1 [1991] 4 All ER 937; [1991] 2 EGLR 152, following the same judge's identical award in *Syrett* v *Carr & Neave* [1990] 2 EGLR 161.
2 *Heatley* v *William H Brown Ltd* [1992] 1 EGLR 289.
3 *Ezekiel* v *McDade* [1994] 1 EGLR 255; reduced on appeal to £4000 ([1994] EGCS 194).
4 [1990] 1 EGLR 170.
5 See pp132–139.
6 See p219.
7 See, for example, *Collard* v *Saunders* (1972) 221 EG 797.

surveyor or valuer may be held responsible for more specific consequences (such as hypertension leading to loss of the plaintiff's employment) depends upon whether such drastic consequences could reasonably have been foreseen. In *Drinnan v CW Ingram & Sons*[1] a Scottish judge was not prepared to strike out such a claim at a preliminary stage, although he expressed his "gravest doubts" as to its chance of success at trial.

B Lender

Where a mortgage lender relies on a negligent over-valuation of property which is offered as security for a loan, the damages payable by the negligent valuer should reflect all losses which flow from that negligence. In addition to the capital sum which is lent and lost (together with interest on that sum for the period over which the lender is deprived of it), there may be a claim for certain incidental losses, such as the costs involved in repossessing and reselling the property. It may also be necessary to set against these losses the value of any rights which the lender has against a defaulting borrower.

1 The basic measure

In defining the basic loss suffered by a mortgage lender who relies on a negligent over-valuation of the mortgaged property, the courts in recent years have emphasised that there is an important distinction to be drawn between cases where, given an accurate valuation, there would still have been a mortgage advance, albeit at a lower level, and those where no loan transaction at all would have resulted. These two categories are commonly described as "transaction" and "non-transaction" cases. It is worth noting at the outset that a court's decision as to the category into which a particular case falls does not depend exclusively upon the attitude of the lender; a number of recent cases have been classified as "non-transaction" on the basis of evidence that a smaller loan would not have been acceptable to the borrower.[2] It appears that a lender

---

1 1967 SLT 205.
2 *Banque Bruxelles Lambert SA v Eagle Star Insurance Co Ltd* [1994] 2 EGLR 108; *Nyckeln Finance Co Ltd v Stumpbrook Continuation Ltd* [1994] 2 EGLR 143; *HIT Finance Ltd v Lewis & Tucker Ltd* [1993] 2 EGLR 231.

who seeks damages on a "non-transaction" basis bears the onus of proving that the case falls into that category.[1]

(a) "Transaction" cases

The basic measure of damages in a "transaction" case consists of the difference between: (i) what has been lent and lost in reliance on the negligent valuation; and (ii) what would have been lent and lost if the valuer had not been negligent. If the latter situation would not have resulted in any loss at all (because the smaller loan would have remained fully secured), then the valuer is liable for the full amount of the loan, less whatever the lender is able to recover from the borrower or from repossession and resale of the property. If, however, falling property values mean that even the smaller loan would have been partly unsecured at the time of the borrower's default, this hypothetical loss is offset against the loss which the lender has actually suffered. In such circumstances (ie where the property would have provided insufficient security even for the smaller loan), the basic measure of damages becomes simply the difference between the loan which has been made and that which would have been made. This measure, which was agreed by the parties in *Singer & Friedlander Ltd* v *John D Wood & Co*,[2] was applied in *Corisand Investments Ltd* v *Druce & Co*[3] and *Allied Trust Bank Ltd* v *Edward Symmons & Partners*.[4]

These principles may be illustrated by two simple examples.

Example 1
A	Valuation of property	£1,000,000
B	Mortgage loan (at 70%)	£700,000
C	True value at date of valuation	£500,000
D	Loan if true value had been known	£350,000
E	Value at date of borrower's default	£500,000

Here the basic measure of damages against the negligent valuer is £200,000 (ie B − E). There is no hypothetical loss to be offset, since (D − E) is not greater than zero.

---

1 *Mount Banking Corporation Ltd* v *Brian Cooper & Co* [1992] 2 EGLR 142 at p144, *per* RM Stewart QC.
2 (1977) 243 EG 212.
3 (1978) 248 EG 315.
4 [1994] 1 EGLR 165.

Example 2

A	Valuation of property	£1,000,000
B	Mortgage loan (at 70%)	£700,000
C	True value at date of valuation	£500,000
D	Loan if true value had been known	£350,000
E	Value at date of borrower's default	£250,000

Here the basic measure of damages is £350,000 (B − E) − (D − E). The lender has actually lost £450,000, but would have lost £100,000 in any event. In effect, therefore, the figure E (which appears in both elements of the equation) can be cancelled out, and the measure stated simply as B − D.

It may be noted that this method of assessment places the risk of a fall in the value of the security, as a result of movements in the property market generally, on the lender rather than the valuer. However, this is not done explicitly (by identifying that element in the overall loss and excluding it from the computation); it simply comes about as a result of the formulae used.

(b) "Non-transaction" cases

The basic measure of damages in a "non-transaction" case consists of everything which has been lent and lost in reliance on the negligent valuation. Here there is no "hypothetical loss" to be offset since, by definition, there would have been no mortgage loan at all if the true value of the property had been known. Nevertheless, a question of crucial importance which has been debated in a number of recent cases is whether, even in such circumstances, it is appropriate to hold the valuer responsible for losses which result from a fall in the property market subsequent to the making of the loan.

The lender's argument in such cases is a straightforward one. It is that since, but for the valuer's negligence, there would have been no mortgage loan at all, the valuer must accept liability for all the losses which flow from the making of that loan. These losses consist simply of the amount of the loan less whatever is recovered by the lender, and there is no justification for making any further deduction. This measure of damages was applied so as to throw market losses on to the defendant valuers in *United Bank of Kuwait* v *Prudential Property Services Ltd*,[1] where Gage J regarded himself as bound by the earlier decision of the Court of Appeal in *Baxter* v *FW Gapp & Co Ltd*.[2]

The counter-argument raised by valuers is that, while a negligent valuation may have resulted in a loan being less than fully secured, it has not *caused* (in a legal sense) that part of the lender's overexposure which results from a fall in market values.[3] Moreover, since lenders do not rely on valuers to offer any sort of protection against market movements, such movements cannot legitimately be regarded as within the risk to which a particular lender has been exposed *by the valuer's negligence*.

It appears that, for the moment at least, it is the valuers' arguments which represent the law. The leading case is *Banque Bruxelles Lambert SA* v *Eagle Star Insurance Co Ltd*[4] where Phillips J, relying heavily on the decision of the House of Lords in *Banque Keyser Ullmann SA* v *Skandia (UK) Insurance Co*,[5] stated:[6]

Whether the cause of the loss of an advance is clearly foreseen or not reasonably foreseeable I do not see how the negligent adviser can fairly be said to have caused that loss unless his advice has been relied upon as providing protection against the risk of that loss.

His lordship moreover felt strongly that market losses should in principle fall on the lender rather than on the negligent valuer:[7]

Where a party is contemplating a commercial venture that involves a number of risks and obtains professional advice in respect of one head of risk before embarking on the adventure, I do not see why negligent advice in respect of that head of risk should, in effect, make the adviser the underwriter of the entire adventure. More particularly, where the negligent advice relates to the existence or amount of some security against risk in the adventure, I do not see why the adviser should be liable for all the consequences of the adventure, whether or not the security in question would have protected against them.

---

1 [1994] 2 EGLR 100.
2 [1939] 2 KB 271 (significantly more fully reported at [1939] 2 All ER 752).
3 For the difference between factual and legal causation, see p134.
4 [1994] 2 EGLR 108.
5 [1991] 2 AC 249.
6 [1994] 2 EGLR 108 at p133.
7 [1994] 2 EGLR 108 at p132.

Having thus set out his views as to where the risks *ought* to lie, Phillips J concluded that there was nothing in the case law to prevent him from excluding market losses from the damages awarded against a negligent mortgage valuer. His lordship pointed out that in *HIT Finance Ltd* v *Lewis & Tucker Ltd*,[1] where the lenders' damages included market losses, this measure was expressly conceded by the defendants.

The precise ground on which Phillips J in *BBL* felt justified in not following *Baxter* v *FW Gapp & Co Ltd*[2] is not at all clear. However, it was pointed out by Judge Fawcus in *Nyckeln Finance Co Ltd* v *Stumpbrook Continuation Ltd*[3] that *Baxter* v *Gapp* "was not a case where there had been evidence of any fall in the property market, let alone a catastrophic one, so that the present issue did not really fall for consideration".[4] Having decided that, as matter of common sense, the negligent mortgage valuation was a mere scene-setter and could not be said to have *caused* losses due to a falling market, Judge Fawcus expressly chose to follow *BBL* in preference to *United Bank of Kuwait* v *Prudential Property Services Ltd*.[5]

Judges in a number of subsequent cases have shown a clear preference for the view expressed in *BBL* and *Nyckeln* as against that taken in *United Bank of Kuwait*.[6] It appears therefore that, subject to what an appeal court might say, a negligent mortgage valuer is not liable for that part of the lender's losses which can be traced to a fall in the property market, even where it is established that, given a competent valuation, no mortgage transaction would have taken place.

2 Incidental items of loss

The distinction between "transaction" and "non-transaction" cases

---

1 [1993] 2 EGLR 231.
2 [1939] 2 KB 271.
3 [1994] 2 EGLR 143.
4 [1994] 2 EGLR 143 at p154.
5 [1994] 2 EGLR 100.
6 *Axa Equity & Law Home Loans Ltd* v *Goldsack & Freeman* [1994] 1 EGLR 175; *Axa Equity & Law Home Loans Ltd* v *Hirani Watson* May 12 1994, Queen's Bench, unreported; *BNP Mortgages Ltd* v *Goadsby & Harding Ltd* [1994] 2 EGLR 169. See also *Mortgage Express Ltd* v *Bowerman & Partners* [1994] 2 EGLR 156 (a solicitors' negligence case).

which was described above[1] may also be of importance where a lender seeks damages for incidental losses and expenses which arise out of the loan transaction, notably the costs involved in taking proceedings against a defaulting borrower to repossess and sell the mortgaged property. In a case where, had the true value of the property been known, a smaller loan would nevertheless have been made, it seems that such damages should not be awarded. This is because, as was pointed out by Gibson J in *Corisand Investments Ltd* v *Druce & Co*:[2] "The plaintiffs would have been taking proceedings with equal lack of utility in respect of the smaller loan they would have made if they had received a valuation which was not in breach of the defendants' duty."

In "non-transaction" cases, the legal and other costs incurred in repossessing and reselling the security have normally been included in the damages payable by a negligent valuer.[3] Indeed, while defendants have on occasion disputed individual items of loss (such as an overpayment to the estate agents who were handling the resale),[4] no defendant appears seriously to have challenged the lender's entitlement in principle to recover such costs.

Notwithstanding this general acceptance, however, one might perhaps question whether the risk of having to take proceedings against a defaulting mortgagor is really one against which a lender relies on a valuer for protection. If it is not, then, as with losses resulting from a fall in the property market,[5] it is suggested that this cost should not be included in the damages awarded for the valuer's negligence. Furthermore, the lender cannot evade this issue by arguing: "I relied on you for an assurance that the value of the property would be sufficient to cover such costs in addition to the amount of the outstanding loan". If this argument were accepted, it could equally be used to hold the valuer liable for the borrower's failure to pay interest at the contractual rate, something which was flatly denied by the House of Lords in *Swingcastle Ltd* v *Alastair Gibson*.[6]

---

1 See p164.
2 (1978) 248 EG 315 at p506.
3 See, for example, *Baxter* v *FW Gapp & Co Ltd* [1939] 2 KB 271; *Swingcastle Ltd* v *Alastair Gibson* [1991] 2 AC 223; [1991] 1 EGLR 157.
4 *HIT Finance Ltd* v *Lewis & Tucker Ltd* [1993] 2 EGLR 231.
5 See pp166–168.
6 [1991] 2 AC 223; [1991] 1 EGLR 157: see p171.

3 Interest

In addition to the capital sum lost which forms the basic measure of damages,[1] a lender is entitled to compensation from a negligent valuer for having been deprived of interest on that capital. According to Phillips J in *Banque Bruxelles Lambert SA* v *Eagle Star Insurance Co Ltd*,[2] that entitlement in truth comprises two separate claims: first, from the date of the loan to the date on which the security was realised, damages reflecting the unearned interest on the entire capital sum; and second, from the date on which the security was realised to the date of judgment, interest on the capital lost in accordance with the court's statutory discretion under the Supreme Court Act 1981, section 35A(1).[3] While other judges have not explicitly divided the lender's claim in this way, it appears that their view of the lender's overall entitlement is not substantially different from that of Phillips J.[4] In any event, it seems that what should be awarded is simple rather than compound interest.

The most important question in this context concerns the rate of interest which is to be adopted, and the leading authority is the decision of the House of Lords in *Swingcastle Ltd* v *Alastair Gibson*.[5] That case concerned a remortgage agreement under which the plaintiff finance company lent £10,000 on the security of a house which was (negligently) valued by the defendant at £18,000. Because the plaintiffs regarded the borrowers as "non-status" (or high risk), the rate of interest payable under the mortgage contract was more than 36%, rising to some 45% on any default in repayment. When the borrowers fell into arrears, the plaintiffs repossessed the property and sold it for £12,000. They then sued the defendant for everything which they had lost in consequence of the mortgage, including accrued interest at the default rate. This claim succeeded in the county court; the Court of Appeal,[6] despite an acknowledgment by Neill LJ that "to award damages on this basis is in effect to treat the valuer as the guarantor of the contract of loan", held unanimously that it was

---

1 See p164.
2 [1994] 2 EGLR 108.
3 As to interest on the judgment debt itself, see p144.
4 See, for example, *HIT Finance Ltd* v *Lewis & Tucker Ltd* [1993] 2 EGLR 231.
5 [1991] 2 AC 223; [1991] 1 EGLR 157.
6 [1990] 3 All ER 463; [1990] 2 EGLR 149.

bound by the authority of *Baxter v FW Gapp & Co Ltd*[1] to uphold the judge's award.

On further appeal by the defendant valuer, the House of Lords unanimously overturned the decision of the Court of Appeal and overruled *Baxter v Gapp* on the point in issue. As Lord Lowry (who delivered the only speech) pointed out:[2]

The approach [ie in *Baxter v Gapp*], if carefully scrutinised, seems contrary to principle: the aggrieved party was entitled to be placed in the same position as if the wrong had not occurred, and not to receive from the wrongdoer compensation for lost interest at the rate which the borrower had contracted to observe ... What the lenders lost, in addition to their other damages, was the use of the £10,000 while it was perforce locked up in the loan.

His lordship then expanded upon these points:

My Lords, it is clear that the lenders ought to have presented their claim on the basis that, if the valuer had advised properly, they would not have lent the money. Where they went wrong was to claim not only correctly that they had to spend all the money which they did but incorrectly that the valuer by his negligence deprived them of the interest which they would have received from the borrowers if the borrowers had paid up. The security for the loan was the property, but the lenders did not have a further security consisting of a guarantee by the valuer that the borrowers would pay everything, or indeed anything, that was due from them to the lenders at the date, whenever it occurred, on which the loan transaction terminated. The fallacy of the lenders' case is that they have been trying to obtain from the valuer compensation for the borrowers' failure and not the proper damages for the valuer's negligence.

The principle inherent in this decision was applied in *HIT Finance Ltd v Lewis & Tucker Ltd*,[3] where the plaintiff lender was a wholly owned subsidiary of two public companies, which were the only source of funds for its mortgage lending operations. In an action against a negligent valuer the plaintiff claimed that, since it was obliged to account to its parents for all interest received from the borrower, its loss in a "non-transaction" case consisted of everything

---

1 [1939] 2 KB 271.
2 [1991] 2 AC 223 at p238; [1991] 1 EGLR 157.
3 [1993] 2 EGLR 231.

which the borrower should have paid. This argument was roundly rejected by Wright J who, having examined the underlying realities of the situation, concluded that the plaintiff was a mere puppet and that it was the parent companies which had in truth suffered the relevant loss. And, in the absence of any evidence as to precisely how the parent companies raised the money to fund the plaintiff's activities, they were entitled merely to a rate of interest designed to compensate them for being kept out of their money.

If interest is not to be awarded so as to reflect the borrower's obligations, then what *is* the appropriate rate to adopt? Although the courts have not returned a consistent answer to this question, there is some authority to suggest that, in the absence of any evidence as to how a lender funded an advance, something close to the Special Account (the successor to the Short Term Investment Account) rate will be selected. In *Swingcastle Ltd* v *Alastair Gibson*[1] this produced a rate of 12%; in the earlier "transaction" case of *Corisand Investments Ltd* v *Druce & Co*[2] it resulted in an award of 9%.[3]

These cases, however, may perhaps be regarded as exceptional. Where a lender can provide evidence as to how it raised the money needed to finance the loan, it should be entitled to recover interest based on either its actual borrowing rate (as in *Nykredit Mortgage Bank plc* v *Edward Erdman Group Ltd*[4]) or normal commercial borrowing rates. In *Banque Bruxelles Lambert SA* v *Eagle Star Insurance Co Ltd*,[5] for example, the plaintiffs were awarded base rate + 1% ("fair compensation for being deprived of the use of money"), despite the valuers' claim that the Special Account rate should be used. Indeed, a court may even select such a rate where no specific evidence has been proffered, on the basis that commercial organisations can be presumed to fund their activities on a normal commercial basis.[6] Moreover, if a lender can satisfy the court that, had it not lent on this transaction, it would have lent

---

1 [1991] 2 AC 223; [1991] 1 EGLR 157; see also *BNP Mortgages Ltd* v *Chadwick Bird* July 1994, Official Referees' Business, unreported.
2 (1978) 248 EG 315.
3 This was based on the Short Term Investment Account, the predecessor of the Special Account.
4 October 1 1993, Mayors and City of London Court, unreported.
5 [1994] 2 EGLR 108.
6 *HIT Finance Ltd* v *Lewis & Tucker Ltd* [1993] 2 EGLR 231.

on another and would have received interest at a high contractual rate, there may be the basis for an award at that rate. Such cases, however, are likely to be rare. As Neill LJ pointed out when *Swingcastle Ltd* v *Alastair Gibson* was before the Court of Appeal:[1]

The lender could be awarded a sum equivalent to the amount he would have earned on another loan if he had had the money available for this purpose. In my view, however, such an award should not be made in the absence of evidence that the money lent would have been used for another transaction. This evidence would have to be directed to proving an unsatisfied demand for loans and I anticipate that such evidence might seldom be forthcoming.

4 Offsets against damages

In assessing the totality of a lender's loss, credit must be given for any sums which the lender has received under the mortgage agreement.[2] The most important of these are the money which is recovered by the lender on sale of the repossessed property, and any repayments of capital and/or interest made by the borrower prior to default. It is suggested that, in a "transaction" case, repayments by the borrower ought logically to be ignored, on the assumption that these would equally have been made in the event of a smaller loan. However, a lender's damages were reduced to take account of interest repayments made by the borrower in *Corisand Investments Ltd* v *Druce & Co*,[3] a ruling rather unsatisfactorily "explained" in the later case of *Assured Advances Ltd* v *Ashbee & Co*[4] as based on the impossibility of knowing for certain what would have happened if a smaller loan had been made.

Other sums falling to be offset include any income, such as rent, which is produced by the property between the dates of its repossession and its resale. In *Banque Bruxelles Lambert SA* v *Eagle Star Insurance Co Ltd*[5] the plaintiffs claimed to give credit for all the income which they had received (though not for the capital sum on sale of the property) "simply by totalling it without regard to when it was received and setting the total against the total of the

---

1 [1990] 3 All ER 463 at p469; [1990] 2 EGLR 149.
2 *London & South of England Building Society* v *Stone* (1983) 267 EG 69 at p77, *per* Stephenson LJ; *cf* the (untenable) view of O'Connor LJ in the same case (at p73).
3 (1978) 248 EG 315.
4 [1994] EGCS 169.
5 [1994] 2 EGLR 108.

damages recoverable for loss of use of the loans advanced". This was criticised by the valuers, who argued that credit should be given on a running account basis, so that early receipts would operate so as to reduce the capital outstanding. Nevertheless, the plaintiffs' approach was accepted by Phillips J as appropriate and fair, given that they were claiming interest on a simple and not a compound basis.

5 The borrower's covenant

It is clear from what is stated above that a mortgage lender's damages against a negligent valuer fall to be reduced on account of any sums which are actually recovered by the lender from the borrower. A more controversial question concerns what account, if any, is to be taken of sums which *might* be so recovered, most importantly by taking action against the borrower to enforce his or her personal covenant to repay the loan.

This question first arose in *Eagle Star Insurance Co Ltd* v *Gale and Power*,[1] where the plaintiffs lent £3,015 on the security of a house valued by the defendants at £3,350, on terms that the mortgagor would after four years repay £1,500 of the loan out of his retirement gratuity. The house, which had been negligently overvalued, was in truth worth only £1,600; however, if the mortgagor duly made the promised repayment, the outstanding loan would be fully secured on the property. When the plaintiffs brought an action for negligence against the defendants, Devlin J denied that the mortgagor's covenant could be ignored in assessing the damages. On the other hand, his lordship rejected the defendants' argument that this was a case for nominal damages, and awarded the plaintiffs damages of £100 as an indemnity against such contingencies as the house collapsing or the borrower proving unable to fulfil his covenant.

The *Eagle Star* case is unusual, in that the lenders took action against the valuers at a time when the borrower had not defaulted in repaying the mortgage loan. A more common version of the problem, which arose in *London & South of England Building Society* v *Stone*,[2] provoked a remarkable diversity of opinions among the four judges who were involved in the proceedings. The

---

1 (1955) 166 EG 37.
2 (1983) 267 EG 69.

case arose out of a mortgage loan of £11,880 which was made by the plaintiffs in reliance on a valuation carried out by the defendant. Unfortunately, in carrying out his inspection the defendant had negligently failed to discover that the house, which was built on the site of a filled quarry on a hillside, was in danger of collapsing as the quarry fill slid downwards. The plaintiffs paid for the necessary repairs (which cost more than the total value of the house); then, partly from a sense of moral responsibility for the conduct of a valuer whom they had chosen, and partly as a public relations exercise, they announced that they would take no action whatsoever against the purchasers on their personal covenant to repay the loan.

In the plaintiffs' action against the valuer, Russell J held that the basic measure of damages to be awarded to the plaintiffs was the amount of their loan, but that from this figure a sum should be deducted to take account of the alternative means by which the plaintiffs might have protected their position. The judge thought that, in terms of honour and commercial good sense, the plaintiffs might reasonably choose not to pursue the purchasers for the full amount of their debt, but that they should not have let them off completely; he therefore deducted £3,000.

In the Court of Appeal, Sir Denys Buckley agreed with the trial judge's deduction on the basis that the contingency of repayment or non-repayment by the purchasers had to be taken into account in evaluating what the plaintiffs had lost. However, O'Connor LJ disagreed, holding that money owing from the mortgagor (or even actually repaid by him!) did nothing to diminish the plaintiff's loss. A middle course was steered by Stephenson LJ, who felt that the question resolved itself into one relating to mitigation of damage:[1]

[Valuing the chance of repayment] can be justified only if it was reasonable for the respective plaintiffs to enforce the borrowers' covenant to pay; for what the borrowers might pay could only be taken into account in mitigation of the plaintiffs' damage if the plaintiffs ought to have mitigated that loss and damage by enforcing the borrowers' covenants ... It seems to me the wrongdoer must show that the wronged party's reasoned choice to waive his contractual rights against the third party is unreasonable in the ordinary course of events in the particular field of commercial business and in all the circumstances, it may be some special, of the particular case.

---

1 (1983) 267 EG 69 at p77.

On the facts before him, Stephenson LJ held that the plaintiffs' refusal to enforce the borrowers' covenant was not "an act of unreasonable benevolence or forgiveness". He therefore agreed with O'Connor LJ (though for different reasons) that no deduction should be made from the damages awarded.

The view that the borrower's covenant becomes significant in the context of the lender's duty to mitigate gains support from the decision of Judge Byrt QC in *Nykredit Mortgage Bank plc* v *Edward Erdman Group Ltd*.[1] There too, however, the lender's decision not to pursue the borrower was held to be reasonable, since the latter was "engulfed in debt with no significant assets" and was thus not worth suing.

C Vendor

Where a valuer advising a potential vendor negligently undervalues the property concerned, the probable consequence is that the property will be sold for less than it is worth. In such circumstances it appears, by analogy with the case of a purchaser,[2] that the basic measure of damages will be the difference between the sale price and the true market value of the property at the time when it is sold. Although direct authority for this proposition is surprisingly difficult to find, it was accepted as correct in *Shacklock* v *Chas Osenton, Lockwood & Co*[3] where, however, the allegation of negligence failed on the facts. Furthermore, it was applied in the case of *Weedon* v *Hindwood, Clarke & Esplin*,[4] where valuers conducting compulsory negotiations on behalf of a landowner negligently allowed themselves to be persuaded by the local authority to accept too low a figure based on out of date legal principles. This measure of damages has also been accepted as appropriate in cases where the negligence of a mortgagee's valuer causes repossessed property to be sold for less than its true value, to the detriment of the mortgagor.[5]

---

1 October 1 1993, Mayors and City of London Court, unreported.
2 See p146.
3 (1964) 192 EG 819.
4 (1974) 234 EG 121.
5 See *Cuckmere Brick Co Ltd* v *Mutual Finance Ltd* [1971] Ch 949; *Garland* v *Ralph Pay & Ransom* (1984) 271 EG 106.

Ironically, in the only reported case to have raised the issue of a vendor's damages directly, the court appears to have used an incorrect basis of assessment. This was in *Bell Hotels (1935) Ltd* v *Motion*,[1] where the defendant valuer told the plaintiffs that their hotel and its contents were worth approximately £20,000 and that it would not attract brewery companies as potential purchasers. Relying on this advice, the plaintiffs sold the property for £21,730 to a private purchaser, who resold it within a week to a brewery company for £25,000. Having held that the defendant's advice was negligent, Byrne J awarded the plaintiffs £5,000 damages, though without stating explicitly how this figure was arrived at. If (as seems likely) it represents the difference between the resale price and the defendant's valuation, it is suggested that the decision is incorrect; the plaintiff's loss was in fact £3,270, that being the difference between what they actually received and what they should have received on the sale.

In the unusual case of *Kenney* v *Hall, Pain & Foster*,[2] a vendor complained of an allegedly negligently *overvaluation* of his property. Relying on the defendants' assurances as to the price which could be obtained for his house, and leaving what appeared to be a sensible safety margin, the plaintiff obtained a bridging loan in order to purchase and renovate two other properties. When the plaintiff's house, which had been greatly overvalued, proved virtually impossible to sell, the plaintiff's venture overstretched him to the verge of bankruptcy. The difficult task of assessing damages in this situation was eased by the parties agreeing that, had the plaintiff been properly advised, he would have sold his house and purchased a replacement at much lower prices, thus losing only some £10,000 as a result of a fall in the property market. The plaintiff's damages were accordingly assessed so as to cover all the losses resulting from his disastrous course of action, less the £10,000 which he would have lost in any event.

D Other claimants

If there is a single principle underlying the assessment of damages in respect of negligence by a surveyor or valuer, it is probably that the court should attempt to place the claimant, so far

---

1 (1952) 159 EG 496.
2 (1976) 239 EG 355.

as money can achieve this, in a position as if the professional work had been properly carried out. In *Beaumont* v *Humberts*,[1] for example, it was alleged that a surveyor had negligently advised a client to insure a property against fire damage for too low a figure. This allegation was not substantiated;[2] had it been, the damages would have reflected the difference between what the client received when claiming on the insurance policy and what would have been received had the property been insured for its true value. Similarly in *Whitley (FG) & Sons Co Ltd* v *Thomas Bickerton*,[3] where surveyors negligently failed to pursue appeals on behalf of their clients against a refusal of planning permission, the resulting damage was perceived as the depreciation in value of the clients' site at the moment when it became too late to rectify the situation.

The *Whitley* case is illustrative of the judicial tendency to adopt, wherever possible, a "capitalisation" approach to the question of damages, by comparing the capital value of what the plaintiff has with what he or she ought to have had. This approach was adopted in the context of rent review work in *Rajdev* v *Becketts*,[4] where the defendant surveyor's negligent failure to make proper representations on behalf of a tenant resulted in the determination, by an independent surveyor acting as expert, of a surprisingly high rent. It was held that the tenant's damages should reflect the difference in value of a lease at this rent and a lease at the rent which ought to have been fixed if the defendants had duly performed their work. A similar starting point was also used in *Knight* v *Lawrence*,[5] which involved the negligent failure, on the part of a receiver appointed by mortgagee's receiver, to trigger certain rent reviews. It was held that the landlords were held entitled to the extra value which their properties would have realised if the rent reviews had been carried out. In fact the judge in this case went further, by investigating how, if the properties in fact been sold at that higher price, the plaintiffs' resulting financial position would have differed.

It should not be thought, however, that a capitalisation approach

---

1 [1990] 2 EGLR 166.
2 See p130.
3 [1993] 1 EGLR 139.
4 [1989] 2 EGLR 144.
5 [1991] 1 EGLR 143.

of this kind will inariably be applied; indeed, the Court of Appeal has warned that it "should not be mechanically applied in circumstances where it may appear inappropriate".[1] The flexibility thus offered has been utilised in rent review cases involving negligent surveyors and solicitors so as to base damages on the amount of rent lost to a landlord over the rental period,[2] the loss to a landlord of the *chance* of obtaining a higher rent,[3] and the cost to a tenant company of extracting itself from the disadvantageous underlease into which it had entered on its solicitors' advice.[4]

As we have stressed, the basic legal position is that a plaintiff who seeks damages from a surveyor or valuer must show that loss has resulted from the latter's negligence. This principle may serve to rule out claims by house owners who seek to remortgage the property or to obtain a further advance upon its security. No doubt a valuer who is instructed by the lender will owe a duty of care to the house owner but, if the property is negligently overvalued and the loan is duly made, what loss does the house owner suffer as a result?

Although there are as yet no reported cases involving remortgages or further advances, one claim pending at the time of writing concerns a married couple who sought to remortgage their house in order to raise funds for the husband's business. Following what the wife alleged to be a negligent over-valuation, the loan was made and the money duly invested in the business which rapidly declined into insolvency. The wife thereupon brought an action for negligence against the valuer concerned, arguing that, but for his negligence, there would have been no loan and therefore no loss!

It is suggested that this claim should in principle be rejected, since the loss in question is surely attributable to the failure of the business rather than to the negligence of the valuer. However, it appears that a court has refused to strike out the claim at the preliminary stage, holding that the plaintiff has at least an arguable case.

---

1 *County Personnel (Employment Agency) Ltd* v *Alan R Pulver* [1987] 1 All ER 289 at p297; [1986] 2 EGLR 246, *per* Bingham LJ.
2 *CIL Securities Ltd* v *Briant Champion Long* [1993] 2 EGLR 164.
3 *Corfield* v *DS Bosher & Co* [1992] 1 EGLR 163.
4 *County Personnel (Employment Agency) Ltd* v *Alan R Pulver* [1987] 1 All ER 289; [1986] 2 EGLR 246.

CHAPTER 8

Defences to liability

A Limitation periods

A succession of statutory provisions dating back to 1623 has established the principle that all civil actions must be commenced within a specified period. Failure to start proceedings within the relevant period (which means either issuing a writ or, where appropriate, taking the necessary steps to begin arbitration) results in the action becoming statute-barred. Where this occurs, the effect in some exceptional circumstances is that the plaintiff's legal right is extinguished altogether.[1] In most cases, however, the effect is merely that, if the defendant pleads the limitation point, the plaintiff's right may no longer be enforced by legal action.

The current law on this subject is largely contained in the Limitation Act 1980 (as amended). This specifies both the periods within which different types of action must be commenced and the circumstances in which those periods may be extended. We now turn to consider how those statutory provisions affect claims for professional negligence against surveyors and valuers.

1 Claims in contract

Where a client sues a surveyor or valuer for breach of contract, the relevant statutory provision is usually the Limitation Act 1980, section 5:

An action founded on simple contract shall not be brought after the expiration of six years from the date on which the cause of action accrued.

If (very unusually) the contract between surveyor and client is in the form of a deed, a limitation period of 12 years is substituted.[2]

For the purpose of these provisions, a cause of action "accrues" as soon as a breach of contract is committed. It is irrelevant whether the client has suffered any damage or loss at that stage,

---

1 See Limitation Act 1980, sections 3, 11A(3) and 17.
2 Limitation Act 1980, section 8.

let alone whether or not the client is aware of either the breach of contract or any resulting loss. All that matters is that the defendant has acted (or has omitted to act) in a way which contravenes the express or implied terms on which he or she is engaged.

In the context of surveys and valuations, the first breach of contract will often occur through an inadequate inspection of a property or an inaccurate calculation of its value. In respect of that particular breach of contract, the six-year period will immediately begin to run. However, it is suggested that, in the vast majority of cases, a negligent valuer or surveyor will also commit a second breach of contract when a misleading report (based on the negligent inspection or calculation) is submitted to the client. In practice, therefore, a client may (by basing an action on this second breach) obtain a contractual limitation period of six years from the date of the report.

A problem which has emerged in actions against solicitors, though not as yet in connection with surveyors or valuers, concerns the accrual of a cause of action where the defendant's breach of contract consists of a failure to act. In *Midland Bank Trust Co Ltd v Hett, Stubbs & Kemp*[1] it was held that a solicitor's breach of contract, in failing to register a land charge on behalf of his client, was a "continuing breach", and that the limitation period did not begin to run until the land in question was sold to a third party and subsequent registration of the charge became pointless. However, in *Bell v Peter Browne & Co*,[2] the Court of Appeal rejected the idea of a "continuing breach" in similar circumstances, ruling that a solicitor's basic obligation involves carrying our the client's instructions within a reasonable time, and that there is a sufficient breach of contract to trigger the limitation period as soon as that reasonable time has elapsed.

2 Claims in tort

Where a surveyor or valuer is sued in the tort of negligence by a third party, or where a client chooses to frame an action in tort rather than in contract,[3] the starting point for limitation purposes is the Limitation Act 1980, section 2:

---

1 [1979] Ch 384.
2 [1990] 2 QB 495.
3 See p28.

An action founded on tort shall not be brought after the expiration of six years from the date on which the cause of action accrued.

Although the wording of this provision appears very similar to that which governs claims in contract,[1] there is a crucial distinction. A cause of action in tort accrues, not when the defendant commits a negligent act, but when the plaintiff suffers loss or damage as a result. As with claims in contract, however, the limitation period begins to run irrespective of whether or not the plaintiff is aware of the loss or damage, subject to certain exceptions which are discussed below.

There are very few reported cases dealing with the application of section 2 to negligent surveys or valuations, but the legal position appears fairly straightforward. The great majority of legal actions against surveyors and valuers arise out of a negligent report on which the plaintiff (either the client, or a sufficiently "proximate" third party) has relied in deciding to enter into some transaction, such as a purchase or a loan on mortgage. It was held in *Secretary of State for the Environment* v *Essex, Goodman & Suggitt*[2] that a cause of action accrues to such a plaintiff as soon as the transaction in question becomes legally binding, for example on the exchange of contracts to purchase a property. The case itself concerned a survey of commercial property on behalf of the prospective tenants, but the same principle has been assumed to apply to a purchaser's survey[3] and to a mortgage valuation commissioned by a building society but relied on by the purchaser.[4]

The reasoning which underlies the courts' ruling is that the transaction into which the plaintiff has entered is less valuable in reality than it appeared to be. Even though the contingencies which make it less valuable (such as the *possibility* that expensive repairs will be needed) may never happen, the mere existence of those contingencies means that the plaintiff's interest is immediately worth less in capital terms, so that sufficient "loss" has been suffered to start the tort limitation clock running. It may be noted that this reasoning is consistent with the courts' insistence that a purchaser's

---

1 See p180.
2 [1985] 2 EGLR 168.
3 *Horbury* v *Craig Hall & Rutley* [1991] EGCS 81.
4 *Felton* v *Gaskill Osbourne & Co* [1993] 2 EGLR 176; *Campbell* v *Meacocks* [1993] CILL 886.

basic loss is not "cost of repair", but the difference between the price paid for the property and its true value *on the date of purchase*.[1]

A similar approach has been adopted in professional negligence cases involving solicitors; the courts have almost invariably[2] ruled that, if a "capitalised" view of the transaction shows it to be less valuable to the client because of the solicitor's negligence, then the limitation period in tort begins immediately.[3] Thus, for example, where a solicitor negligently fails to ensure that the client has security of tenure in a property which is being acquired, the client suffers loss immediately, not when he or she is subsequently evicted from the property.

It has recently been held that a mortgagee who lends too much in reliance on a negligent valuation suffers loss as soon as the loan agreement becomes binding, and that the limitation period for a claim in tort thus runs from that date.[4] This is in spite of the fact that, in this situation, the court may prefer to assess the mortgagee's damages at the date of trial, so as to take into account such matters as repayments made by the borrower.[5]

In cases where the work of a surveyor or valuer does not lead to a "transaction" as such, the identification of sufficient loss or damage to start the limitation period in tort will be a question of fact to be deduced from all the evidence. In *Kitney* v *Jones Lang Wootton*,[6] for example, the plaintiff tenant of certain commercial premises instructed the defendants to identify and supervise whatever works were required to comply with the tenant's repairing covenant (such compliance being a condition precedent to the tenant's right to renew his lease). The works were carried out to the defendants' specification but, when the plaintiff's lease expired in December 1974, the landlords refused to renew it, claiming that certain breaches of the repairing covenant remained. The plaintiff duly challenged this claim in legal proceedings, a course which

---

1 See p146.
2 See, however, *UBAF Ltd* v *European American Banking Corporation* [1984] QB 713.
3 See, for example, *Forster* v *Outred & Co* [1982] 2 All ER 753; *Bell* v *Peter Browne & Co* [1990] 2 QB 495; *Lee* v *Thompson* [1989] 2 EGLR 151.
4 *First National Commercial Bank plc* v *Humberts* (1993) 10 Const LJ 141.
5 *Banque Bruxelles Lambert SA* v *Eagle Star Insurance Co Ltd* [1994] 2 EGLR 108.
6 [1988] 1 EGLR 145.

resulted (in May 1984) in a decision in favour of the landlords. The plaintiff thereupon issued a writ for negligence against the defendants, on the ground that they had failed to ensure that all necessary work was done, but this action was held to be barred by time. Nolan J ruled that the plaintiff's cause of action against the defendants had accrued, not when the 1984 court *declared* that his right to renew his lease was lost, but 10 years earlier when that right had *actually* been lost![1]

Another example of "loss" in a non-transaction case may be seen in *Whitley (FG) & Sons Co Ltd* v *Thomas Bickerton*,[2] which concerned planning advice. In 1976 the plaintiffs purchased a site with the benefit of conditional planning permission for mineral extraction (which was due to expire on November 30 1978), and retained the defendant surveyors to act for them in obtaining the county council's agreement to a scheme of working in accordance with the conditions in the planning permission. The defendants' attempts to reach agreement with the county council were thwarted by the latter's implacable opposition to all suggested schemes; the planning permission lapsed; and on November 28 1984 the plaintiffs issued a writ for professional negligence, alleging that the defendants had not tried hard enough. The gist of the claim was that the defendants should have referred the matter to the Secretary of State leaving sufficient time (about a year) for a determination to be made which would prevent the planning permission from lapsing.

In upholding the defendants' claim that this action was statute-barred, Douglas Brown J rejected the plaintiffs' argument that they had suffered no loss until the planning permission actually expired (on November 30 1978), and had issued their writ within six years of that date. The judge's view was that, as soon as it had become too late in practice to obtain an effective determination from the Secretary of State (December 1 1977), any valuation of the site would take its deteriorating planning prospects into account, so that it was from that date that the tort limitation period began to run.

The rules contained in section 2 of the 1980 Act are subject, at least in principle, to a "longstop" time bar by virtue of section 14B.

---

1 Similar facts would probably now attract the operation of the Latent Damage Act: see p185.
2 [1993] 1 EGLR 139.

This provides that an action in tort for negligence (other than one which includes personal injuries) will be barred 15 years after the last *breach of duty* by the defendant on which it is based. The longstop will bar a claim where less than six years have elapsed since the cause of action accrued. It will also operate where the cause of action has not yet accrued at all (because no loss or damage has yet been suffered).

In the context of actions against surveyors and valuers, the longstop may well be relevant in cases involving the extended limitation period for claims based on "latent damage".[1] However, although in theory this provision can also override the basic principles laid down by section 2, it appears improbable that it will have such an effect in practice. This is because the necessary factual situation would require a gap of no less than nine years between the surveyor's last breach of duty and the accrual of a cause of action (ie the first occurrence of damage resulting from that breach of duty), something which must be regarded as highly unlikely to occur.

3 Latent damage

The principles described above are clearly capable of causing severe hardship to plaintiffs, who may lose the right to bring an action before becoming aware of its existence. However, it should not be overlooked that seeking to alleviate this hardship by relating limitation periods to plaintiffs' knowledge will inevitably create a risk of hardship to defendants, in that ancient claims (when witnesses and other evidence may be unavailable) are potentially more difficult to defend. None the less, the legislative history shows Parliament becoming increasingly sympathetic to the plight of plaintiffs. Reform in respect of personal injury claims was introduced in 1963, and this was extended to negligence cases not involving personal injuries by the Latent Damage Act 1986.

The Latent Damage Act inserts two new provisions (sections 14A and 14B) into the Limitation Act 1980. These sections, which came into operation on September 18 1986, do not operate so as to revive any action which was already statute-barred (under the then existing rules) on that date;[2] nor do they apply to actions which

---

1 See below.
2 Latent Damage Act 1986, section 4(1)(a).

had already been commenced.[1] Very importantly, it has been held both at first instance[2] and in the Court of Appeal[3] that the phrase "action for damages for negligence" in section 14A(1) refers only to actions *in tort*; the extended limitation period created by this section thus has no application to claims for breach of a purely contractual duty of care.

(a) The requirement of knowledge

The effect of section 14A is to permit a plaintiff to commence proceedings *either* within six years from the date on which the cause of action accrues (ie the date on which loss or damages is suffered)[4] *or*, if this would be later, within three years of the "starting date". This crucial date is defined by section 14A(5) as:

The earliest date on which the plaintiff or any person in whom the cause of action was vested before him first had both the knowledge required for bringing an action for damages in respect of the relevant damage and a right to bring such an action.

According to section 14A(6), "knowledge" for this purpose refers to two separate things. First, there is knowledge of "the material facts about the damage in respect of which damages are claimed. This means:[5]

Such facts about the damage as would lead a reasonable person who had suffered such damage to consider it sufficiently serious to justify his instituting proceedings for damages against a defendant who did not dispute liability and was able to satisfy a judgment.

Second, there is knowledge of certain "other facts":[6]

(a) that the damage was attributable in whole or in part to the act or omission which is alleged to constitute negligence; and
(b) the identity of the defendant; and
(c) if it is alleged that the act or omission was that of a person other than

---

1 *Ibid*, section 4(1)(b).
2 *Iron Trades Mutual Insurance Co Ltd* v *JK Buckenham Ltd* [1990] 1 All ER 808.
3 *Re ERAS EIL appeals* [1992] 2 All ER 82.
4 See p182.
5 Limitation Act 1980, section 14A(7).
6 *Ibid*, section 14A(8).

the defendant, the identity of that person and the additional facts supporting the bringing of an action against the defendant.

However, knowledge that any acts or omissions did or did not, as a matter of law, involve negligence is irrelevant for this purpose.[1]

It is important to appreciate that "knowledge", the concept which is at the centre of the extended limitation period, is not restricted to those things of which the plaintiff is actually (ie subjectively) aware. Section 14A(10) provides:

For the purposes of this section a person's knowledge includes knowledge which he might reasonably have been expected to acquire –
(a) from facts observable or ascertainable by him; or
(b) from facts ascertainable by him with the help of appropriate expert advice which is reasonable for him to seek;
but a person shall not be taken by virtue of this subsection to have knowledge of a fact ascertainable only with the help of expert advice so long as he has taken all reasonable steps to obtain (and, where appropriate, to act on) that advice.

The effect of this provision, which appears highly relevant to claims against surveyors or valuers, is as follows:

1. A plaintiff will be deemed to know about any defects in the property whose existence and significance are sufficiently obvious to be appreciated by a lay person.
2. The plaintiff will also be deemed to know about those defects which are sufficiently visible that a reasonable lay person, while not appreciating their significance, would at least seek expert advice. Thus, for example, substantial cracking in walls might well be regarded as something which should lead a lay person to seek expert advice; if so, the plaintiff will in effect be fixed with knowledge of what that hypothetical expert would have discovered and reported.
3. However, a plaintiff who *does* call in expert advice will not then be fixed with knowledge of anything which that expert negligently fails to discover, so that the plaintiff's original claim remains unbarred. If this were not so, the expert would presumably be liable in a professional negligence action for depriving the plaintiff of the original claim.

---

1 Limitation Act 1980, section 14A(9).

Before considering how the latent damage rules affect actions against surveyors and valuers, it may be noted that the question whether they are even capable of applying to such actions has generated some dispute. In *Horbury* v *Craig Hall & Rutley*,[1] which involved a negligent survey carried out for a house purchaser, Judge Bowsher QC referred to "some feeling in the professions that the [Latent Damage] Act was intended to refer only to the liabilities of people with responsibility for the construction of buildings or machinery and not to refer to negligent misstatements by professionals about buildings after their construction". The judge made it clear that he did not share this feeling, and his views were echoed by Judge Lewis QC in *Campbell* v *Meacocks*.[2] The defendants in that case, who were sued by house buyers in respect of a mortgage valuation which they had carried out for a building society, argued that section 14A, which refers to "damage" rather than "loss", is thereby restricted to cases where the defendant negligently causes physical damage to the fabric of a building. The judge however, fortified by dictionary definitions of the word "damage" which include "loss", rejected this argument and held that claims against surveyors and valuers are indeed subject to the latent damage principles. If further support is needed for this proposition, it may be found in *Spencer-Ward* v *Humberts*,[3] where the Court of Appeal held that an action against mortgage valuers was barred under section 14A; the possibility that the section might be inapplicable was apparently not even considered.

As to the "knowledge" which is required to start the three-year period running in such cases, this was held in *Horbury* v *Craig Hall & Rutley*[4] to include knowledge that a surveyor had failed to detect the removal of chimney breasts and consequent lack of support for the flues. This defect could have been (and indeed was) rectified at a cost of £132, and the judge held that a plaintiff, knowing that he or she had a claim for that small amount (at 1984 prices) "against a defendant who did not dispute liability and was able to satisfy a judgment", would regard it as "sufficiently serious to justify ... instituting proceedings for damages" against that defendant. In

---

1 [1991] EGCS 81.
2 [1993] CILL 886.
3 [1994] EGCS 129.
4 [1991] EGCS 81.

Campbell v *Meacocks*,[1] on the other hand, receipt by the plaintiffs of a letter from loss adjusters about subsidence damage suffered by an adjoining property (with which the plaintiffs' house shared a concrete raft foundation) did not give them sufficient "knowledge" of negligence by a mortgage valuer. The letter did not actually suggest that the plaintiffs' property was damaged, nor were there any observable signs of subsidence in that property; moreover, the plaintiffs had the benefit of the defendants' recent mortgage valuation report which assured them that the property was in good order.

The recent decision of the Court of Appeal in *Spencer-Ward* v *Humberts*[2] provides some useful guidance on what is meant by "knowledge" in this context. That case arose out of a residential mortgage valuation carried out by the defendants (instructed by a building society) in March 1984, on which the plaintiffs relied in deciding to purchase. When in 1988 the plaintiffs decided to resell, they discovered that the house was of a non-standard "Woolaway" construction consisting of concrete blocks, something which the valuer's report had not revealed. On June 27 1988 the plaintiffs wrote to the building society complaining that the valuer's report contained a "grossly misleading and inaccurate statement", that the concrete construction was suspect and that the house was consequently devalued by at least £30,000. On June 28 1991 (ie three years *and one day* later), the plaintiffs issued a writ against the defendants, alleging negligence.

The defendants' plea that the action was statute-barred was argued as a preliminary issue and was in due course taken to the Court of Appeal. In seeking to define "knowledge" for the purpose of section 14A of the Limitation Act 1980, their lordships relied heavily on two previous decisions concerning personal injury, which turned on similar words used in section 14.[3] Particular weight was given to remarks of Lord Donaldson MR in *Halford* v *Brookes*:[4]

In this context "knowledge" clearly does not mean "know for certain and beyond possibility of contradiction". It does, however, mean "know with sufficient confidence to justify embarking on the preliminaries to the issue of

---

1 [1993] CILL 886.
2 [1994] EGCS 129.
3 *Halford* v *Brookes* [1991] 3 All ER 559; *Nash* v *Eli Lilly & Co* [1993] 4 All ER 383.
4 [1991] 3 All ER 559 at p573.

a writ, such as submitting a claim to the proposed defendant, taking legal and other advice and collecting evidence". Suspicion, particularly if it is vague and unsupported, will indeed not be enough, but reasonable belief will normally suffice.

Applying these principles to the facts of *Spencer-Ward* v *Humberts*, the Court of Appeal was in no doubt that the plaintiffs had sufficient "knowledge" on the date at which they wrote to the building society; their action was accordingly barred by time.

A very important point of interpretation in respect of section 14A, which has given rise to conflicting judicial decisions, concerns the legal position where a plaintiff acquires the relevant "knowledge" in stages, for example by discovering a succession of defects which a surveyor or valuer has overlooked in the course of inspecting a property. The question which then arises is whether the plaintiff's claim in respect of all those defects is barred under section 14A three years after the plaintiff discovers the first of them, or whether the plaintiff may always bring an action in respect of defects discovered within the last three years, while if necessary abandoning any claim in respect of those discovered earlier.

In *Horbury* v *Craig Hall & Rutley*,[1] it was held by an Official Referee that the former view was the correct one, on the basis that a plaintiff's cause of action against a negligent surveyor is "one single cause of action, not a bundle of causes of action relating to different defects in the house and different elements of inconvenience as they arise". In consequence, the plaintiff's knowledge of her surveyor's failure to notice that chimney breasts had been removed (a defect rectified at a cost of only £132) ultimately barred her claim in respect of devastating dry rot, also missed by the surveyor, which required the house to be virtually demolished and rebuilt at a cost of more than £75,000!

In *Felton* v *Gaskill Osbourne & Co*,[2] a county court judge came to a totally different conclusion as to the correct interpretation of section 14A. Pointing out that the section refers to knowledge of *the damage* in respect of which damages are claimed, the judge ruled that a plaintiff's knowledge of other items of damage cannot debar him or her from claiming in respect of something which has come

---

1 [1991] EGCS 81.
2 [1993] 2 EGLR 176.

to light only within the last three years. It was accordingly held that the plaintiff's awareness, when exchanging contracts to purchase a house, that the mortgage valuer had failed to notice and report on dampness and a leaning chimney, did not operate to bar a claim in respect of a bulging gable and a defective bressummer beam, matters which were not discovered until some six years later.

It is suggested with respect that, while the "single cause of action" principle adopted in *Horbury* is correct, both decisions are in fact based upon an erroneous approach to the problem. As we have seen earlier,[1] the "damage" in respect of which damages are claimed from a negligent surveyor or valuer lies, *not* in the physical damage suffered by the property, but rather in the overpayment which the purchaser makes in reliance on the misleading report. It follows therefore that the crucial question is when the purchaser first had "knowledge" that the report was misleading and that he or she had consequently paid more for the property than it was really worth. If this is correct, it means that the "starting date", for the purposes of section 14A, is the date on which the plaintiff becomes aware of some defect which has been overlooked by the surveyor or valuer and which is of sufficient importance to have affected the value of the property concerned.

(b) The longstop

The knowledge-based limitation period for latent damage claims, and indeed the basic period applicable to actions in tort, may both be overridden by a "longstop" time bar which is laid down by the Limitation Act 1980, section 14B(1). This provides:

An action for damages for negligence, other than one [involving personal injuries], shall not be brought after the expiration of fifteen years from the date (or, if more than one, from the last of the dates) on which there occurred any act or omission –
(a) which is alleged to constitute negligence and
(b) to which the damage in respect of which damages are claimed is alleged to be attributable (in whole or in part).

It is made clear by section 14B(2) that a claim in tort will be barred 15 years after the defendant's last *breach of duty*, whether

---

1 Pp146–154.

or not the limitation periods laid down by section 2 or section 14A have expired or even begun. The only cases to which the longstop does not apply are those involving fraud or deliberate concealment.[1]

4 Personal injuries

Although negligence actions against surveyors involving personal injuries are mercifully rare, they are not unheard of.[2] Where they do arise, they are subject to a different limitation period from those described above. The Limitation Act 1980, section 11(1) prescribes a special time-limit for "any action for damages for negligence, nuisance or breach of duty" in which the damages claimed "consist of or include damages in respect of personal injuries to the plaintiff or any other person". The subsection also makes clear that this provision, unlike the rules on latent damage described above, applies "whether the duty exists by virtue of a contract or of provision made by or under a statute or independently of any contract or any such provision".

The basic limitation period for claims falling under section 11 is three years from either the date on which the cause of action accrued or (if later) the date of knowledge of the person injured. The statutory definition of "knowledge" for this purpose[3] is very similar to that used in the context of latent damage claims; it thus includes not only what the plaintiff actually knows, but also what could have been deduced from the observable or ascertainable facts (with medical or other appropriate expert assistance, if it would have been reasonable for the plaintiff to seek this). Moreover, and quite apart from this extended basic period, the court has a general discretion under section 33 of the Limitation Act simply to disapply the limitation rules in any action involving personal injuries, having first considered the degree to which each of the parties would be prejudiced by its decision whether or not to do so.

It is important to note that section 11 applies to actions where the damages claimed "consist of *or include*" damages for personal injuries. This means that where a purchaser, for instance, sues in respect of injury which can be attributed to a negligent survey, he

---

1 See p194.
2 See, for example, *Allen* v *Ellis & Co* [1990] 1 EGLR 170.
3 Limitation Act 1980, section 14.

or she may at the same time recover damages for the economic loss resulting from the purchase, *even where the time-limit normally applicable to that claim has expired*. No doubt the importance of this apparent loophole has decreased since the introduction of an extended limitation period in cases of latent damage,[1] but it may in principle operate to revive a claim which appeared to be statute-barred.

What of the converse case, in which the limitation period applicable to personal injuries has expired, but not the period applicable to a plaintiff's other losses? This may come about because, while the personal injury period is simply three years from the date of knowledge, a claim in respect of latent damage *cannot* be barred until at least six years from when the damage occurs. The question which then arises is whether the plaintiff can, on the court's refusal to exercise its discretion under section 33, abandon the claim in respect of personal injuries but continue with the remainder.

It appears on the basis of the Scottish case of *Drinnan v CW Ingram & Sons*[2] (which concerned an earlier statute) that such tactics are indeed possible. It was there held that, since a plaintiff who suffers different categories of injury, loss or damage arising out of the same incident has a separate cause of action for each type,[3] each of these is subject to its own limitation period. The net result appears to be that a plaintiff is entitled either to *combine* claims or to *separate* them, in order to gain an advantageous limitation period. However, the plaintiff does not have similar room for manoeuvre in respect of different items of damage within a single category, since these are covered by a single cause of action.[4]

5 Contribution claims

As we shall see in the next chapter,[5] it is possible in certain circumstances for one person (A) who is liable for damage suffered by another (B) to recover a contribution from a third party (C), who is (or who would be if sued) also liable for that damage.[6] Where

---

1 See pp185–191.
2 1967 SLT 205.
3 *Brunsden v Humphrey* (1884) 14 QBD 141.
4 See p190.
5 Pp228–231.
6 Civil Liability (Contribution) Act 1978, section 1(1).

such a right to contribution arises, it is not affected by the fact that the limitation period applicable to B's claims against either A or C has expired.[1] Instead, a special time-limit is prescribed by the Limitation Act 1980, section 10(1):

> Where under section 1 of the Civil Liability (Contribution) Act 1978 any person becomes entitled to a right to recover contribution in respect of damage from any other person, no action to recover contribution by virtue of that right shall be brought after the expiration of two years from the date on which that right accrued.

The remainder of section 10 makes clear that, for this purpose, the right to recover contribution "accrues" on the date that A is held liable by a court or an arbitrator for the damage to B, or when A agrees to pay B in respect of that damage.

6 Fraud and concealment

The rules on limitation discussed above are subject to an important exception, designed to ensure that they are not used as an instrument of fraud. According to the Limitation Act 1980, section 32:

> (1) . . . where in the case of any action for which a period of limitation is prescribed by this Act, either –
> (a) the action is based upon the fraud of the defendant; or
> (b) any fact relevant to the plaintiff's right of action has been deliberately concealed from him by the defendant; . . .
> the period of limitation shall not begin to run until the plaintiff has discovered the fraud or concealment . . . or could with reasonable diligence have discovered it.
> References in this subsection to the defendant include references to the defendant's agent and to any person through whom the defendant claims and his agent.
> (2) For the purposes of subsection (1) above, deliberate commission of a breach of duty in circumstances in which it is unlikely to be discovered for some time amount to deliberate concealment of the facts involved in that breach of duty.

The effect of this provision is, with one exception, not to alter the limitation periods described above for the various causes of action,

---

1 *Ibid*, section 1(2) and (3).

but to postpone the date on which each of those periods begins to run. Thus, for example, an action in the tort of deceit must still be commenced within six years. However, that six-year period will begin, not when the defendant's deceit caused loss to the plaintiff, but when the fraud was or should have been discovered.

The exceptional situation, in which section 32 affects the primary limitation period itself, concerns cases of latent damage. As we have seen,[1] such cases are normally subject to special rules involving a principle of discoverability and a "longstop", but these special rules are neither necessary nor desirable in a case of fraud or deliberate concealment. It is accordingly provided that, in any case to which section 32 applies, sections 14A and 14B are replaced by the normal six-year limitation period for claims in tort.

In considering the relevance of section 32 to surveyors and valuers, it should be emphasised that reported cases of a survey or valuation being fraudulently carried out are extremely rare, though not entirely unknown.[2] However, the case of *Westlake* v *Bracknell District Council*[3] suggests that the statutory provision may have a wider field of operation. The plaintiffs in that case purchased a house in 1975 with the aid of a 95% mortgage from the defendant local authority, which was offered to them after the defendants had received a satisfactory report on the property (not shown to the plaintiffs) from one of their staff surveyors. Shortly after moving in, the plaintiffs became worried by evidence of gaps between skirting boards and floors. They thereupon contacted the defendants and were visited by the same staff surveyor, who told them that the cracks were due to settlement and assured them that there was no cause for concern. In 1981, when the plaintiffs attempted to sell the house, they discovered that the concrete floor slab was seriously defective and that the property was unmortgageable and thus effectively unsaleable.

The plaintiff's writ alleging negligence against the defendants was issued in 1983, whereupon the defendants pleaded that the action was statute-barred.[4] The judge, however, held that the statements

---

1 Pp185–192.
2 See, for example, *Alliance & Leicester Building Society* v *Edgestop Ltd (No 3)* [1994] 2 EGLR 229.
3 [1987] 1 EGLR 161.
4 The latent damage rules had not yet been enacted.

made by the surveyor on his second visit to the property amounted to "deliberate concealment" of facts relevant to the plaintiffs' cause of action, so that the period of limitation did not begin to run until 1982, when the plaintiffs learned the truth about the defects. In so ruling, the judge expressed the opinion that, while deliberate concealment requires something more than mere "neglect of duty", it includes such matters as "conduct involving recklessness or turning a blind eye or unconscionable conduct".

The decision in *Westlake* seems, with respect, eminently fair and reasonable; nevertheless, a recent pronouncement by the Court of Appeal casts serious doubts upon its correctness. In *Sheldon* v *RHM Outhwaite (Underwriting Agencies) Ltd*[1] it was held by a majority of the Court of Appeal that, on a true interpretation, section 32 does not apply to cases where the defendant's "deliberate concealment" of a relevant fact occurs *after the plaintiff's cause of action has already arisen*. If this is decision is correct, it means that section 32 will hardly ever apply to surveys or valuations which are not themselves fraudulently carried out. This is because the cause of action in such cases arises in contract when the report is sent to the client, and in tort when the client acts in reliance upon it. According to *Sheldon*, any subsequent concealment is irrelevant.

B Exemption clauses and disclaimers

1 Types of disclaimer

In any discussion as to the extent to which it is possible to exclude or restrict a person's liability for negligence, it must be acknowledged from the outset that the word "disclaimer" has no single precise meaning in law. It is often used in this context in rather a loose sense, to describe a whole range of terms and notices, both written and oral, some but not all of which are incorporated as terms of a contract. These clauses may share a common overall objective (the limitation of liability), but there are considerable differences of both legal analysis and effectiveness between the main categories.

The simplest type of "disclaimer" consists of a contract term which purports to exclude altogether the potential liability of one party to the other for a breach of that contract. Less draconian are those

---

1 [1994] 4 All ER 481.

contract terms which seek merely to place some limit on a party's liability for breach, for example by imposing a financial ceiling on claims, or by making liability subject to a time-limit shorter than that which would be imposed by statute.[1] In principle, it is thought that such terms would probably govern not only a professional person's *contractual* duty to use reasonable care and skill, but also whatever duty is owed concurrently to the client *in tort*.[2] However, this is presently a matter of conjecture, since there are as yet no reported cases involving surveyors or valuers in which such a provision has fallen for interpretation. Indeed, it is extremely rare to encounter an attempt by a surveyor or valuer to exclude liability towards the client, perhaps because it is felt within the surveying profession that the exercise of due care and skill is the very essence of what a professional undertakes to provide and that, if this duty is excluded, the service given (and paid for) would be of little value. Nevertheless, it remains to be seen whether, in the light of the enormous claims which have arisen out of commercial valuations, some firms may in future seek to *restrict* their liability, perhaps to an amount which can be covered by professional indemnity insurance.

Exemption clauses aimed at the client may be seldom found in the surveying world, but the same is certainly not true of notices or statements which seek to avoid liability in tort to third parties. Reports from surveyors and valuers to their clients frequently contain a provision to the effect that they are for the use only of the client (and sometimes also the client's other professional advisers), and that no responsibility is undertaken towards any other person. Similarly, standard form correspondence between mortgagees and house buyers often attempts to ensure that, even if the latter is shown a copy of the mortgage valuation report, the valuer concerned cannot be held liable for its content. As a general principle, such exclusions of liability do not seem an unreasonable tactic for a professional person to adopt, since the essence of a claim by a third party is often in effect a complaint about the inadequacy of a survey or valuation by someone who has relied on it, but who has not paid for it.

Notwithstanding their differences, the types of disclaimer described above are similar in that they purport to meet head-on an

---

1 See pp180–196.
2 See p28.

obligation which might otherwise arise, and to exclude or restrict that obligation. However, there is also a more subtle form of disclaimer, one which attempts to avoid liability by preventing one or more of the essential elements of that liability from coming into existence. A valuation report, for example, might (and indeed should) make clear the assumptions on which it is based and should identify those underlying facts, such as site conditions, planning consents or questions of title, which have not been personally checked by the valuer. Likewise, a survey report might state that it had proved impossible to obtain access to, or to inspect thoroughly, certain parts of the property. Such qualifications may undoubtedly serve to restrict the matters in respect of which anyone may justifiably claim to rely on the report, and thus to limit the scope of any future negligence action against the surveyor or valuer in question. However, the wording must be very clear if it is to have this effect; thus in *Lowy* v *Woodroffe, Buchanan and Coulter*,[1] surveyors who failed to make a proper inspection of parts of a property where dry rot might be inspected were not protected by a statement in their report that "in view of the prevalence of dry rot in London it is impossible to guarantee every property is free".

Closely linked to this "warning" type of disclaimer is the role of a professional person's contract of engagement in defining the service which is to be provided. A term in that contract which makes clear that a surveyor will not test a building's services, or which defines the basis on which a property is to be valued, is *not* an exemption clause and is accordingly not subject to the legal principles which are about to be discussed. Such a term operates instead to limit the area within which the principles of professional negligence can operate, by defining the task to which the professional must bring due care and skill. This will be binding upon the client as a matter of contract; it will also bind third parties, who cannot reasonably expect to be in a better position than the client in this respect. It is therefore of the utmost importance for all professionals to ensure that their standard terms of engagement set out clearly and unequivocally the service which is to be undertaken and, where appropriate, any limitations upon that service.

---

1 (1950) 156 EG 375.

2 General effectiveness of disclaimers

Contract terms which seek to exclude or restrict the liability of a party for breach have long been treated by the courts in a restrictive way. This is not the place for a detailed discussion of the rules governing such exemption clauses, but two of the main requirements are worthy of mention. First, the term in question must be incorporated into the contract between the parties, which means either that it is contained in a signed document[1] or that reasonable steps are taken to bring it to the attention of the other party[2] before or at the time the contract is made.[3] It follows that a term in a surveyor's report will be ineffective as an exemption clause, though it may conceivably take effect as a warning sufficient to prevent reliance.[4]

The second main requirement mentioned above is that the wording of the exemption clause should clearly cover the breach of contract which has occurred. In the context of liability for negligence the courts have adopted a particularly rigorous approach, with the result that, unless an exemption clause refers explicitly to negligence or a synonym for it, it is very unlikely to be effective in excluding liability.[5] However, it appears that a somewhat less rigid view is taken of clauses which purport merely to place a limit on the amount of compensation payable in respect of negligence.[6]

As regards the avoidance of liability *in tort* to third parties, it is obvious that, under the doctrine of privity of contract, an exemption clause in a contract (such as a surveyor's terms of engagement) will be binding only upon the client. Nevertheless, it has been generally accepted since the decision of the House of Lords in *Hedley Byrne & Co Ltd* v *Heller & Partners Ltd*[7] that liability to those who are not linked by contract may be excluded by a non-contractual notice of disclaimer, although the precise legal basis on which such a disclaimer operates is not altogether clear.

In *Hedley Byrne* itself, where a bank was held to owe no duty of

---

1 *L'Estrange* v *F Graucob Ltd* [1934] 2 KB 394.
2 *Parker* v *South Eastern Ry* (1877) 2 CPD 416.
3 *Olley* v *Marlborough Court Ltd* [1949] 1 KB 532.
4 See p135.
5 *Canada Steamship Lines Ltd* v *R* [1952] AC 192 at p208, *per* Lord Morton; *Smith* v *South Wales Switchgear Co Ltd* [1978] 1 All ER 18.
6 *Ailsa Craig Fishing Co Ltd* v *Malvern Fishing Co Ltd* [1983] 1 All ER 101.
7 [1964] AC 465.

care in respect of references because it had given them expressly "without responsibility", Lord Devlin regarded it as obvious that "a man cannot be said voluntarily to be undertaking a responsibility if at the very moment when he is said to be accepting it he declares that in fact he is not".[1] The other judges likewise treated the disclaimer as preventing any inference that the bank had "assumed responsibility".[2] However, this explanation now appears insufficient to justify the effectiveness of disclaimers since, as explained earlier,[3] the law no longer bases liability in tort for negligent advice upon a "voluntary assumption of responsibility".

Notwithstanding this change of emphasis in negligent advice cases, it appears that non-contractual disclaimers are still in principle effective, though they may be vulnerable to attack under the Unfair Contract Terms Act 1977.[4] In the Scottish case of *Hadden* v *City of Glasgow District Council*,[5] where a local authority mortgagee brought a clear disclaimer to the attention of a house buyer at the time when the latter applied for a mortgage, this was held to prevent any implication of a duty of care owed by the mortgage valuer. Nor was that all; the judge held that, since the parties were not in a contractual relationship,[6] the disclaimer was subject neither to the Unfair Contract Terms Act[7] nor to the rigorous principles of construction normally given to exemption clauses, since those principles are applicable only to contract terms!

The ruling in *Hadden* was applied in the later Scottish case of *Commercial Financial Services Ltd* v *McBeth & Co*,[8] which concerned a valuation of a holiday complex development. The defendant valuers' report, which they supplied to the developers who had instructed them, included a clause stating that "this valuation is for the use only of the parties to whom it is addressed and no responsibility is accepted to any third party for the whole or any part of its contents". The valuation was shown to and relied on

---

1 [1964] AC 465 at p533.
2 [1964] AC 465 at pp492 (*per* Lord Reid); 504 (*per* Lord Morris); 511 (*per* Lord Hodson); 540 (*per* Lord Pearce).
3 See p37.
4 See p201.
5 1986 SLT 557.
6 See p8.
7 See p211.
8 January 15 1988, Court of Session, unreported.

by a mortgagee, who subsequently brought an action for negligence, but it was held that the defendants had successfully disclaimed any responsibility which they might otherwise have had.

Timing, however, is crucial to the effectiveness of a disclaimer. As with contractual exemption clauses, a disclaimer must be communicated to the plaintiff before any liability has arisen. In *Martin* v *Bell-Ingram*[1] the plaintiff house buyer, having applied to a building society for a loan on mortgage, was informed by the building society that, in the light of the defendant valuer's report on the property, the loan would be forthcoming, whereupon the plaintiff committed himself to the purchase. When the plaintiff subsequently received the building society's formal offer of mortgage, this contained purported disclaimers of liability on the part of the valuer, but it was held that these came too late to protect the valuer from liability for negligence.

3 The Unfair Contract Terms Act
(a) The statutory provisions

The Unfair Contract Terms Act 1977 represents the first attempt to impose statutory controls on exemption clauses generally. The Act identifies various types of legal liability which may arise. In respect of some of these, any attempt at exclusion or restriction is declared to be void; for others, exclusion or restriction is made subject to a test of reasonableness. In the present context, the most important statutory provisions are those which govern liability for "negligence", which is defined so as to include both contractual and tortious duties of care.[2] However, the application of the Act is limited to duties arising in the course of a business,[3] which is defined so as to include a profession and the activities of any government department or public authority.[4]

Reported claims against surveyors and valuers which involve personal injuries are mercifully rare, though not completely unknown.[5] Should one arise, any disclaimer would be completely irrelevant, for section 2(1) of the Act provides:

---

1 1986 SLT 575.
2 Unfair Contract Terms Act 1977, section 1(1).
3 *Ibid*, section 1(3).
4 *Ibid*, section 14.
5 See *Allen* v *Ellis & Co* [1990] 1 EGLR 170; p163.

A person cannot by reference to any contract term or to a notice given to persons generally or to particular persons exclude or restrict his liability for death or personal injury resulting from negligence.

Of more practical significance to surveyors and valuers is section 2(2), which provides:

In the case of other loss or damage,[1] a person cannot so exclude or restrict his liability for negligence except in so far as the term or notice satisfies the requirement of reasonableness.

It is moreover for the person seeking to rely on such a term or notice to prove its reasonableness.[2]

This crucial concept of "reasonableness" is defined in section 11, which distinguishes between those disclaimers which are contained in a contract and those which are not. As to the former, section 11(1) provides:

In relation to a contract term, the requirement of reasonableness . . . is that the term shall have been a fair and reasonable one to be included having regard to the circumstances which were, or ought reasonably to have been, known to or in the contemplation of the parties when the contract was made.

Non-contractual disclaimers are governed by section 11(3):

In relation to a notice (not being a notice having contractual effect), the requirement of reasonableness ... is that it should be fair and reasonable to allow reliance on it, having regard to all the circumstances obtaining when the liability arose or (but for the notice) would have arisen.

The wording of these two provisions gives rise to a distinction which may be of considerable importance in practice. The reasonableness or otherwise of a contract term is to be assessed in the light of the parties' knowledge at the time of making the contract; thus, the circumstances surrounding the defendant's subsequent breach of contract (the nature and degree of the professional negligence, the loss suffered etc) cannot be taken into account. However, such factors *can* be considered (and may

---

1 Ie property damage or economic loss.
2 Unfair Contract Terms Act 1977, section 11(5).

indeed be of great significance) in deciding whether reliance on a non-contractual notice would be reasonable, since this falls to be assessed at a later stage.

Finally, section 11(4) makes special provision for those disclaimers which attempt to place a financial limit on liability:

Where by reference to a contract term or notice a person seeks to restrict liability to a specified sum of money, and the question arises ... whether the term or notice satisfies the requirement of reasonableness, regard shall be had in particular . . . to –
(a) the resources which he could expect to be available to him for the purpose of meeting the liability should it arise; and
(b) how far it was open to him to cover himself by insurance.

Thus, where the extent of potential liability is very great, and professional indemnity insurance cover either unobtainable or ruinously expensive, it might be reasonable for a professional person to limit liability to an amount no greater than can be reasonably covered by such insurance.[1]

(b) The scope of the Unfair Contract Terms Act

At the time when *Yianni v Edwin Evans & Sons*[2] was decided, mortgage application forms and other documents issued by building societies to house buyers commonly contained provisions designed to exclude any implied warranty on the part of the society that the purchase price of the property was reasonable. Many also specifically advised purchasers to obtain their own survey before agreeing to purchase. After *Yianni*, when it became clear that a mortgage valuer could be liable for negligence to the purchaser, many mortgagees revised their standard documentation so as to include express disclaimers of responsibility, both for themselves and for the valuer appointed to carry out an inspection of the property.

The effectiveness of such disclaimers, and in particular their susceptibility to attack under the Unfair Contract Terms Act, arose for consideration in *Smith v Eric S Bush*; *Harris v Wyre Forest District*

---

1 See *Smith v Eric S Bush*; *Harris v Wyre Forest District Council* [1990] 1 AC 831 at p859; [1989] 1 EGLR 169, *per* Lord Griffiths; p206.
2 [1982] QB 438.

Council,[1] where the House of Lords was required to decide between two conflicting decisions of the Court of Appeal. In *Smith v Eric S Bush*,[2] which arose out of a mortgage valuation carried out on behalf of a building society by an independent surveyor, the plaintiff purchaser had signed an application form which stated:

I understand that the society is not the agent of the surveyor or firm of surveyors and that I am making no agreement with the surveyor or firm of surveyors. I understand that neither the society nor the surveyor or the firm of surveyors will warrant, represent or give any assurance to me that the statements, conclusions and opinions expressed or implied in the report and mortgage valuation will be accurate or valid and the surveyor's report will be supplied without any acceptance of responsibility on their part to me.

The Court of Appeal held unanimously that this disclaimer constituted a "notice" within the meaning of section 2(2) of the Unfair Contract Terms Act and, moreover, that it failed the "reasonableness" test and could not therefore exclude the valuer's liability.

In *Harris* v *Wyre Forest District Council*,[3] which concerned a local authority mortgage and a valuation carried out by a staff valuer, the plaintiff purchasers had signed an application form which stated:

I/We understand . . . that the valuation is confidential and is intended solely for the benefit of Wyre Forest District Council in determining what advance, if any, may be made on the security and that no responsibility whatsoever is implied or accepted by the council for the value or condition of the property by reason of such inspection and report.

On this occasion, a differently constituted Court of Appeal held unanimously that the Unfair Contract Terms Act was limited in its application to contract terms and notices which purported to exclude or restrict *liability*; it thus had no impact whatever on a disclaimer such as the present one, the effect of which was to prevent a *duty of care* from ever coming into existence by indicating that the required "voluntary assumption of responsibility" was missing.[4]

---

1 [1990] 1 AC 831; [1989] 1 EGLR 169.
2 [1987] 1 EGLR 157.
3 [1987] 1 EGLR 231.
4 See p37.

As Lord Templeman pointed out when the two cases reached the House of Lords, the *Harris* interpretation "would not give effect to the manifest intention of the Act but would emasculate the Act".[1] Lord Griffiths, too, was worried that "the result of taking the notice into account when assessing the existence of a duty of care would result in removing all liability for negligent misstatements from the protection of the Act".[2] Fortunately for their lordships' concerns, relief from such a conclusion lay within the Unfair Contract Terms Act itself. Section 13(1) of the Act, a provision which was inexplicably not mentioned by the Court of Appeal in *Harris* v *Wyre Forest*, provides that, to the extent that section 2 prevents the exclusion or restriction of any liability, it also prevents "excluding or restricting liability by reference to terms and notices which exclude or restrict the relevant obligation or duty". In the unanimous view of the House of Lords, this provision was conclusive. As Lord Jauncey remarked:[3] "These words are unambiguous and are entirely appropriate to cover a disclaimer which prevents a duty coming into existence. It follows that the disclaimers here given are subject to the provisions of the Act."

(c) The requirement of "reasonableness"
(i) General principles

As mentioned above,[4] it is extremely rare to encounter an attempt by surveyors or valuers at an outright exclusion of liability for negligence towards a client. It is suggested, moreover, that a court would be quick to treat any such attempt as "unreasonable" and thus ineffective by virtue of the Act. This is because, once the obligation to exercise due care and skill is removed from the contract under which a professional person is retained, it is difficult to see that much remains which is of any real value.

However, this argument does not necessarily apply with equal force to an attempt by a professional person to place a financial limit on liability. It is well known that surveyors and valuers, like other professionals, operate against a background of indemnity

---

1 [1990] 1 AC 831 at p848; [1989] 1 EGLR 169. The conflict between the Court of Appeal decisions had earlier been faced in *Davies* v *Parry* [1988] 1 EGLR 147 by McNeill J, who followed *Smith* v *Bush*.
2 [1990] 1 AC 831 at p 857.
3 [1990] 1 AC 831 at p 873.
4 See p197.

insurance dealing with their potential liability for negligence, and that the cost of obtaining such insurance prevents most if not all firms from obtaining unlimited cover. It might well be regarded as reasonable, therefore, for a firm to restrict its liability, even to clients, to a level at which it can secure professional indemnity insurance at a cost which is not wholly uneconomic.

Such suggestions gain some support from the speech of Lord Griffiths in *Smith* v *Eric S Bush*; *Harris* v *Wyre Forest District Council*:[1]

> I would not, however, wish it to be thought that I would consider it unreasonable for professional men in all circumstances to seek to exclude or limit their liability for negligence. Sometimes breathtaking sums of money may turn on professional advice against which it would be impossible for the adviser to obtain adequate insurance cover and which would ruin him if he were to be held personally liable. In these circumstances it may indeed be reasonable to give the advice on a basis of no liability or possibly of liability limited to the extent of the adviser's insurance cover.

On turning to consider the "reasonableness" of attempts by surveyors or valuers to exclude or restrict liability towards third parties, it is suggested that, as a general principle, these would (and indeed should) be more sympathetically received by the courts. After all, complaints about the quality of professional advice are inherently less convincing when voiced by those who have not paid for it, and this is surely even more so where the advice in question is accompanied by a clear disclaimer of responsibility. It appears therefore that a surveyor or valuer (at least in the commercial sphere) may avoid liability to third parties by stating expressly that a valuation report is for the use of the client alone, and is not to be disclosed to or relied on by anyone else.[2]

(ii) Mortgage valuations

Whether or not these suggestions are correct, it is now clear that they have no relevance to an attempt by a mortgage valuer (or by the mortgagee) to exclude liability to a house buyer. This situation is indeed the one in which disclaimers by surveyors and valuers

---

1 [1990] 1 AC 831 at p859; [1989] 1 EGLR 169.
2 See *Commercial Financial Services Ltd* v *McBeth & Co* January 15 1988, Court of Session, unreported; p42.

have most frequently been discussed by the courts, and the decision of the House of Lords in *Smith* v *Eric S Bush*; *Harris* v *Wyre Forest District Council*[1] means that, save in exceptional circumstances, such disclaimers will fail the statutory test of reasonableness and will thus provide no defence to the house buyer's claim. The terms of the disclaimers in those cases, and their lordships' ruling that they were subject to the Unfair Contract Terms Act, are discussed above;[2] at this point we consider the House of Lords' grounds for deciding that they did not satisfy the test of "reasonableness".

Lord Templeman's approach to this question began by listing the reasons given by defending counsel for arguing that the disclaimers should be upheld:[3]

(1) The exclusion clause is clear and understandable and reiterated and is forcefully drawn to the attention of the purchaser.
(2) The purchaser's solicitors should reinforce the warning and should urge the purchaser to appreciate that he cannot rely on a mortgage valuation and should obtain and pay for his own survey.
(3) If valuers cannot disclaim liability they will be faced by more claims from purchasers some of which will be unmeritorious but difficult and expensive to resist.
(4) A valuer will become more cautious, take more time and produce more gloomy reports which will make house transactions more difficult.
(5) If a duty of care cannot be disclaimed the cost of negligence insurance for valuers and therefore the cost of valuation fees to the public will be increased.

[Counsel for the valuers] also submitted that there was no contract between a valuer and a purchaser and that, so far as the purchaser was concerned, the valuation was "gratuitous", and the valuer should not be forced to accept a liability he was unwilling to undertake.

Having thus summarised counsel's argument, Lord Templeman moved swiftly to demolish it:

All these submissions are, in my view, inconsistent with the ambit and thrust of the Act of 1977. The valuer is a professional man who offers his services for reward. He is paid for those services. The valuer knows that 90 per cent

---

1 [1990] 1 AC 831; [1989] 1 EGLR 169.
2 See pp203–205.
3 [1990] 1 AC 831 at pp851–852.

of purchasers in fact rely on a mortgage valuation and do not commission their own survey. There is great pressure on a purchaser to rely on the mortgage valuation. Many purchasers cannot afford a second valuation. If a purchaser obtains a second valuation the sale may go off and then both valuation fees will be wasted. Moreover, he knows that mortgagees ... are trustworthy and that they appoint careful and competent valuers and he trusts the professional man so appointed. Finally, the valuer knows full well that failure on his part to exercise reasonable skill and care may be disastrous to the purchaser. If, in reliance on a valuation, the purchaser contracts to buy for £50,000 a house valued and mortgaged for £40,000 but in fact worth nothing and needing thousands more to be spent on it, the purchaser stands to lose his home and to remain in debt to the building society for up to £40,000.

Returning to this issue at the end of his speech, Lord Templeman added a final blow:[1]

The public are exhorted to purchase their homes and cannot find houses to rent. A typical London suburban house, constructed in the 1930s for less than £1,000 is now bought for more than £150,000 with money largely borrowed at high rates of interest and repayable over a period of a quarter of a century. In these circumstances it is not fair and reasonable for building societies and valuers to agree together to impose on purchasers the risk of loss arising as a result of incompetence.

Lord Griffiths, whose remarks on this issue were endorsed by Lord Jauncey,[2] rejected as impossible any attempt to draw up an exhaustive list of the factors to be taken into account when deciding on the "reasonableness" of a disclaimer. None the less, his lordship suggested[3] that certain factors will always be relevant. These include:

1. Whether the parties are of equal bargaining power.
2. In cases of advice, whether it would have been reasonably practicable to obtain the advice from an alternative source, taking into account considerations of costs and time. His lordship noted that a house buyer commissioning his own inspection and report would in effect have to pay twice for the same advice and that this would place a considerable financial strain on young buyers at the

---

1 [1990] 1 AC 831 at p854; [1989] 1 EGLR 169.
2 [1990] 1 AC 831 at pp873–874.
3 [1990] 1 AC 831 at pp858–859.

bottom of the market.

3. The difficulty of the task being undertaken for which liability is being excluded. In this context his lordship regarded a mortgage valuation as "work at the lower end of the surveyor's field of professional expertise".

4. The practical consequences of the decision on reasonableness (in particular the availability of insurance and its effect in spreading the risk of negligence over a wider area and thus lessening its impact).

Additionally, in the present context, Lord Griffiths regarded it as very important that:

The surveyor is only appointed in the first place because the purchaser wishes to buy the house and the purchaser in fact provides or contributes to the surveyor's fees. No one has argued that, if the purchaser had employed and paid the surveyor himself, it would have been reasonable for the surveyor to exclude liability for negligence, and the present situation is not far removed from that of a direct contract between the surveyor and the purchaser.

Although the House of Lords was thus very firm in its opinion that reliance upon the disclaimers under consideration would not be reasonable, it was at pains to point out that this would not necessarily always be the case. Lord Griffiths, with whose remarks Lord Templeman expressly agreed, suggested an important limitation upon the scope of their decision:[1]

It must, however, be remembered that this is a decision in respect of a dwelling house of modest value in which it is widely recognised by surveyors that purchasers are in fact relying on their care and skill. It will obviously be of general application in broadly similar circumstances. But I expressly reserve my position in respect of valuations of quite different types of property for mortgage purposes, such as industrial property, large blocks of flats or very expensive houses. In such cases it may well be that the general expectation of the behaviour of the purchaser is quite different. With very large sums of money at stake prudence would seem to demand that the purchaser obtain his own structural survey to guide him in his purchase and, in such circumstances with very much larger sums of money at stake, it may be reasonable for the surveyors valuing on behalf of those who are providing the finance either to exclude or limit their liability to the purchaser.

---

1 [1990] 1 AC 831 at pp859–860; [1989] 1 EGLR 169.

The House of Lords' ruling on disclaimers in *Smith* v *Bush* appears to have been generally accepted by both the surveying and the legal profession, to the extent that very few mortgage valuers or mortgagees have since attempted to rely on a disclaimer when sued by a house buyer. Indeed, in *Henley* v *Cloke & Sons*,[1] counsel for the defendant valuers conceded (with the approval of the judge) that a standard disclaimer in building society literature provided them with no defence, even though the property in question was a substantial four-bedroomed detached house in a pleasant residential area of Maidstone, which was purchased by the plaintiff in 1984 for £74,000. Moreover, in *Beaton* v *Nationwide Building Society*,[2] the one reported case in which reliance was placed on a disclaimer, the defence failed. It was held that neither the fact that the house buyers had been advised by their solicitors to have a full survey, nor that they had been told by the estate agents of previous underpinning work, was a sufficient ground on which to distinguish *Smith* v *Bush*. The judge also rejected the defendants' argument that a notice, given to a house buyer so as to exclude the warranty as to the reasonableness of the purchase price which would otherwise be implied,[3] was also effective to exclude a duty of care at common law.

The strength of the views expressed in *Smith* v *Bush*, and the wide-ranging nature of the decision, make it unnecessary to examine earlier cases in which courts of first instance had similarly struck down mortgage valuers' disclaimers as unreasonable.[4] However, one case which merits a little more discussion is that of *Stevenson* v *Nationwide Building Society*,[5] which was cited in argument in *Smith* v *Bush* but was not referred to in their lordships' speeches, where a similar disclaimer was held to be effective in barring a purchaser's claim against a building society in respect of an in house mortgage valuation. The wording of the disclaimer was for the most part almost identical to that used in *Harris* v *Wyre Forest District Council*, but it went on to emphasise that the

---

1 [1991] 2 EGLR 141.
2 [1991] 2 EGLR 145.
3 Under the Building Societies Act 1962, section 30 (repealed by the Building Societies Act 1986).
4 See *Davies* v *Idris Parry* [1988] 1 EGLR 147; *Green* v *Ipswich Borough Council* [1988] 1 EGLR 239; *Roberts* v *J Hampson & Co* [1988] 2 EGLR 181.
5 (1984) 272 EG 663.

inspection by the building society's valuer was not a structural survey and to state that such a survey could be provided by the society, albeit at an additional cost to the purchaser.

There were two crucial facts in the *Stevenson* case which convinced the judge that, the Unfair Contract Terms Act notwithstanding, it was reasonable for the mortgagee to rely on the disclaimer and thus to exclude its liability. The first of these was that the plaintiff himself was an estate agent who was familiar with such disclaimers and with the range of surveys and valuations which were available. Second, and perhaps more significant, what was purchased in this case was not "a dwelling house of modest value", but a relatively expensive (£52,000) property consisting of two shops, a maisonette and a flat. Given this "commercial" element, it seems that there is no conflict between *Stevenson* and *Smith* v *Bush*.

(d) The Scottish dimension

Although the statutory principles described above now apply to Scotland as they do to England and Wales, this has not always been the case. As originally drafted, Part II of the Unfair Contract Terms Act 1977 (which applies only to Scotland) did not cover the exclusion or restriction of liability by a non-contractual notice. However, Part II was amended by section 68 of the Law Reform (Miscellaneous Provisions) (Scotland) Act 1990, so as to bring it into line with the English law. The reform came into operation on April 1 1991, and applies only to liability for loss or damage which is suffered on or after that date.

The legal position in Scotland prior to 1991 gave rise to an interesting conflict of judicial opinion in respect of reliance by mortgage valuers upon disclaimers contained in building society literature. In *Robbie* v *Graham & Sibbald*,[1] it was reluctantly held by a Scottish judge that, since such a disclaimer was not contained in a contract, it was not subject to challenge under the Unfair Contract Terms Act; a house buyer in Scotland was accordingly not entitled to the protection given by *Smith* v *Eric S Bush*; *Harris* v *Wyre Forest District Council*.[2] However, this ruling was (somewhat ingeniously)

---

1 [1989] 2 EGLR 148.
2 [1990] 1 AC 831; [1989] 1 EGLR 169.

circumvented in *Melrose v Davidson & Robertson*,[1] where a similar disclaimer was held to be a term of the contract between a house buyer and a building society, a ruling which was sufficient to bring the disclaimer within the statutory rules!

---

1 1993 SLT 611; see p9.

CHAPTER 9

Sharing the blame

In this chapter we consider two statutory provisions which may be of relevance where the negligence of a surveyor or valuer is a cause, but not the only cause, of loss which is suffered by a client or a third party. The first of these statutes, the Law Reform (Contributory Negligence) Act 1945, applies where the other cause of loss is the plaintiff's own fault; here the damages payable may be reduced to take account of this fact, so that the Act operates as a partial defence for the surveyor or valuer concerned. The second statute, the Civil Liability (Contribution) Act 1978, applies where the other cause of loss is the default of a third party (such as the plaintiff's solicitor). In such circumstances the liability of the surveyor or valuer to the plaintiff is not reduced, but that defendant may, if sued by the plaintiff, then recover from the third party in question a contribution towards the damages payable. Of course, the converse is also true; if it is the third party whom the plaintiff chooses to sue, he or she may then recover contribution from the surveyor or valuer.

A Contributory negligence

1 General principles

Until 1945, English law treated a plaintiff's contributory negligence as a complete defence to liability. Thus, where loss resulted partly from the defendant's negligence and partly from the plaintiff's failure to take reasonable steps to protect his or her own interests, a claim by the plaintiff would fail altogether. This principle was obviously capable of producing harsh and unjust results, and recognition of potential harshness led to its frequent evasion by the courts on somewhat artificial grounds. However, the problem was not properly solved until the enactment of the Law Reform (Contributory Negligence) Act 1945, which provides in effect for the sharing of responsibility between the parties.

Section 1 of the 1945 Act provides:

Where any person suffers damage as the result partly of his own fault and partly of the fault of any other person or persons, a claim in respect of that damage shall not be defeated by reason of the fault of the person suffering the damage, but the damage recoverable in respect thereof shall be reduced to such extent as the court thinks just and equitable having regard to the claimant's share in the responsibility for the damage.

The concept of "fault" is clearly of central importance to this provision, and this is defined by the Act to include more than just "negligence" in the strict sense of the word. According to section 4, "fault means negligence, breach of statutory duty or other act or omission which gives rise to liability in tort or would, apart from this Act, give rise to the defence of contributory negligence".

A defendant who seeks to rely on the defence of contributory negligence is not required to establish that the plaintiff owed the defendant a duty to take care of his or her own interests; the statute effectively means that everyone is assumed to be under such a duty at all times. What the defendant must prove is that the plaintiff was guilty of "fault" and that this fault was a contributory cause of the loss in respect of which damages are claimed. It follows from this that those principles of law which determine a defendant's breach of duty in negligence cases,[1] and those which govern the causation of damage,[2] are applied in contributory negligence cases to the conduct of the plaintiff.

Where a defendant succeeds in a plea of contributory negligence, it is for the court to decide what reduction in the damages payable would be just and equitable, having regard to the plaintiff's "share in the responsibility for the damage". The Act gives no indications as to how this judicial discretion is to be exercised, but decided cases[3] suggest that two factors are likely to be of the greatest importance. These are, first, the relative "blameworthiness" of the parties and, second, the relative "causative potency" of their respective conduct, which requires the court to make a judgment as to which of the causes of the plaintiff's loss might be regarded as more "significant".

2 Scope of the Law Reform (Contributory Negligence) Act

While it is well settled that the 1945 Act governs those actions for

---

[1] See Chapter 3.
[2] See Chapter 6.
[3] Notably *Davies* v *Swan Motor Co (Swansea) Ltd* [1949] 2 KB 291.

"negligence" which are based on tort, some doubts remain as to its relevance in claims for breach of contract, at least those in which a claim might alternatively be brought in tort. If it is not applicable to such claims, the question which arises is whether a client who complains of "negligence" but who is partly to blame can, by the simple expedient of framing the action in contract rather than in tort, evade a possible reduction of the damages payable.

This question can only be finally answered by the House of Lords, but it appears in the meantime that lower courts will not permit the principle of shared responsibility to be outflanked in this way. This was certainly the view expressed in *Forsikringsaktieselskapet Vesta v Butcher*,[1] where Hobhouse J divided breaches of contract into three categories:

(1) Where the defendant's liability arises from some contractual provision which does not depend on negligence on the part of the defendant.

(2) Where the defendant's liability arises from a contractual obligation which is expressed in terms of taking care (or its equivalent) but does not correspond to a common law duty to take care which would exist in the given case independently of contract.

(3) Where the defendant's liability in contract is the same as his liability in the tort of negligence independently of the existence of any contract.

His lordship's view, which was endorsed by the Court of Appeal,[2] was that apportionment under the 1945 Act would be possible in cases within category (3), with the result that a client in such a case could not evade the statutory provisions by framing the claim in contract rather than in tort. It has subsequently been confirmed by the Court of Appeal that no apportionment is possible in a category (1) case;[3] the legal position in a category (2) case remains unsettled.

The *Vesta* decision is of considerable practical importance in the context of claims for professional negligence, since the vast majority of such actions fall into category (3). It thus appears that surveyors and valuers can in principle raise the defence of contributory negligence against their clients, irrespective of whether the action against them is based on contract or tort. Indeed, it has been

---

1 [1986] 2 All ER 488.
2 [1988] 2 All ER 43.
3 *Barclays Bank plc* v *Fairclough Building Ltd* Times, May 11 1994.

conceded by plaintiffs in several recent actions against valuers that this is the law at High Court level, although some have specifically reserved the point for possible challenge on appeal.[1]

Whatever may be the final outcome of the debate over the applicability of the 1945 Act to claims for breach of contract, it is settled that contributory negligence can never be a defence to an action in the tort of deceit. This principle seems self-evident where an action is brought against the fraudulent person, for it would be ridiculous to allow that person to argue: "It is true that I lied to you, but you could and should have discovered my deceit"! However, it is important to appreciate that the defence of contributory negligence is equally unavailable in cases where a morally innocent employer is held vicariously liable for an employee's fraud. It was on this basis that in *Alliance & Leicester Building Society* v *Edgestop Ltd (No 1)*,[2] where a firm of estate agents incurred liability for a series of mortgage frauds committed by one of its staff, it was held to be no defence for the firm to argue that the lending institutions ought reasonably to have discovered the fraud in time to avoid making the loans in question.

3 Professional negligence cases

The central allegation in most actions for professional negligence, and virtually all of those which involve surveyors or valuers, is that the plaintiff has relied on some misleading report from the defendant and has in consequence entered into some disadvantageous transaction. Faced with such a claim, a defendant who pleads contributory negligence will attempt to establish one of two things: either that it was unreasonable for the plaintiff to rely on the advice in question; or that, while the reliance itself may have been reasonable, the plaintiff's ultimate decision to enter into the transaction was not.

To take the second of these possibilities first, it was acknowledged by Judge Fawcus QC in *Nyckeln Finance Co Ltd* v *Stumpbrook Continuation Ltd*[3] that "it might at first blush seem

---

1 See, for example, *Banque Bruxelles Lambert SA* v *Eagle Star Insurance Co Ltd* [1994] 2 EGLR 108; *Nyckeln Finance Co Ltd* v *Stumpbrook Continuation Ltd* [1994] 2 EGLR 143.
2 [1994] 2 All ER 38.
3 [1994] 2 EGLR 143.

conceptually difficult to envisage a finding that a particular course of conduct was reasonable and at the same time to attribute fault, in the sense of negligence, to the person taking that reasonable course". Nevertheless, as the judge pointed out, "there is clearly a distinction between a finding that a person reasonably relies on a valuation, and a consideration of whether that person is then at fault in lending a particular sum of money in the light of that valuation". Such a distinction might be drawn, for example, in the case of a lender who has no reason to doubt the accuracy of a valuation but who is independently negligent in failing to appreciate that the borrower is financially unsound.[1]

The other possible ground of contributory negligence, that the plaintiff ought not to have relied on the defendant' advice, is more contentious. Indeed, one might question whether it should in principle be effective at all. On one reading at least, liability for negligent advice under *Hedley Byrne* v *Heller* requires, not only reliance by the plaintiff on that advice, but *reasonable* reliance; thus, if the plaintiff's reliance is not reasonable, it might be argued that this should completely negate the defendant's liability, rather than providing scope for a sharing of responsibility.

It may be that some such thoughts were in the mind of McNeill J in *Davies* v *Idris Parry*[2] when, in rejecting a mortgage valuer's claim that a house buyer was contributorily negligent for not commissioning his own survey, his lordship said: "Either the defendant was to blame or the plaintiffs were wholly responsible. There is, in my view, no middle way such as a division of fault would imply."

As we shall see, certain cases involving commercial lending transactions have indeed adopted this "middle way". Nevertheless, it is suggested that a reduction of damages for "unreasonable reliance" by the plaintiff will seldom be appropriate. As observed by Judge Fawcus QC in *Nyckeln Finance Co Ltd* v *Stumpbrook Continuation Ltd*:[3] "It lies ill in the mouth of a professional valuer, who is giving a valuation for mortgage lending purposes, to say that it was unreasonable for the party to whom such valuation was given to rely on it".

---

1 See p223.
2 [1988] 1 EGLR 147.
3 [1994] 2 EGLR 143 at p148.

In similar vein, though more generally expressed, are the remarks of Phillips J in *Banque Bruxelles Lambert SA* v *Eagle Star Insurance Co Ltd*:[1] "No court will lightly hold a plaintiff at fault for relying on advice given by a professional adviser who owes a duty of care to the plaintiff". However, as his lordship acknowledged: "It does not follow from this that there is no scope for a finding that [the plaintiffs] were at fault in failing to question the valuations. Whether they should have done so must depend upon the conduct to be expected of a reasonably prudent merchant bank in the circumstances prevailing".

4 Contributory negligence by house buyers

Reported attempts by mortgage valuers (and, in one case, by a building surveyor) to raise the defence of contributory negligence against a house purchaser have invariably failed. Nor is this surprising; it would surely require very exceptional circumstances to convince a court that a lay person (whether a client or a sufficiently "proximate" third party) had acted unreasonably in placing reliance on a report undertaken by a qualified professional. In the absence of such circumstances, it seems likely that the reaction of most judges would be similar to that of Park J in *Yianni* v *Edwin Evans & Sons*,[2] where the argument was first put forward:

[Counsel] says that the plaintiffs should be held guilty of contributory negligence, because they failed to have an independent survey; made no inquiries with the object of discovering what had been done to the house before they decided to buy it; also failed to read the literature provided by the building society, and generally took no steps to discover the true condition of the house. It is true that the plaintiffs failed in all these respects, *but that failure was due to the fact that they relied on the defendants to make a competent valuation of the house. I have been given no reason why they were unwise to do so.*[3]

Subsequent attempts by mortgage valuers to argue that a house buyer should have commissioned a structural survey of the property have proved no more successful. In *Davies* v *Idris Parry*,[4] McNeill J

---

1 [1994] 2 EGLR 108 at p138.
2 [1982] QB 438 at p457.
3 Emphasis supplied.
4 [1988] 1 EGLR 147.

pointed out that such an argument was inconsistent with one of the bases of the valuer's liability, namely his or her awareness that house buyers are unlikely to have an independent survey, but that they will instead rely on their mortgage valuation. On a more practical level, Auld J in *Whalley* v *Roberts & Roberts*[1] found that the plaintiffs "were not fully aware of the different types of survey or report that were available to them or of the precise shortcomings of the mortgage valuation report when considered with the other more detailed surveys and reports on offer". Nor was his lordship persuaded to find contributory negligence either by the warnings on the mortgage valuer's report form or by the fact that many purchasers do in fact commission their own survey.

The most extreme illustration of judicial reluctance to hold a lay person guilty of contributory negligence *vis-à-vis* a professional adviser is to be found in *Allen* v *Ellis & Co.*[2] The plaintiff there purchased a house in reliance on the defendants' negligent survey report. A year later the plaintiff, in seeking to investigate a leak, placed a piece of wooden board on the roof, stepped on to it and fell through, sustaining fairly severe injuries.

In holding the defendants liable for the plaintiff's injuries (on the ground that their report had given him a misleading impression as to the state of the roof), Garland J rejected their argument that anyone who climbs on to an asbestos roof is guilty of contributory negligence. As his lordship pointed out:

The plaintiff is a layman. He knows nothing, or virtually nothing, about building or property . . . I find it impossible to hold him contributorily negligent. If he were unaware of the risk – and I accept his evidence that he was unaware of the risk – then it cannot be said that he was negligent in failing to comprehend it.

While it is clear from the above discussion that a negligent surveyor or valuer will have great difficulty in obtaining a finding of contributory negligence against a lay person, it appears that this will not be altogether impossible. Indeed, certain remarks of Park J in *Yianni* v *Edwin Evans & Sons*[3] suggest that this particular door is at least slightly ajar. Referring to the standard form disclaimers

---

1 [1990] 1 EGLR 164.
2 [1990] 1 EGLR 170.
3 [1982] QB 438 at p457.

contained in the building society's documentation, his lordship stated: "No doubt if the paragraph had been in stronger terms, and had included a warning that it would be dangerous to rely on the valuer's report, then I think that the plaintiffs might well have been held to be negligent."

5 Contributory negligence by commercial lenders

Where an action for professional negligence is brought against a surveyor or valuer by a lay person such as a house buyer, the imbalance of knowledge and expertise between the parties militates strongly against a finding of contributory negligence. While it may still exist, such imbalance is of far less significance in cases where the plaintiff is a commercial organisation, such as a bank or finance house, whose normal business activities include the lending of large sums of money on the security of property. Furthermore, it is surely reasonable to expect that such an organisation, before committing itself to a loan transaction, will make a careful appraisal of all the risks involved (not merely the adequacy of the security, but also the financial stability of the borrower, the state of the property market and so on). In principle, therefore, it might appear that the defence of contributory negligence would be more readily invoked where a commercial lender seeks damages in respect of a negligent valuation.

It is certainly true that, in the plethora of cases which have resulted from the collapse of the commercial property market in the late 1980s, pleas of contributory negligence have become increasingly common. As lenders seek damages from the valuers whose over-optimistic view of a property (against the background of a booming market) has left them unsecured, so those valuers counter by claiming that the lenders themselves have negligently under-estimated the risks involved in a particular transaction. The success rate of the defence to date remains fairly low; none the less, the high level of damages which are claimed in many of these cases means that even slender straws are to be clutched at, and it thus seems likely that allegations of contributory negligence will become even more of a routine feature in commercial lending cases.

(a) Valuation in excess of recent purchase price

Of the reported English cases in this area, the most significant is undoubtedly the decision of Phillips J in *Banque Bruxelles Lambert*

SA v *Eagle Star Insurance Co Ltd*.[1] That case concerned two separate transactions, each consisting of a large loan made by the plaintiff bank to a property company, on the security of property which represented the borrowers' only significant asset. On each occasion the plaintiffs relied on a valuation of the property submitted to them by John D Wood & Co, lending 90% of that valuation but obtaining mortgage indemnity guarantee insurance policies to cover the full amount of the loan. When the property market slumped and the borrowers became insolvent, the plaintiffs discovered that the value of each property was far less than the amount of the outstanding loan. They accordingly sought redress from the valuers, alleging negligence on the ground that the valuations, without any real justification or explanation, had far exceeded the price at which each borrower had within the previous month acquired the property in question. In one case a property acquired for £25.5m was valued at £44.35m; in the other a property acquired for £73m was valued at £103m. Negligence was duly established in each case, but the valuers sought to limit their liability by pleading contributory negligence.

In seeking to set up this defence, John D Wood & Co relied on a number of aspects of the transactions in question, all but one of which were rejected by the judge. Among the points which were held *not* to constitute negligence by the lenders were the fact that they had lent 90% of the perceived value (thus leaving them with an insufficient "cushion" against a market fall); that the loans were in breach of the lenders' own internal procedures; that the borrowers in each case had injected no cash (and were thus carrying none of the risk); that the intermediary who had negotiated the loans had a conflict of interests; and that the valuers had been selected to give the valuations in question because, out of several valuers approached by the intermediary for an "armchair valuation", they had provided the highest figure. It is worth noting that the plaintiffs were not shown to have known about these multiple "armchair valuations"; had they done so, a finding of contributory negligence would probably have resulted.

The remaining allegation, and the basis on which the valuers succeeded in establishing their defence, was a very simple one. It was that the plaintiffs, no less than the valuers, were aware of the

---

1 [1994] 2 EGLR 108.

substantial discrepancy between the valuations and the purchase prices of the properties, and that they should have not have entered into the loan transactions unless and until they were given a convincing explanation of how this had come about (such as that the property had not been properly marketed, or that the vendor had been forced to sell at very short notice). Convinced by expert evidence that a reasonably prudent banker would indeed have demanded such an explanation, the judge ruled that the plaintiffs were guilty of contributory negligence in this respect and that they must accordingly forfeit 30% of their damages.

The arguments which led to a finding of contributory negligence in *Banque Bruxelles Lambert SA* v *Eagle Star Insurance Co Ltd* were also successfully relied on by the defendant valuers in *Nyckeln Finance Co Ltd* v *Stumpbrook Continuation Ltd*,[1] although the reduction in the damages on that occasion was only 20%, because the plaintiff lenders had made at least some attempt to investigate the discrepancy between purchase price and valuation. Nevertheless, while it appears highly likely to be used in more cases in future, it is worth pointing out the paradox which lies at the heart of this defence and which might well lead other judges to reach a different conclusion. Since the plaintiff's alleged negligence consists of failing to realise that the defendant has over-valued the property, the crucial question is whether a reasonable plaintiff would have come to this conclusion. It follows that, the greater and more obvious the defendant's negligence, the more likely it is that the plaintiff should have detected it and thus the more chance there is that the defendant will succeed in avoiding at least part of his or her responsibility!

The judgment of Phillips J in *Banque Bruxelles Lambert SA* v *Eagle Star Insurance Co Ltd* contains a further ruling on contributory negligence which is both significant and controversial. His lordship held that, since the protection given to the plaintiffs by their mortgage indemnity guarantee insurance was to be ignored (as *res inter alios acta*) in computing their damages,[2] it must also be ignored in deciding whether or not they were guilty of contributory negligence. It followed, in the judge's opinion, that the question whether a reasonably prudent merchant bank would have made the

---

1 [1994] 2 EGLR 143.
2 See p142.

loans in question should be answered on the hypothetical basis that they had no such insurance cover.

While acknowledging his lordship's unease at the prospect that a valuer might be held liable in full, notwithstanding clear evidence of contributory negligence on the part of either the lender or the insurer, it is suggested that there is an alternative means of preventing this which is to be preferred, since it avoids the need to assess contributory negligence on a commercially unrealistic basis. It would surely be better to recognise that it is the insurer who is the true plaintiff in cases of this kind, and to decide whether or not there has been contributory negligence by asking the question whether or not a reasonable insurer would have provided a mortgage indemnity guarantee policy in these circumstances.

(b) Failure to investigate the borrower

It was suggested earlier that, as a matter of principle, it should be somewhat easier for a valuer to base contributory negligence on the part of a commercial lender upon some conduct by the lender which is quite independent of the valuation itself. The example given was that of a lender who, while quite reasonably relying on the valuation of the property, unreasonably fails to carry out a proper investigation of the borrower's financial stability. Ironically, perhaps, while the English courts have acknowledged on at least four occasions that such a failure might indeed support a finding of contributory negligence, none of the valuers concerned in those cases actually succeeded in establishing the defence.

The most thorough judicial consideration of this issue is to be found in *HIT Finance Ltd* v *Lewis & Tucker Ltd*,[1] where the judgment of Wright J typifies the courts' cautious approach. The plaintiffs there had lent £1.54m on the security of a property which the defendants had valued at £2.2m, but which was in truth at the date of valuation worth no more than £1.35m. When the plaintiffs claimed damages for professional negligence, the defendants argued that the plaintiffs should have realised that the property had been sold several times in quick succession to inflate its value, and that they should therefore have subjected the borrowers to close scrutiny before agreeing to lend.

In rejecting these allegations, Wright J made some telling

---

1 [1993] 2 EGLR 231.

observations as to the relative importance of the steps taken by commercial lenders to protect their interests:

Obviously, a sensible commercial finance house would wish, in an ideal world, to make loans only to borrowers who would meet their obligations thereunder both as to repayment of capital and interest on time and in all respects exactly in compliance with the contractual terms so that the lender would never have to have recourse to the underlying security ... By contrast, the whole purpose of the taking of security, and the valuation of that security, is to ensure that the lender has an adequate safety net in the event that the borrower defaults, whether that default should have been foreseeable by the lender had he taken appropriate precautions, or not.

As the judge then pointed out:

The "cushion" apparently provided by the property on the basis of the defendants' valuation was accordingly £660,000. In such circumstances, even if the borrowers turned out to be complete men of straw, the lenders were entitled to regard themselves as being more than adequately covered not merely in respect of the capital sum lent, but also any likely loss of interest, and indeed all the costs and expenses likely to be incurred in foreclosing upon and realising the security. In such circumstances, although the hypothetical lender might not unreasonably feel irritated at being put to the trouble of having to realise his security rather than enjoying the fruits of his investment in a peaceful manner and in accordance with the terms of his contract, it is very difficult to see how such a lender could properly be characterised as "imprudent".

His lordship's emphasis on the value of the property as the lender's primary security was subject to only one qualification:

I am not suggesting that the prudent lender, merely because he has the comfort of more than adequate security, is entitled to shut his eyes to any obviously unsatisfactory characteristics of the proposed borrower. Plainly a lender would not be acting prudently if he made a loan in circumstances where he had substantial reason for suspecting the honesty of the borrower. Such circumstances might well call into question the provenance of the security itself, quite apart from the possibility that the lender might be put at risk by some other form of fraudulent behaviour on the part of his borrower.

This question of the borrower's honesty surfaced again when the judge offered his view of the underlying commercial realities of the situation:

I accept that a prudent lender must not shut his eyes to any obvious lack of integrity or substance in his borrower; but, subject to that, I find it difficult to see how [the borrower's financial position] is of any relevance in the case of a commercial lender who is, by definition and to the knowledge of the valuer, in business to take a degree of risk. The whole purpose of taking the security is . . . to provide protection against loss for the lender in the event that the risk in question ripens into actuality.

In refusing to hold the plaintiffs guilty of contributory negligence, his lordship paid some attention to the apparently conflicting decision of the New Zealand Court of Appeal in *Kendall Wilson Securities* v *Barraclough*.[1] The plaintiff there, a solicitors' nominee company, made substantial losses by lending on the security of land which the defendant had negligently over-valued, but was held to have contributed to its losses by negligently failing to investigate the borrower. Wright J regarded this case as distinguishable, on the basis of the extra obligations of prudence and caution imposed on those (like the plaintiffs) who act as trustees in investing clients' money. Moreover, he felt that, even if the New Zealand case supported the idea of a general duty on lenders, the *extent* to which they would be expected to investigate a borrower would depend on all the facts of a given particular case, and in particular the apparent safety margin offered by the security.

The views expressed by Wright J in *HIT Finance Ltd* v *Lewis & Tucker Ltd* were endorsed by Gage J in *United Bank of Kuwait* v *Prudential Property Services Ltd*.[2] The judge in the later case had no doubt that, in an appropriate case, a commercial lender could be held contributorily negligent for failing properly to investigate the borrower, but was satisfied that, on the facts, the plaintiffs had not fallen below the standards required of reasonably competent bankers. And, in *Nykredit Mortgage Bank plc* v *Edward Erdman Group Ltd*,[3] a similar conclusion was reached by Judge Byrt QC on the basis of expert evidence which suggested that the plaintiffs' investigation of the borrower was in fact more extensive and more thorough than would have been undertaken by most mortgage lenders.

A point of some difficulty which has been discussed in recent

---

1 [1986] 1 NZLR 576.
2 [1994] 2 EGLR 100.
3 October 1 1993, Mayors and City of London Court, unreported.

commercial lending cases concerns the role of the lender's solicitors. It has twice been argued[1] by a negligent valuer that the lender's solicitors were aware, either actually or constructively, of the unsatisfactory characteristics of the borrower, and that this knowledge could be attributed to the lender so as to support a finding of contributory negligence. On each occasion the defendant's argument failed, on the ground that the solicitors' duty to the lender was limited to ensuring that the mortgage was effective. As Wright J put it:[2] "The solicitors were not required to make any investigation of or give any advice upon the general, commercial or financial implications of the loan". Similarly, Judge Marr Johnson QC said that it was not the solicitors' function "to act as detectives on the plaintiffs' behalf".[3] However, neither judge appeared to doubt that, in an appropriate case, contributory negligence on the part of a lender could be established in this way.

It is suggested, with respect, that to base contributory negligence on such imputed knowledge would be a thoroughly undesirable development in the law. It is one thing to deem a client to have notice of things which his or her agent knows and has a duty to pass on; it is quite another to stigmatise that client as "negligent" for failing to act upon knowledge which they do not in fact possess. A finding of contributory negligence, at least in the context under discussion, should reflect an assessment of a lender's commercial decisions against a real, not a hypothetical, background.

If it is argued that this is unfair on the valuer, since the lender's loss is caused by the solicitor's negligence as well as by the valuer's, the remedy must surely lie in an action by the valuer against the solicitor for contribution under the Civil Liability (Contribution) Act 1978.[4] Except where the solicitor is actually an employee of the lender, holding the latter contributorily negligent on the basis of what the former ought to have done would seem a wholly unjustified extension of the doctrine of vicarious liability beyond the relationship of employer and employee.

---

1 *HIT Finance Ltd* v *Lewis & Tucker Ltd* [1993] 2 EGLR 231; *Axa Equity & Law Home Loans Ltd* v *Goldsack & Freeman* [1994] 1 EGLR 175.
2 *HIT Finance Ltd* v *Lewis & Tucker Ltd* [1993] 2 EGLR 231 at p235.
3 *Axa Equity & Law Home Loans Ltd* v *Goldsack & Freeman* [1994] 1 EGLR 175 at p178.
4 See pp228–231.

(c) Other cases

The issue of contributory negligence by a commercial lender has arisen in two more recent cases in circumstances very different from those so far described. On each occasion, what was said on the subject was *obiter*, since the lenders in both cases failed in their attempts to establish negligence against the valuers concerned. Nevertheless, the judge in each case made it clear that, had negligence been established, a reduction of damages on the ground of contributory negligence would have been appropriate.

In *PK Finans International (UK) Ltd* v *Andrew Downs & Co Ltd*,[1] the crucial question was whether the defendants should have emphasised to their clients the need to verify the planning assumptions on which their valuation was based (and which turned out to be incorrect). The judge held that the defendants' failure to do this did not amount to negligence, since they were entitled to assume that the plaintiffs, a financial institution considering a loan of £1m, would be well aware of this.[2] Had the judge reached the opposite conclusion, he would have deducted no less than 80% of the plaintiffs' damages for their failure to send the valuation report to their solicitors, who would undoubtedly have carried out the necessary investigations.

In *Craneheath Securities Ltd* v *York Montague Ltd*[3] the plaintiff finance company, having lent money on the security of a restaurant business, alleged that the defendant valuers, on whose report they had relied, had based their "profits" valuation on unrealistic turnover figures. In the course of the trial it emerged that, not only had the defendants not been shown any recent accounts of the business, the plaintiffs themselves had obtained a recent set of accounts but had not shown them to the defendants! It was held by Jacob J that the defendants had not been negligent and were thus not liable at all, but his lordship had something more to say about the conduct of the plaintiffs:

Where a valuation has been given to a man, and that man has, and knows he has, more information affecting the valuation than the valuer had, he is very likely to find himself at least partly at fault if he seeks to place reliance on the valuation without first giving the valuer that information for comment.

---

1 [1992] 1 EGLR 172.
2 See p119.
3 [1994] 1 EGLR 159.

B Contribution among wrongdoers

A person who is preparing to enter into a transaction may well seek professional advice from more than one source before doing so. If the transaction turns out to be disadvantageous and loss is suffered, the questions which then arise are which (if any) of the professional advisers can be held responsible, and what are their respective liabilities.

It may of course be that, when the roles of the various professionals are examined, it becomes clear that one or more of them has not been negligent at all. Thus, for example, surveyors seeking office accommodation for a client were held not to have been negligent in failing to discover that apparently suitable premises were in fact burdened by an onerous planning condition, since they were entitled to assume that the client's solicitors would investigate the planning position.[1] Similarly, a surveyor inspecting a house for a prospective purchaser was held reasonably entitled to take the vendor's word that the property enjoyed main drainage, since the surveyor could expect this to be confirmed by the purchaser's solicitors through preliminary inquiries.[2] Again, where a mortgagee's solicitors discovered that the property had previously changed hands at wildly different prices, it was held that they were not negligent in failing to inform their clients of this fact; they had told the valuer who was assessing the security, and it was the negligence of the latter (in failing to take account of the discrepancies) which was the sole cause of the mortgagee's loss.[3]

Assuming that negligence either is or could be established against more than one person, their respective liabilities will depend initially upon how the plaintiff chooses to proceed. Where the plaintiff joins more than one defendant in the same action and is successful against more than one, the plaintiff is entitled (under the principle of joint and several liability) to enforce judgment against any or all of those defendants for the full amount awarded. If this enforcement results in one defendant bearing a disproportionate share of the damages, that defendant may then claim contribution from the others.

---

1 *GP & P Ltd* v *Bulcraig & Davis* [1988] 1 EGLR 138.
2 *Strover* v *Harrington* [1988] 1 EGLR 173.
3 *Scholes* v *Brook* (1891) 63 LT 837: affirmed (1892) 64 LT 674.

Where, instead of joining multiple defendants, the plaintiff chooses to sue only one of them, the one who is selected and held liable may in turn demand contribution from the others. This may be done either by joining them as third parties to the original suit, or in separate contribution proceedings. In either event, the claimant is required to show that the other person *could* have been liable to the original plaintiff; in effect. Therefore the claimant fights the plaintiff's case against the second wrongdoer.

By whichever of these routes a claim for contribution arises, it will be governed by the Civil Liability (Contribution) Act 1978. Section 1(1) of that Act provides that "any person liable in respect of any damage suffered by another person may recover contribution from any other person liable in respect of the same damage (whether jointly with him or otherwise)". For the purposes of this provision, all that matters is that the person seeking contribution has been found liable to the original plaintiff by a court, or has bona fide settled or compromised a claim on which liability *could* have been established.[1] However, the *basis* of that original liability (and, for that matter, the original liability of the person from whom contribution is demanded) is irrelevant; it may arise from "tort, breach of contract, breach of trust or otherwise".[2] all that matter is that he or she has been found liable by a court, or has bona fide settled or compromised a claim on which liability *could* have been established.[3]

It is important to note that a claim for contribution is subject to a special limitation period of two years from the date on which the right to contribution arises (that is the date on which the claimant is held liable in court or settles the original claim).[4] This period applies to the exclusion of the normal limitation periods.[5] Thus, a person who has acquired a right to recover contribution may exercise that right notwithstanding that he or she has ceased to be liable.[6] What is more, contribution may be recovered from a person whose original liability for the damage in question is now barred by

---

1 Civil Liability (Contribution) Act 1978, section 1(4).
2 *Ibid*, section 6(1).
3 *Ibid*, section 1(4).
4 Limitation Act 1980, section 10.
5 See pp193–194.
6 Civil Liability (Contribution) Act 1978, section 1(2).

limitation.[1] In effect, therefore, where more than one professional adviser is involved in the same transaction, all remain at risk until the last limitation period has expired.[2]

Where a claim under the 1978 Act is successful, section 2(1) provides that "the amount of the contribution recoverable from any person shall be such as may be found by the court to be just and equitable having regard to the extent of that person's responsibility for the damage in question". However, the court's discretion is subject to one restriction; a person whose liability to the person originally suffering damage would have been reduced (eg because of contributory negligence on the part of the latter[3]) cannot be ordered to pay more in contribution than they would have had to pay if sued directly.[4]

Reported cases of contribution among property professionals are few and far between, but note may be taken of two which concerned valuers and solicitors acting for mortgagees. In *Anglia Hastings & Thanet Building Society* v *House & Son*[5] the defendants, when sued by the building society for negligent mortgage valuations of two flats, admitted their liability but joined the society's solicitors as third parties to the proceedings. The court found that, if either of the professional parties had done their job properly, the building society would never have agreed to lend to the particular borrower and would therefore not have lost money. However, the fault of the solicitors was held to be greater than that of the valuers, because it included a failure to disclose conflicts of interest and not merely negligence, and so they were ordered to contribute 70% of the damages.

The second case, this time involving commercial property, is *UCB* v *Dundas & Wilson*.[6] The plaintiff bank there sued its solicitors for failing to discover, from title deeds and planning permissions, that the development land which was to be security for a loan was subject to a serious risk of subsidence. It was held that the solicitors

---

1 *Ibid*, section 1(3).
2 See *Secretary of State for the Environment* v *Essex, Goodman & Suggitt* [1985] 2 EGLR 168.
3 See pp213–227.
4 Civil Liability (Contribution) Act 1978, section 2(3).
5 (1981) 260 EG 1128. This case concerned the Law Reform (Married Women and Tortfeasors) Act 1935, which was the forerunner of the 1978 Act.
6 1989 SLT 243.

were entitled to join as third parties a firm of valuers who, although instructed by the borrowers, owed a duty of care to the plaintiff lenders. However, the case provides no assistance as to how contribution should be assessed in such circumstances, since it was fought only on the preliminary issue of whether the valuers could indeed be liable for "the same damage".

The case of *Computastaff Ltd* v *Ingledew Brown Bennison & Garrett*,[1] though not involving surveys or valuations, offers an interesting example of the contribution provisions in operation. The plaintiffs there retained a firm of agents to seek office accommodation for them to rent. The agents found suitable premises and, taking the information from particulars drawn up by the landlords' estate agents, told their clients that the rateable value of the property was £3,305. The correct figure was in fact £8,305 but, when the discrepancy was noticed (the landlords' solicitors quoted the correct figure in reply to a preliminary enquiry), the plaintiffs' solicitors and the two firms of agents investigated the matter in such a negligent fashion that the plaintiffs were still given the wrong answer. The plaintiffs duly took the lease and, on finding that the burden of the rates was far heavier than they had been led to expect, sued their own agents and solicitors in negligence. These defendants brought in the landlords' agents on the ground that, since they too could have been directly liable in tort to the plaintiffs, they were liable under the 1978 Act to contribute towards the damages payable by the defendants. It was held by McNeill J held that, as between the plaintiff's own advisers, liability should be apportioned at 40% to the solicitors and 60% to the agents; however, each of these defendants was then entitled to recoup one-half of what they had to pay from the landlords' agents.

---

1 (1983) 268 EG 906.

CHAPTER 10

Professional indemnity insurance

A The general background

It is the common practice of those bodies which govern professions to require their members, as a condition of membership, to obtain and maintain professional indemnity ("PI") insurance. As far as surveyors and valuers are concerned, both the RICS and the ISVA insist that their members take out such insurance. In describing the operation of PI insurance, we shall concentrate in this chapter on the RICS scheme; that of the ISVA is largely similar, though not identical in every respect.

The RICS lays down PI insurance requirements for those of its members who are principals in private practice. The requirements, which are contained in a byelaw and associated regulations (together known as the Compulsory PII Regulations), impose minimum standards as to the level and quality of insurance cover which must be obtained. The most important provisions are as follows:

i cover must provide indemnity at or above a prescribed minimum level;
ii cover must be on an "each and every claim" basis;
iii the uninsured excess must not exceed the maximum permitted amount;
iv "run off" cover must be maintained for at least six years after ceasing to practise;
v the member must provide annual confirmation that the requisite insurance is in place.

B The nature of PI insurance

A PI policy is one of "liability" rather than "loss" insurance. Its function is to indemnify the insured person (the professional) against his or her liability to third parties. It does *not* provide any direct remedy to a third party who claims to be the victim of professional negligence.[1]

Until the 1970s, PI insurance was normally written upon an "acts occurring" basis, meaning that any claim arising in respect of a particular survey or valuation would be covered by the insurance policy which was in force at the time the work was carried out. This system could create problems in that, if a claim took many years to be either litigated or settled (and 10 years is not uncommon), the insurance cover might then be found to be completely inadequate. Accordingly, the practice of insurers changed and policies were written on a "claims made" basis, which means that the relevant policy is that which is in force when the claim is made, not when the work in question was carried out.

The PI insurance market is cyclical in nature. The 1970s was a period of strong demand for high-quality insurance cover against professional liability, to be provided upon an "each and every claim", as opposed to an "aggregate", basis. In response to this demand, a number of new insurers entered the market, and the resulting competition between insurers forced premiums down to what many observers believe was an artificially low level. During the same period, claims made on PI policies increased considerably in both number and size, partly at least because the courts took a wider view of the scope of professional liability.

An inevitable consequence of these increases was that some insurers withdrew from the PI insurance market altogether, while others took a much firmer line on claims submitted. In particular, many disputes arose where surveyors and valuers, seeking to obtain cheaper insurance cover, found that the "new" insurer would seek to avoid liability on the ground that the claim in question should have been notified to the previous insurer.

The case of *Thorman* v *New Hampshire Insurance Company (UK) Ltd*[2] is a good example of "the problems which can arise when professional men, in this case a firm of architects, transfer their professional negligence insurance cover from one set of underwriters to another".[3] The plaintiff architects were insured with New Hampshire until September 1983 and thereafter with Home Insurance, who were the second defendants to the proceedings. In

---

1 See p241.
2 (1987) 39 BLR 41.
3 (1987) 39 BLR 41 at p45, *per* Sir John Donaldson MR.

July 1979, the architects gave New Hampshire notice of a claim concerning defective brickwork on a housing development which they had carried out for a housing association. A few months later a settlement was reached and the architects and insurers filed their papers, but no full discharge was obtained for this settlement. In May 1982, the Housing Association notified the architects of its intention to issue a generally endorsed writ referring, among other things, to defective brickwork. It was only after Home Insurance had taken over the risk that the Housing Association's allegations were particularised in a Statement of Claim and Scott Schedule, at which point it became clear that the brickwork was not the only complaint. A dispute then arose as to which insurer was under an obligation to indemnify the architects in respect of the other allegations.

The Court of Appeal held that all the items in the Scott Schedule constituted a single claim, which was the responsibility of New Hampshire, the earlier insurer. The issue of the writ constituted a claim covering all the matters subsequently particularised in the Statement of Claim and Scott Schedule. Sir John Donaldson MR, while making clear that the question of what would fall within a single claim was a matter of fact depending upon the circumstances of each individual case, gave some examples:[1]

i separate contracts for separate building owners but the same negligent mistake: separate claims;
ii a single contract for two houses on separate sites, with complaints about the window design of one and the foundations of the other: separate claims;
iii as ii above, but the same complaint about both houses: one claim;
iv a single contract in relation to a number of houses on the same development and a single complaint regarding a wide range of unrelated defects: one claim;
v as iv above, but with defects manifesting themselves individually and leading to separate complaints: depending on the precise facts, this might be regarded as separate claims or as enlargements of the original claim.

The RICS professional indemnity collective policy, effective from August 1993, attempts to deal with this problem by including the following provisions within its General Conditions:

---

1 (1987) 39 BLR 41 at pp51–52.

2. The Insured shall give to the Insurers as soon as possible details in writing of:
   (a) any claim or claims made against them;
   (b) the discovery of any loss to them which may be the subject of indemnity hereunder.
3. The Insured shall give to Insurers notice in writing as soon as possible during the Policy Period of:
   (a) any circumstance of which the Insured shall first become aware during the Policy Period which may give rise to a claim against them;
   (b) the discovery of a reasonable cause for suspicion of dishonesty or fraud on the part of a present Partner, Director or Employee of the Firm(s) whether giving rise to a claim or loss under this Policy or not . . .

Provided notice has been given in accordance with this Condition then any subsequent claim the Insured or any loss discovered by the Insured shall be deemed to have been made or discovered during the Policy Period.

C Invalid claims

1 Material non-disclosure

Like all contracts of insurance, PI policies are based upon the principle of the utmost good faith between the insurer and the insured. This principle relates not only to the inception of the risk but also in the steps taken to carry out the contract. However, its most important application lies in the duty which is imposed upon an insured person to make full disclosure of all material facts that might influence a prudent insurer in fixing the premium or determining whether he will take on the risk. This duty is set out in the Marine Insurance Act 1906, section 18(1) which, despite its name, has been held also to govern contracts of non-marine insurance and reinsurance. Compliance with this duty is of critical importance since, if there has been non-disclosure of a material fact, the insurer is entitled to avoid the policy and thus to reject any claims made under it.

It should be noted that PI policies normally last for a period of 12 months only. They are subject to annual renewal by the insurer, which is dependent upon a renewal application being completed by the insured. The renewal application constitutes an offer by the insured for a new contract for the following 12-month period, and it is consequently subject to the duty of disclosure.

In relation to survey and valuation work, it is hardly surprising (in view of the level of claims settlements) that insurers currently require a great deal of information in a proposal form for PI insurance. Specific questions asked by insurers now include the following:

i   nature of activity(ies);
ii qualifications and experience of staff;
iii location;
iv number of offices;
v   claims experience, including fraud or dishonesty;
vi retroactive cover;
vii fee income;
viii overseas operations/activity;
ix insurance history;
x   internal controls and checking procedures;
xi amount of indemnity required;
xii level of uninsured excess;
xiii size of projects/contracts;
xiv partner to staff ratio;
xv number of valuations undertaken per partner; and
xvi geographical spread of work.

This list, while covering most of the matters on which PI insurers routinely require information, is not exhaustive. Additional information, such as the conditions of engagement used by the surveyor or valuer, may be asked for. Also, particularly in relation to valuation work, some insurers now wish to know the identity of the companies for whom the surveyor or valuer is working, since there is evidence that a greater exposure to claims exists when work is undertaken for certain lenders.[1]

It should be emphasised that the duty of a person seeking insurance (whether for the first time or on an annual renewal) is not merely to answer the insurer's questions; it is to disclose all material facts. Thus, for example, a firm of surveyors which failed to disclose that one of its partners had served a term of imprisonment following a conviction for assault could find its PI policy avoided by the insurers, even though this matter was not covered by a specific question on the proposal form.

The question of what kind of non-disclosure is "material", in the

---

[1] *Information Paper on Professional Indemnity Insurance, the Notification of Valuation Claims*, published jointly by the RICS, the Council of Mortgage Lenders and PI Insurers, February 1994.

sense of entitling the insurer to avoid liability under the policy, was addressed by the House of Lords in *Pan Atlantic Insurance Co Ltd v Pine Top Insurance Co.*[1] That case arose when one insurer sought to avoid the reinsurance of the other on the ground that, at the time that the reinsurance was placed, the claims figures were misrepresented. In holding that the misrepresentation satisfied the test of materiality, so that the reinsurers were entitled to avoid liability, the House of Lords explained and modified the much-criticised decision of the Court of Appeal in *CTI v Oceanus Mutual Underwriting Association (Bermuda).*[2]

The *Pan Atlantic* decision lays down two important principles with regard to "materiality". First, it was decided by a bare majority of the House of Lords that a circumstance could be "material", even though full and accurate disclosure of it would not in itself have been the *decisive* factor in the insurer's decision whether to accept the risk and,if so, at what premium. Second, the House of Lords held that it was not sufficient to show that the non-disclosed or misrepresented matter would be considered material by a *prudent* insurer; that matter must have in fact induced the making of the contract by the *actual* insurer.

The reason underlying the second point was explained by Lord Mustill:[3]

True, the inequalities of knowledge between assured and underwriter have led to the creation of a special duty to make accurate disclosure of sufficient facts to restore the balance and remedy the injustice of holding the underwriter to a speculation which he had been unable fairly to assess; but the consideration cannot in logic or justice require courts to go further and declare the contract to be vitiated when the underwriter, having paid no attention to the matters not properly stated and disclosed, has suffered no injustice thereby.

Although this represents an extra hurdle for an insurer to surmount in order to avoid liability, common sense suggests that it will not usually prove too difficult to do so. As Lord Mustill went on to point out:

---

1 [1994] 3 All ER 581.
2 [1984] 1 Lloyd's Rep 476.
3 [1994] 3 All ER 581 at p610.

The assured will have an uphill task in persuading the court that the withholding or mis-statement of circumstances satisfying the test of materiality has made no difference.

In such a case, the insurer's evidence will be all the more credible where a full written record has been made and kept of all the information required and given when the risk was accepted.

2 Non-compliance with policy terms and conditions

In addition to the general duty of disclosure described above, PI insurance policies usually impose a number of other obligations upon the insured, non-compliance with which will enable the insurer to avoid liability under the policy. Of particular importance in this respect are those provisions, found in every policy, which require the insured to give notice of actual or potential claims. The wording of General Conditions 2 and 3 of the RICS professional indemnity collective policy has already been set out;[1] however, different policies impose different requirements, and it is crucial for surveyors and valuers to examine their own policy so as to ensure that all relevant requirements are met.

An illustration of the problems which may arise in this context is provided by *Tilley & Noad* v *Dominion Insurance Co Ltd*.[2] During the 1985 policy year of PI insurance, a firm of valuers notified their insurers of two claims made against them, relating to valuations of farming assets which the firm had provided in 1982 and 1984. The relevant valuations had been carried out by a consultant valuer whose age was given as 81 on the insurance proposal form dated November 27 1984. On the evidence, it was apparent that this consultant's abilities had declined between March 1982, when he carried out the first valuation, and April and November 1984, when he carried out further valuations of the same property.

In seeking to avoid liability, the insurers relied on two separate provisions of the policy: an *exclusion* of liability resulting from any circumstance known to the insured at inception of the policy and likely to give rise to a claim; and a *condition* requiring the insured to give immediate notice of any claim or occurrence of which the insured might become aware which might subsequently give rise to

---

1 See p235.
2 [1987] 2 EGLR 34.

a claim. According to the insurers, the firm knew that the consultant had been furnishing some unreliable valuations, and their failure to notify the insurers of this fact was sufficient to invalidate their claim under the policy.

In considering these arguments, Mervyn Davies J explained the difference between these two provisions. The *condition* was concerned with the notification of which occurred during the current policy, not with past events; it consequently had no application to the present case, since all the relevant events had taken place before the policy was issued. The *exclusion*, on the other hand, was concerned with the insured's knowledge at the time when the policy was issued. Since, on the evidence, the firm had not become aware of any unreliable valuations from its consultant carried out before April 1984, it followed that claims based on the 1982 valuation were not excluded. However, the insurers were entitled to resist claims based wholly on the 1984 valuations.

A very different kind of policy exclusion was interpreted by the courts in *Summers* v *Congreve Horner & Co (a firm) and Independent Insurance Co Ltd*.[1] That case arose out of a structural survey of a house, carried out by an employee of the defendant firm, which failed (allegedly through negligence) to discover damp and dry rot. The employee in question, who had been with the firm for some five months, was not professionally qualified; however, he was a law graduate who had been a trainee building surveyor for more than three years, had passed all the RICS examinations and was in his final year of preparing for the test of professional competence (which he subsequently passed).

When the client made a claim against the firm, the PI insurers sought to deny liability on the basis of Exclusion 11 of the RICS Professional Indemnity Collective Policy wording. This reads as follows:

The Policy shall not indemnify the Assured against any claim or loss:–
11 arising from survey/inspection and/or valuation reports of real property unless such surveys/inspections and/or valuations shall have been made:–
   (a) by a Fellow or Associate of the RICS or of the ISVA or of [certain named Architectural Faculties and Institutes]; or

---

1 [1992] 2 EGLR 152.

(b) by anyone who has not less than five years experience of such work or such other person nominated by the Assured to execute such work subject always to supervision of such work by a person qualified in accordance with (a) above.

Since the employee in question did not fall within either the first or the second group of persons covered, the crucial question was whether his work had been "supervised" within the meaning of this provision.

The firm's evidence as to its supervision of the particular employee was as follows:

i   to begin with, he had merely accompanied a partner on surveys, watching what was done and having potential problems pointed out and explained;
ii he then progressed to carrying out inspections under the constant supervision of the same partner, who listened to his dictation of reports and gave advice and guidance;
iii the next stage was for the partner merely to visit the site with the employee for 30 minutes or so, to check that there were no problems;
iv finally, when the firm was satisfied as to his competence, the employee was allowed to carry out some inspections on his own on the basis of a checklist provided by the partner who then discussed the report with the employee and signed it.

The claim in question arose out of the third survey for which the final procedure had been adopted. The principal did not visit the surveyed premises at any material time, although he had recently surveyed a neighbouring property.

By a majority, the Court of Appeal (reversing the judgment of Judge Fox-Andrews QC) held that the degree of control exercised by the partner of the defendant firm was sufficient to justify a finding of supervision. The Court of Appeal was satisfied that it was enough if the unqualified person received that degree of supervision which good practice required in the profession of surveying for a person of his training and experience. However, somewhat illogically, the court also stated that the policy would always require *some* supervision, even if "good practice" might regard an employee as competent to carry out surveys without any supervision at all.

With effect from August 1993, the wording of the appropriate exclusion of the RICS professional indemnity collective policy wording includes an additional subpara (c), which reads as follows:

Any other person delegated by the Insured to execute such work as part of their training subject always to:
(i) supervision of such work by a person qualified in accordance with (a) above; or
(ii) agreement in writing having been obtained from the Insurers prior to cover being granted.

This amended wording still makes no reference to the degree of supervision required, although the wording of another PI policy available for surveyors states specifically that physical supervision will not be required. If there is any doubt, this is a matter which should be checked with the insurer concerned before any relevant professional work is undertaken.

D PI insurance and third party rights

As noted at the start of this chapter, PI insurance policies provide cover for a professional person in respect of liabilities incurred, rather than direct cover for any person to whom such liabilities may be incurred. This point is clearly illustrated by the case of *Normid Housing Association Ltd v Ralphs & Mansell Ltd*,[1] in which the defendant architects were sued by their clients for defective design and execution of works. The total amount claimed was some £5.7m, and disputes arose between the defendants and their PI insurers as to the extent of cover under the policy. When the insurers offered to settle the claim for £250,000, the defendants proposed to accept this, whereupon the plaintiffs sought an injunction to restrain the defendants from doing so.

The Court of Appeal held that, in the absence of any allegation of bad faith or collusion between the architects and the insurers, the plaintiffs had no right to interfere with the proposed settlement. As the court pointed out, the architects were under no specific contractual obligation to their clients to take out or maintain PI insurance, and so they were free to exercise their own judgment as to what benefits they would attempt to obtain from their policy. Nor could the plaintiffs rely on the Third Parties (Rights Against Insurers) Act 1930,[2] since that Act applies only where the insured person

---

1 (1988) 43 BLR 18.
2 See p242.

has become insolvent.

An inevitable consequence of this decision has been that many clients insist, as a condition of appointment of a surveyor or valuer, that the latter undertakes not to settle any claim with insurers without the prior written consent of the client. Although the effect of such a provision has not yet been tested in court, it would probably entitle the client to restrain any proposed settlement to which he or she did not consent. Moreover, it is possible that the decision in the *Normid Housing* case itself would have been different if the architects there had specifically undertaken to take out and maintain PI insurance to a specified level.

The principle that a person making a claim against an insured has no direct rights against the insurer is subject to a statutory exception. The Third Parties (Rights Against Insurers) Act 1930, section 1 provides that, where a person becomes insolvent, any rights which that person has against liability insurers are transferred to those third parties to whom the insured person may be liable within the terms of the relevant policy. This provision is clearly designed to enable the third party to claim directly against the insurers, but it has been interpreted in a limited way which deprives it of much force. It was held by the Court of Appeal in *Post Office v Norwich Union Fire Insurance Society Ltd*[1] that, unless and until the insured person's liability to the plaintiff has been established (by legal action, arbitration or agreement), the insured person has no "rights" against the insurers, and there is consequently nothing to be transferred to the third party at that stage.

Section 2 of the 1930 Act requires insurers, liquidators and insolvency practitioners to divulge to third parties such information as they might reasonably require for the purpose of ascertaining what rights if any have been transferred under the Act. This appears potentially to be a very useful provision, since claimants will frequently want to investigate the PI position before deciding whether or not it is worthwhile bringing legal proceedings. However, the courts have given it a similarly restrictive interpretation to that given to section 1. In *Woolwich Building Society v Taylor*[2] a firm of valuers went into liquidation with enormous potential liabilities (many

---

1 [1967] 2 QB 363.
2 Times, May 17 1994: see also *Nigel Upchurch Associates v Aldridge Estates Investment Co Ltd* [1993] 1 Lloyd's Rep 535.

of which arose out of allegedly negligent valuations). The plaintiffs, who had made certain claims against the firm, demanded from the firm's liquidator and its PI insurers information as to whether the PI insurance policy covered those claims and whether the policy was valid or voidable. The plaintiffs also sought an order permitting them to inspect all documents relevant to the firm's insurance position. In rejecting the plaintiffs' demands, Lindsay J pointed out that any ascertainment of whether the firm had incurred legal liability to the plaintiffs depended upon future events: a judgment not yet given, an award not yet embarked upon or an agreement not yet made. Since, therefore, no such liability had been established, the plaintiffs were not entitled to the information sought. The judge's view was that it would be odd if the position were otherwise, for a third party would then have sweeping rights of information against insurers, even if no proceedings were actually brought.

E Fraud

Public policy prevents a person from obtaining insurance cover for liability which arises out of his or her own fraud. In consequence, where there is any suspicion that fraud may have been involved, a surveyor or valuer who practises as a sole principal may find that the PI insurers attempt to deny liability under the policy. On the other hand, where allegations of fraud are made against a partner or an employee, the firm or company will normally, if innocent, be entitled to indemnity under the PI policy.

Lending institutions in particular are aware that, if they make allegations of fraud against a valuer, the consequence may be that the PI insurers seek to avoid liability. However, this risk must be offset against the possibility that proof of fraud could result in a higher award of damages, and the certainty that it would defeat any possible defence of contributory negligence.[1]

Where an allegation of fraud is made, the courts demand a very high standard of proof, as may be seen from the recent case of *BNP Mortgages Ltd* v *Goadsby & Harding Ltd*.[2] An employee of the the defendants there valued a residential property for remortgage purposes on February 21 1990 at £245,000, confirming this

---

1 See p216.
2 [1994] 2 EGLR 169.

valuation in a letter to the plaintiff lenders on May 23 1990. It was alleged by the plaintiffs that the valuer, in collusion with the owner of the property, had made the valuation fraudulently, in that he either knew that it was false or was reckless as to whether it was true or false.

In rejecting this allegation, Judge Fox-Andrews QC drew attention to what was said by Lord Herschell in *Derry* v *Peek*:[1]

And it is surely conceivable that a man may believe what he states is the fact, although he may be so wanting in care that the Court may think that there were no sufficient grounds to warrant his belief.

In holding that the representation in this case was false, but that the valuer neither knew it to be false nor was reckless as to whether it was true or false, Judge Fox-Andrews QC said:

I had the advantage of seeing the valuer under sustained but fair cross-examination. I concluded that whilst he was prepared to make statements which were not true in order to exculpate himself from a charge of negligence, the plaintiffs have not satisfied me that at the time he had no honest belief in giving the figure that he did. Why he acted in the way he did, which may well be out of character, will not be known. A possibility is the approach of his holiday. There are a number of "keep free" entries in the diary at about this time. But of course I make no finding about that. The fact that he cut many corners eg failing to visit the site, failing to ascertain the sale position of units 3 and 4, the failure to ascertain the then asking prices for the unsold units and the fact that almost contemporaneously he was accurately reflecting the depressed state of the market in [another] valuation are all factors from which a dishonest belief could be determined. Indeed as a paper exercise it may be that I would have made such a finding. But the overwhelming impression I had of him in the witness box was of a man who had no intention of acting dishonestly but who did unfortunately show unusual negligence.

F Current problems

A paper published in February 1994 by the RICS[2] estimated that claims in respect of residential and commercial mortgage valuations

---

1 (1889) 14 App Cas 337 at p361.
2 *Information Paper on Professional Indemnity Insurance, the Notification of Valuation Claims.*

amounted to between £500m and £750m, while the insurance premiums paid in respect of that work were no more than 5% of this figure. It was suggested that to provide full cover would cost in the region of £50 for every valuation carried out. The paper noted that, for some surveyors and valuers, PI insurance had become impossible to obtain at any cost. For others, available cover was restricted to an "aggregate" rather than an "each and every claim" basis, or by making the cover inclusive of legal costs in respect of both the limit of cover and the uninsured excess.

A practice which has grown up in recent years is that of providing insurers with notification of what are known as "shopping lists" of claims. These may allege merely that a property which has been valued by the insured has subsequently been sold at a figure less than the valuation. Similarly, where it is believed that one valuation may have been negligent, all other valuations carried out by that particular surveyor or valuer are automatically notified as potential claims. These "shopping lists" are notified to insurers even though they are not "claims circumstances" as normally understood.

One of the problems caused by such "shopping lists" is that, without any proper evidence of negligence, PI insurers may decide that, when the policy is due for renewal, they will refuse to renew cover, or do so only upon a limited basis or at a greatly increased premium. Worse, they may lead to considerable uncertainty as to what is covered. This is because, when a new PI policy is issued, it will invariably exclude from its cover all claims circumstances reported in the previous policy year. However, it is common for insurers receiving "shopping lists" of claims to note these without prejudice to their position, and it may be a long time before an insurer confirms whether these are covered under the terms of the policy applying at the time the notification was made. By then, a different insurer may be involved and the new policy may contain an exclusion of certain claims circumstances. The consequence of this is that, when a lender subsequently endeavours to pursue a claim against a surveyor or valuer, it may be discovered that PI insurance cover is not effective, even though it appeared to be so at the time when the valuation in question was carried out.

Any consideration of the problems arising out of valuation claims in recent years would be incomplete without reference to Mortgage Indemnity Guarantee (MIG) insurance. Such insurance is intended to provide cover for lenders in respect of the "top slice" of a loan (commonly that part of the loan which exceeds 70% of the figure at which the property is valued). According to the RICS Information Paper, MIG insurers lost approximately £1.2 billion in 1991 and £750m in 1992. Not surprisingly, such losses have had a dramatic effect upon the MIG market in relation to residential property. Since 1993 it has been common for domestic MIG policies to contain a specific exclusion of cover where there is negligence or fraud on the part of the surveyor or valuer or of any other party involved in the making of a loan.

Section 5 of the information paper contains helpful advice as to the procedures which should be adopted by lenders prior to giving notice of claim arising out of a valuation. When a lender repossesses a property, it is established practice to obtain at least one professional valuation (preferably two) in addition to the selling agent's market appraisal. Further investigation may be needed to establish whether the current value is affected by vandalism, or by damage caused to the property by the borrower prior to vacating.

Before giving notice of a potential claim against the original mortgage valuer, lenders should consider the following questions:
i   Does the discrepancy between the original and the current valuation take into account market conditions?
ii Where a forced sale has taken place, does the sale price accurately reflect the current value of the property?
iii Was the appropriate form of valuation requested?
iv Did the original advance meet the lender's own lending criteria?
v   Were internal checks made of comparable information on similar properties?
vi Was legal advice sought upon any qualification made in the valuation report, such as disclaimer notices or interpretations of lease provisions?

Apart from considering these questions, lenders should keep clearly in mind the distinction between:
i   a routine audit letter to the original valuer, requesting details of comparable evidence obtained in support of a valuation figure;
ii a letter asking the original valuer to support a valuation figure on a property which has been repossessed and which appears likely to be sold at a loss;
iii a letter before action.

It is hoped that the advice contained in the information paper, if followed, will result in a significant reduction in the number of claims which are notified to PI insurers. This is essential if PI insurance is to remain available to surveyors and valuers upon realistic terms.

Index

A

APPOINTMENT
  terms of (see INSTRUCTIONS)

ARBITRATOR
  immunity of 15–20
  independent expert, distinguished from 16–18

B

BREACH OF DUTY
  general standard 71–73
  inexperience as 74–75
  loss of fees for (see FEES)
  planning advice, in 178, 184
  proof of 81–87
  rent reviews, in (see RENT REVIEWS)
  specialist, of 73–74
  surveyor
    damp (see timber defects)
    death watch beetle (see timber defects)
    Home Buyers Survey and Valuation 72, 98, 102, 106, 107–108, 158
    method of reporting 91–93, 103–104
    roof defects 49, 78, 91, 97–100, 120, 126, 128, 188, 190
    rot (see timber defects)
    services defects 77, 82, 106–107, 108, 228
    subsidence 45, 49, 79, 100–106, 124, 129, 230
    timber defects .. 3, 41, 60, 61, 74, 76, 77, 78, 93–97, 125, 151, 152, 190, 198
    woodworm (see timber defects)
  valuer
    accuracy 110–111
    "bracket" 111–114
    construction defects 82, 126–128, 189
    legal knowledge 122–123
    valuation methods 114–122

BUILDING SOCIETIES OMBUDSMAN (see MORTGAGE LENDER)

C

CAUSATION (see DAMAGES)

CLIENT
  contract with 1–7
  duty to
    contract 10–12
    tort 4–6, 28–33

COMPANY
liability to 65–66

CONTRIBUTION CLAIMS 193–194, 226, 228–231

CONTRIBUTORY NEGLIGENCE
house buyer, of 218–220
mortgage lender, of 220–227
professional negligence cases, in 216–218
scope of 214–216

D

DAMAGES
causation 132–135
collateral benefits 141–143
insurance, effect on 141–142
interest on 144–145
lender
  basic measure
    "non-transaction" cases 166–168
    "transaction" cases 165–166
  incidental losses 168–169
  interest 170–173
  repayment by borrower 173–176
  syndicated loan 143–144
mitigation of loss 139–140, 161, 174–176
assessment of 177–179
purchaser
  cost of repair 147, 149–150
  discomfort, distress, inconvenience (see INCONVENIENCE)
  incidental losses 154–157
  overpayment 146–154
  personal injury 100, 139 163–164
reliance 135–138
remoteness of damage 138–139
vendor
  over-valuation 134, 136, 177
  under-valuation 176–177

DAMP (see TIMBER DEFECTS)

DEATH WATCH BEETLE (see TIMBER DEFECTS)

DISCLAIMER
common law principles 8, 9, 48, 199–201
types 196–198
Unfair Contract Terms Act 201–203
  "reasonableness" test 205–211
  scope of the Act 203–205

DISCOMFORT (see INCONVENIENCE)

DISTRESS (see INCONVENIENCE)

E

EMPLOYER
  liability of (see VICARIOUS LIABILITY)

ENGAGEMENT
  terms of (see INSTRUCTIONS)

ESTATE AGENT
  negligence by 60, 62, 63, 231

EXEMPTION CLAUSE (see DISCLAIMER)

EXPERT
  evidence 83–87
  independent (see INDEPENDENT EXPERT)
  witness 81–83

F

FEES
  contingency 22–23
  express agreement 22–23
  forfeiture of 25–28
  implied agreement 23–25

FIRM
  liability of (see VICARIOUS LIABILITY)

FRAUD
  valuer, by 69, 194–196, 243–244

G

GUIDANCE NOTES
  survey 90
  valuation 75, 117–122

H

HOME BUYERS SURVEY AND VALUATION 72, 98, 102, 106, 107–108, 158

HOUSE BUYER
  contributory negligence of 218–220
  damages for (see DAMAGES)
  mortgage valuer's liability to 45–53

I

INCONVENIENCE
  damages for 157–163

INCORPORATED SOCIETY OF VALUERS AND AUCTIONEERS (ISVA)
  (see GUIDANCE NOTES)

INDEPENDENT EXPERT
  arbitrator, distinguished from 15–20
  challenge to 20–21
  negligence by 15, 17, 19, 64, 129

INSTRUCTIONS
  confirmation of
    surveyor 75–79, 90–91
    valuer 79–80
  model terms
    survey 90–91, 107
    valuation 121

INSURANCE (see also PROFESSIONAL INDEMNITY INSURANCE)
  mortgage indemnity guarantee 43, 136, 142, 222, 245–246
  valuations
    damages for 178
    negligence in 80, 130

INTEREST
  damages, on 144–145
  mortgage lender, entitlement to 170–173

L

LENDER (see MORTGAGE LENDER)

LIMITATION OF LIABILITY (see DISCLAIMER)

LIMITATION PERIODS
  contract 180–181
  contribution 193–194, 229–230
  fraud and concealment 194–196
  latent damage 185–192
  personal injury 192–193
  tort 181–185

M

MALLINSON REPORT 121

MITIGATION (see DAMAGES)

MORTGAGE LENDER
 contributory negligence of 220–227
 damages for (see DAMAGES)
 liability to house buyer
  contract 8–10, 55
  Ombudsman scheme 7–8
  tort 7, 13, 53–59
 valuer's duty to (see MORTGAGE VALUATION)

MORTGAGE VALUATION
 commercial
  duty of care 34, 41–44
  damages (see DAMAGES)
  lender's contributory negligence 220–227
  negligence in 112–113, 115–117, 118–119, 123
 residential
  buyer's contributory negligence 218–220
  disclaimer 206–211
  liability to house buyer 45–53
  negligence in 45, 49, 113–114, 119–121, 123–129

N
NEGLIGENCE (see BREACH OF DUTY)

P
PARTNER
 liability of (see VICARIOUS LIABILITY)

PERSONAL INJURY (see DAMAGES)

PROFESSIONAL INDEMNITY INSURANCE
 fraud 243–244
 nature of 232–235
 non-disclosure 235–238
 policy conditions 238–241
 problems involving 244–246
 professional requirements 232
 third party rights 241–243

PURCHASER (see also HOUSE BUYER)
 liability to, on vendor's survey 59–61

R
RELIANCE (see DAMAGES)

REMOTENESS (see DAMAGES)

RENT REVIEWS
 expert (see INDEPENDENT EXPERT)
 surveyor as advocate 133, 178

REPOSSESSION
duty on sale of property 63–64

ROOF DEFECTS
failure to detect 49, 78, 91, 97–100, 120, 126, 128, 188, 190

ROT (see TIMBER DEFECTS)

ROYAL INSTITUTION OF CHARTERED SURVEYORS (RICS) (see GUIDANCE NOTES)

S

SERVICES
defects in, failure to detect 77, 82, 106–107, 108, 228

STRUCTURAL SURVEY
what is included 89–91

SUBSIDENCE
failure to detect 45, 49, 79, 100–106, 124, 129, 230

SUMMARY JUDGMENT
professional negligence action, in 87–88

T

THIRD PARTIES
liability to
    basis of 34–41
    "down-valuation", for 61–63
    house buyer 45–53
    insurer 43
    joint purchaser 41
    lender 34, 41–44
    sale of repossessed property, on 63–64
    unformed company, to 65–66
    vendor's survey, on 59–61

TIMBER DEFECTS
failure to detect ... 3, 41, 60, 61, 74, 76, 77, 78, 93–97, 125, 151, 152, 190, 198

V

VALUATION
compulsory purchase 123
"crash sale" 79
insurance 80, 130
matrimonial proceedings, in 130–131
meaning of 109–110
mortgage (see MORTGAGE VALUATION)
rating 22, 80
vendor, for (see VENDOR)

VENDOR
  damages (see DAMAGES)
  duty to 79, 130, 176–177
  "down-valuation" 61–63
  survey, liability to purchaser for 59–61

VICARIOUS LIABILITY
  employer, of 12–13, 55–57, 66–67
  fraud, for 69
  partner, of 69–70

W

WOODWORM (see TIMBER DEFECTS)